The Riot Inside Me

BOOKS BY WANDA COLEMAN

Art in the Court of the Blue Fag (1977)

Mad Dog Black Lady (1979)

Imagoes (1983)

Heavy Daughter Blues (1987)

A War of Eyes & Other Stories (1988)

The Dicksboro Hotel & Other Travels (1989)

African Sleeping Sickness (1990)

Hand Dance (1993)

American Sonnets (1994)

Native in a Strange Land: Trials & Tremors (1996)

Bathwater Wine (1998)

Mambo Hips & Make Believe: A Novel (1999)

Love-Ins with Nietzsche: A Memoir (2000)

Mercurochrome (2001)

Ostinato Vamps (2003)

Wanda Coleman—Greatest Hits 1966–2003 (2004)

The Riot Inside Me: More Trials & Tremors (2005)

Wanda Coleman

THE RIOT

INSIDE ME

More Trials & Tremors

A Black Sparrow Book
DAVID R. GODINE
Publisher · Boston

This is
A Black Sparrow Book
published in 2005 by
David R. Godine, Publisher
Post Office Box 450
Jaffrey, New Hampshire 03452
www.blacksparrowbooks.com

Some of the material in this volume is reprinted with the permission of holders of copyright and publication rights. A list of sources and acknowledgments begins on page 259.

Book design and composition by Carl W. Scarbrough
The Black Sparrow Books pressmark is by Julian Waters
www.waterslettering.com

LIBRARY OF CONGRESS
CATALOGING-IN-PUBLICATION DATA

Coleman, Wanda
The riot inside me: more trials & tremors / Wanda Coleman. —1st ed.
p.   cm.
ISBN 1-57423-200-2 (softcover : alk. paper)
"A Black Sparrow Book."
1. Title.
PS3553.047447 R56   2005
818/.5409 22   2004017234

FIRST EDITION
Printed in the United States of America

for Phyllis Clark Williams, John C. Fremont High,
and The Centurions
Summer 1964

Meanwhile, empty space inside the convention center collapses. Cars to cameras. I still see the eyes and mouths of salesmen flash. I don't need satori *on this boulevard. Glad to be with no spare change in my pockets. Everything inside me is broken with nothing left to be cut open.*

—Patrick Bianucci, "Pico Blvd."

CONTENTS

III: The Maya Situation

IV: My Future Is in My Past

Introduction

My Writing Life & Loves

As journalist, poet, writer, and occasional scriptwriter, I find that one of the most difficult of my writerly tasks is deciding *what* becomes *what*. At some point during the writing, it may become *how much of what* becomes the article, the essay, the poem, or the story. In my case, the lines between fact and fiction are irascibly drawn. And I draw them painfully, with my editorial eye focused on a stringent and authentic rendering. My candid appraisals and observations in my fact pieces are usually not intended as insults, even if they may be taken as such by those on whom I focus. Like Wallace Stegner (*Fire and Ice*), I am in the "universal" tradition of writers who concern themselves with The Truth—never mind that it is apt to hurt someone, in some way, most likely me. But allegiance to The Truth need not preclude an impish sense of humor and the satirical, or a romance with the surreal.

Once I've decided on the *what*, all my vision and efforts are turned on the *how*. The actual writing, then, becomes a challenge, a chore, or a joy, depending on the circumstances governing my emotions at the time—what's shaking among those with whom I live in Southern California. Once the decision is made, the issue of *tone* arises, or the *way* I express my *what*.

Introduction

One of the banes of Black authors in the Western United States is our being too frequently left out of the larger cultural dialogues, particularly those on race. (When I speak out, it is never to further the provincial but always *to seek balance and inclusion.*) Speaking out too loudly may net us further isolation. When our voices are heard, it is testimony to our fortitude, genius, and persistence—and, for many, our willingness to travel east if not relocate there. In the introduction to *The African American West: A Century of Short Stories* (University Press of Colorado, 2000), an anthology in which I appear, editors Bruce Glasrud and Laurie Champion aptly summarize The Problem:

> *Because* historically black Americans were denied publication in white journals, *because* American publishers frequently assumed an eastern bias, *because* western African American publishers were too busy exploring opportunities for survival, *because* western writers were less likely to use condescending dialect and to depict stereotypes . . . blacks in the west have too often been neglected.

These words are true to my experience. The editors go on to define "breaking with tradition," and to explore why western writers, Black and White, are frequently in the literary "forefront," and again they seem to be on to something. In the late 1980s, I began to hear the word "experimental" associated with my work. I had always thought of myself as certainly *aspiring* to go beyond the conventional. Had I succeeded beyond my expectations? Or was I being misread vis-à-vis the quote above? Both? Experimentation was a notion I had embraced in my youthful readings as I absorbed the existentialists, particularly the French (de Beauvoir, Genet, Sartre, and Camus, together with the "Negro psychiatrist" Frantz Fanon). I thought I had abandoned it as I matured. Consciously, I no longer cared whether I was avant-garde or not. I wanted to be read, not gather dust on a bookshelf. But the harder I wrote, the more others seemed to cast me outside the mainstream of African American writers—*outside the outside*, as one critical observer put it. Yet, some of my regional cohorts regard me as "predominant" if not completely "establishment." What has come about, then, is my apparent psychosocial *Ma'afa*, my literary middle passage or disjuncture, as I am ever caught between aesthetic devils and deep blue issues.

When reflecting on that part of my psyche claimed by journalism, I am dismayed by how frequently I have been invited to write about the Watts and South Central riots, yet how seldom I've been asked to discuss, in any real depth, other facets of the African American experience in Southern California. The riots may *seem* to be my obsession, but they are not; Los Angeles, however, *is* an unending source of material for my writings. It is a terrain with which I'm fascinated, the birthplace I've yet to abandon. With the aim of showing my Los Angeles whole, I reprint here a couple of interviews and a Q & A, with corrections made where I was heard incorrectly or comments added to passages where my opinions have changed or been better expressed in passing years.

Ceding to current media jargon, I have freely defied geography, using the post-riot names of specific areas of L.A. that conveniently define its entire African American *populus*: "Watts," including Pacoima, thirty-one miles away, in the east San Fernando Valley, and Riverside, fifty-eight miles east; likewise "South Central," including the southern tip of the city proper, Hyde Park, Inglewood, Jefferson Park, and Watts-Willowbrook, despite the steady displacement of Blacks by immigrants of color. While born in Watts, I was, technically, raised not in South Central but in Los Angeles, albeit the southern end, a White enclave where mine was the first Black family. *My* Los Angeles is that city whose boundaries were once rigidly enforced by the Los Angeles Unified School District, a volatile turf ruled by five senior high schools: John C. Fremont, David Starr Jordan, Thomas Jefferson, Manual Arts, and George Washington; it is literally and metaphorically that city which would explode into world headlines twice before the end of the twentieth century.

The Riot Inside Me, then, is the continuation of the nonfictional directions I briefly discuss in my introduction to *Native in a Strange Land: Trials & Tremors* (1996). The first two sections here collect recent essays, interviews, and visitations that encompass my stylistic extremes, from softer moments, as in the open letter to my father, to an encounter with Dr. Roberta Sykes, the Australian author-activist, to "Primal Orb Density," in which actual newspaper headlines, snippets from city desk reports, and a mock quiz underscore my rages. Walking the same ground, I repeatedly meet myself as I hopscotch the decades, skate along relationships, and throw stones into the darkness.

The third section opens with the most controversial text I've ever written: my review of Maya Angelou's *A Song Flung Up to Heaven*, published in the *Los Angeles Times Book Review* on April 14, 2002. Following it are my subsequent articles examining the fallout, insofar as I've been able to assess it. Remarkably, this single book review has made me infamous for far longer than Warhol's fifteen minutes, and even now, two years later, "the trouble" has not quite gone away. To these articles I've added a slightly reflective postscript. There is no such beast as objectivity in this jungle.

"Hollywood was the revolution" is one of my favorite lines; I use it in one of the one hundred jazz poems collectively called the American Sonnets (see *Bathwater Wine* and *Mercurochrome*). In that poem, my Hollywood is simultaneously the topography of Southern California and its impact on world culture from Disneyland to McDonald's (Dizzywizzyland and Mickey D's, as they are known in the ghetto). This sentiment is echoed in the final part of *Riot*, as I return to literal and literary Los Angeles with the playful and bemused spirit that initially inspired this collection. Some of these pieces overlap with or complement those in *Native in a Strange Land*, particularly "Dancer on a Blade," which contains the kind of poetic passages that characterize that book. "I Was a Stand-In Diva for June Jordan," "Letters to E. Ethelbert Miller," and "Wearing My Maturity" illuminate my darkly humorous aspect. "5 Years After," "9/11 Blues," and "The Riot Inside Me" find me back on familiar turf, the implications reaching further —and reverberating globally, I hope.

Finally, I would like to offer my appreciation and gratitude to a few of the advisors, correspondents, friends, mentors, and supporters, new and old, who have watched over me as the decades have thundered by: Linda Albertano, Leatha Scott Bailey, Shelly A. Berger, Malcolm Boyd, Bliss Carnochan, Bibbe and Sean Carrillo, Audrey Christian, Mark Cull and Kate Gale, Fred Dewey, Annie Evans, Elia Evans, Linda Feldman, Neal Fitzpatrick, Jack and Adelle Foley, Myrna and the Family Fortier-Tyson, Maria Gillan, C. S. Giscombe, Jonathan Haft, Anna Halprin, Odie Hawkins, Paul Hoover, Paul Lynel Kalin, Pamala "La Loca" Karol, Stephen Kessler, Lynda Koolish, Lisa Korben, Steve Kowit, Harvey R. Kubernik, La Bob (wherever you are), Jeff Land, Jay Levin, Philomene and Peggarty Long, Ruth Lynch, Tony Magistrale, Mr. Greg and Dieter, Bill Mohr, Earl Ofari-Hutchinson and Zekivu Hutchinson, Steve and Penelope Oshatz, Della Patton, Luis Rodriguez, Sylvia Rickler-Rosen, Michael Roth and Soryl Markowitz, Carol Schwalberg and Eugene Schroerluke, David Trinidad, Quincy Troupe, David Ulin, Jokie X. Wilson, Murray and Charlene Wolfe, and X-Ray (you know who you are). Special thanks to Ishmael Reed for allowing me to squeak my squeak without the censorship and anti-intellectualism that currently threaten civil liberties in post-9/11 America.

WANDA COLEMAN
Los Angeles, California
January 2004

I

MUSIC & MADNESSES

A Girl's Diary

(Excerpts — Summer 1961)

July 22: Another day, another downer. It seems as though all my days are spoiled by something.

July 27: Today was lousy. I've been putting some of that stuff in my Kool-Aid and fruit drinks. I've got to do something to calm my nerves. Music helps. So does rat poison. *Outlaws*—great.

August 2: Didn't go to the library again. Have hard time getting to sleep. Mother sure is unreasonable at times, but I love her all the same. Still, my life is miserable.

August 7: When seven comes on Monday I'm always having bad luck. I got a spankin'. All because I was half asleep when Daddy told me to fix Mom's breakfast.

August 13: Today I got my first *Lois Lane* comic book and a *Batman and Robin* issue. Daddy promised me a quarter before next Sunday.

August 20: Went to the theatre with girlfriends for the first time. The two shows were lousy. We just wasted our money.

August 26: *Kumm Süsser Tod* by Bruch is beautiful. They don't like it. Almost got in trouble because of it.

3

August 28: We register for school September 11th. *Kumm Süsser Tod* is doing something physical to me as well as mental. If only they could hear it through my ears.

Sept. 8: Someone stole mother's purse and all our money. We suspect the dame across the street.

Last Sunday I found out that I am truly a psychic. Psychics have miserable lives. For days I kept getting a weird feeling that someone was looking for me. After Sunday school, I was out bike riding when I looked down the block, all the way to Central Avenue, and a bus pulled up. Two White boys got off, pushing their bikes. They looked exhausted. Suddenly I felt scared inside, took my bike around back, and went into the house. The doorbell rang, and Mother came into the kitchen to say there were some boys in the yard who wanted to see me. I asked her who they were. She said go find out for your lazy self.

It was the same two boys, one blond, one sandy-haired. I stared at them from behind the screen door. They were tall, all sweaty, in khakis and pastel shirts. "Please come out, Wanda," the blond one said. "I came a long way to see you, my buddy 'n' me. All the way from Anaheim."

I went out on the porch.

"You don't remember me," the blond one said.

"Gerald," I said.

He said it had been a hard ride, first on the streets, then by train and by bus. He was worn out but determined to come back to me, just like he promised to that day he and his family moved away from 89th Street. I was eight then, and he was almost twelve. "I'm eighteen now," Gerald said. "My mom couldn't stop me from coming. I've been out here in the world. Things are all messed up. We can't

4

be in love like normal people, or ever get married. You're not strong enough, and I'm not strong enough. One day you'll understand that I'm right."

Funny, I couldn't feel anything inside. Why had I been so scared? I thanked him for coming back to tell me. He wished me luck in life. Then he and the sandy-haired boy turned around, mounted their bikes, and rode off.

Today is Friday. School begins Monday, my first day at Fremont High.

Jabberwocky Baby

The stultifying intellectual loneliness of my 1950s and '60s upbringing was dictated by my looks—dark skin and unconkable kinky hair. Boys gawked at me, and girls tittered behind my back. Black teachers shook their heads in pity, and White teachers stared in amusement or in wonder. I found this rejection unbearable and, encouraged by my parents to read, sought an escape in books, which were usually hard to come by. There were no colored-owned bookstores in our neighborhood. The libraries discouraged Negro readers.

My reading appetite had no limits. At six or seven I was slogging through Papa's dull issues of *National Geographic* and Mama's tepid copies of *Reader's Digest* and her favorite murder mysteries. At age ten I consumed the household copy of the complete works of Shakespeare, and while the violence was striking —and *Hamlet* engrossing, particularly Ophelia—I was too immature to fully appreciate The Bard until frequent rereadings during my mid-teens. In high school I would read Plato's *Dialogues*, Aristotle's *Metaphysics*, Machiavelli's *The Prince*, and Alexander Pope, and my teachers would complain to my parents that I was reading the wrong kind of literature, that my "little learning" was "a dangerous thing."

6

One Christmas, around age ten, I received Johanna Spyri's *Heidi* as a well-intended gift. I had long exhausted our teensy library, including my father's collections of *Knight, Esquire,* and *Playboy* (kept in the garage), and had begun sneaking through my mother's dresser drawers to scarf on unexpurgated Henry Miller. But between my raids on the adults-only stuff, there were only the Sunday funnies (*Brenda Starr*), comic books (*Archie, Little Lulu*), and *Heidi,* reread in desperation until I could quote chunks of the text, mentally squeezing it for what I imagined to be hidden underneath. One early-spring day, my adult first-cousin Rubyline came by the house with a nourishing belated Christmas gift: an illustrated one-volume edition of *Alice's Adventures in Wonderland* and *Through the Looking-Glass.* (Later, on my twelfth birthday, she would also give me my first *Roget's,* which I still use.)

In love with poetry since kindergarten, my "uffish" vows were startlingly renewed with *Alice.* Saved, I promptly retired *Heidi* and steeped myself in *Alice* to an iambic spazz. "Jabberwocky" is one of only about a dozen poems I've ever loved enough to memorize (among the others are Poe's "Raven," Service's "Cremation of Sam McGee," Byron's "Prisoner of Chillon," Coleridge's "Rime of the Ancient Mariner," Henley's "Invictus," and E. A. Robinson's "Richard Cory").

Lewis Carroll's influence on my poetry is easily discerned. I occasionally allude to characters from *Alice* (the White Rabbit, the Cheshire Cat, and my favorite, the Red Queen), dot poems with references to his memorable lines and phrases, and have even written a poem in homage ("Black Alice Laments," in *Mercurochrome*). In one of my poetic fugues, I imagine my own mad tea party, to which I invite deceased surrealist writers and artists whom I admire ("The Ron Narrative Reconstructions," in *Bathwater Wine*).

Many have referred to Carroll's rhymes as nonsense, but in my childhood world—Los Angeles in the '50s—they made perfect sense. It was a city where up was down and down was up. Black adults were always scrounging for money, regardless of how good or how bad they were. White people laughed at things that were not funny. Distances were deceptive and maps untrustworthy. My parents were constantly getting lost and were frightened of asking the police or fireman for assistance, those same authorities White teachers said were friendly and there to protect and serve us. Smiling White adults were instantly and incomprehensibly nasty to us the moment our parents were not around. Waiters, waitresses, and drive-in car hops were hostile, always got our orders wrong, served our food cold, or made us wait until they had attended to everyone else beforehand. Store clerks refused to take our money unless we laid it flat on the counter and would not give us change unless we asked for the correct amount first. White doctors and nurses would never touch us with their bare hands, and seldom with gloves on. White ministers smiled while calling us heathens and pickaninnies. Black and Mexican children were chastised or ignored for behavior that earned White children recognition and praise. All White people lied. Nothing was what it seemed. We were free citizens, yet there were places in the city that we could not visit after sundown.

The daily upheavals in my reality made the Looking-Glass world seem not only logical but somewhere I wished I could go for vacation.

For Dad, On What Would Have Been

His 84th Birthday

An artist and advertising man, George Evans was born in Little Rock, Arkansas, in October 1914, and died in Los Angeles in February 1991. He was educated to the age of eight, then earned his own living by delivering newspapers, shining shoes, and herding cattle. He loved his mother, a minister, and his half sisters, but never knew his father. He left Arkansas as a teenager, when a young colored man there was lynched from a church steeple; he hitchhiked all the way to California. He lived with an aunt until he met and married Lewana Scott. They had four children. He was the sparring partner and longtime friend of Archie Moore, Light Heavyweight Champion of the World 1952–1962.

Just a few days ago I remembered you as you were on the night I nearly died. I felt the tension and the strength in your arms, muscles working to the heft by the rhythm of your steady walk. I have since discovered that the medical name for my "brain fever" was encephalitis.

In my memory, we were once again standing off the admissions' stall of Children's Hospital. It was October 1957. I was ten years old. Your forty-third birthday was days away, and my

9

eleventh soon after. I was sick with delusions and sweats (you know, they've never left me). I was wrapped in my favorite blue rayon blanket. You had pulled it straight off the bed in your panic. Mama had given me a sponge bath and had half-talked, half-forced me into my fresh hand-sewn white flannel jammies peppered with tiny blue and gold flowers. I was so sick I couldn't walk. You carried me through the darkness that night.

(How do I remember all of this? How could I forget? Memory is fluid, and the fever left its strange residue on my psyche.)

As I went in and out of consciousness, I listened to your voices, hear them still, you and Mama weighing our bleak circumstance. Despite the long hours and the hard work, Mama labored as a seamstress. You worked around the clock, as a janitor nights, as a sign painter days. As diligently as you obeyed the maxim of "early to bed, early to rise," you would never achieve wealth, and thirty-three years later, a brain tumor would deprive you of the remnants of your health and wisdom.

You had no money. And no medical insurance. What chance did you have to get the help I needed?

Dr. Rayfield Lewis, one of the few Negro physicians who made house calls in our neighborhood, had sent you across town, from his office to the charity hospital in Hollywood. And now I am listening through my fever to you and Mama as you argue with the cold officious blond admissions nurse. I can see her, Pop. I can see her immaculate starched white collar and uniform, her fine-knit gray-blue sweater. And I can see her helper, the auburn-haired candy striper who keeps sticking the glass thermometer in my mouth. Temperature of 104°. I can see their crisp white caps. Yet there are no angels of mercy here.

Mama doesn't know I'm awake. She thinks I'm sleeping. She cries as she begs for them to let me see a doctor. Her hushed whimpers say that I will die without emergency treatment. You stand behind her, fists rammed into your pockets.

But they don't treat poor colored children here. Not unless the referring physician has privileges. Not even for emergencies.

I am refused admission.

I can still hear the clack of Mama's thick leather heels against the linoleum as she rushes outside to bring the car around to the front. You wait with me. The security guard has been summoned to watch against potential violence. Everyone senses your rage. You are a big man, an ex-boxer, your thick honey-brown arms bulge beneath your worn brown woolen sports jacket, the one you wore home from the shop that evening, the one that makes me itch. The blanket prevents me from coming in contact with it. Once, when my cheek brushes you shoulder, I feel the bite and sting of the wool.

How the guard stares at us. I wonder what he sees. He knows you were once some kind of athlete and is impressed by your size. I can see his badge and his gun. There's the distant honking of the car. You're tired. Your shoulders slump suddenly. You take a deep long breath. And before you bend over to lift me, you look the White security guard in the eyes and say, "Be a man, be decent. My child is dying."

Your words shock him. He holds the double doors open for you. You've shamed him into cooperating. You cradle me in your arms with a grunt. I weigh a hundred pounds. I can hear the scrape of your shoe leather as you carry me outside, into the dark morning, and down the concrete stairs. I look for the moon but can't find it. The old sedan is there, Mama behind the steering wheel. She leaves the motor running, jumps out and opens the door. You lay me in the back, then take the driver's seat. County General is ten minutes away, by Mama's count. But you must be careful not to speed. We can't afford to be stopped by the police.

Your prayers for my recovery ("Jesus, help me, Father") are answered within two weeks. I receive the treatment needed, undergo the spinal taps, the electroencephalograms, the drugs. I live. And now I'm telling about it.

In some strange way, that night—our night—was the most significant of my childhood spent fighting allergies and illnesses. Yet, it is only now, some forty years later, that I've come to recognize this as fact, to examine it, to ask myself why, to grapple for the answer, which still eludes me at this writing. Save to say what

I have never said: No child on Earth could have loved its parents more than I loved mine that night.

And you?

You were magnificent, Pop. You never won the title belt, but at heart you were the truest gentleman champion I've ever known.

My Blues Love Affair

Ol' blues gonna get me
Ol' blues gonna get me high

I grew up in the Southern California of the late 1940s through '50s listening primarily to country-and-western, gospel, and popular music. My mother's relationship to my father, ethnically speaking, was ambivalent—though they both identified as colored. She did not seem to understand or care for the "race music" of the day made by Black folk, or the attendant fashions. I recall one incident where Father brought home a gift for himself, new duds in a large pretty department-store box. He folded back the tissues and lifted out a zoot suit. He even had the wide-brimmed hat and a pair of those exaggerated nines, or kicks (shoes). Mother told him in choice icy terms that she wouldn't be seen with him on the streets "in that silly getup." He closed the box and took the threads back to the store. Her ears were as critical as her eyes when it came to his record collection.

Pop sounds around our household were as diverse as Hoagy Carmichael (*Stardust*), Fats Domino (*Honey Chile*), Peggy Lee (*Mañana*), and Liberace (*September Song*). Al Jarvis's *Make Believe Ballroom* (on KFWB) was one of Mother's radio favorites.

13

Above all, my mother preferred music with a twang: Eddie Arnold, Johnny Cash, Patsy Cline, Tennessee Ernie Ford (on Cliffie Stone's *Hometown Jamboree*, featuring Molly Bee), George Jones, Tex Ritter, The Sons of the Pioneers, Conway Twitty, and Kitty Wells. Mother sang a beautiful soprano along with Patti Page on *Tennessee Waltz*, while *Jezebel* and the wild goose cried regularly through our afternoons on the lips of Frankie Laine.

When we got television in 1951, *Cavalcade of Bands*, *Perry Como*, *Name That Tune*, *It's Polka Time*, *The Frank Sinatra Show*, *The Kate Smith Evening Hour*, Arthur Murray's *Dance Party*, *Stop the Music*, Paul Whiteman's *Goodyear Review*, and *Your Hit Parade* were among the programs that brought the remnants of Tin Pan Alley (1890s to 1950s) and vaudeville (1870s to 1930s) into our living room—the variety shows too numerous to mention except for *The Grand Ole Opry*, *The Hoffman Hayride* (Spade Cooley), and *The Lawrence Welk Show*. Like much of the rest of the nation, no New Year's celebration was complete without Guy Lombardo and His Royal Canadians.

Together with art, literature, and dance, classical music was foremost in my at-home education, echoed in public-school musical appreciation classes where kids were taught to ritually worship the three Bs—Bach, Beethoven, and Brahms. (To them I added a fourth, Max Bruch.) In her efforts to transform me into the debutante I would never become, my mother spent her scrimpings on private piano, violin, and voice lessons. She prepared me for the world as she dreamed it rather than as it existed and would remain, for the working-class poor anyway: a world hostile to the notion of full and complete social parity for those trapped in (and at the bottom of) its African American subculture. In the post-WWII Southern California in which I was raised, there were no traditions, only the growth-industry consumerism that predicted we need only push a button to bring the future (free of racism?) into our homes. Underscoring (undermining?) my mother's Oklahoman colored-lady notions of high society were my father's pugilistic Arkansas pragmatism and love of a music that fascinated me in its aural contradictions. The music my father

14

loved was simple yet complex. I instinctively recognized the difference between eight and twelve notes per bar. The lyrics of Dad's favorite songs seemed unusual, particularly Southern, and used expressions not always easily deciphered by my child's ear.

It did something to you.

Even when I appreciated the double entendres, my knowledge was minus the knowing. My sojourn into the sexual was still more than a decade away. I was also intrigued by the often gender-defying qualities of the voices of various singers beyond the phenomena of Little Willie John (*Fever*), Little Jimmy Scott (*All the Way*), and Ray Charles (particularly his androgynous rendition of *I Didn't Know What Time It Was*). While I could usually tell the difference between Black and White voices, I could not readily distinguish between the male or female voice of Negro singers. This ambiguity seemed, to my ears, deliciously rich. There was something else, profound and magnificent, going on under the surface of language in its marriage to sound. And often the language of the lyric was equally ambivalent, words like "Baby" and "Honey" referring to either a male or female adult. A repressed dialogue!? I puzzled over this phenomenon throughout my childhood, spurred by the fact that my mother would not let my father's music into the house except one day of the year.

Father would frequently skirt Mother's commandment by singing loudly in the bathroom while he shaved or showered. I'm beset by the aromas of shaving cream and after-shave, along with images of him stropping his straight razor and mixing the suds with his shaving brush, whenever I hear *My Blue Heaven*, *St. Louis Blues*, or *Willow Weep for Me*. An admirer of Paul Robeson, he often sang solo at concerts on the then-glamorous stage of the auditorium at the Negro-owned Golden State Insurance Company. When egging his children out of recalcitrance, my father would warp a lyric of *Short'nin' Bread* or *Lazy Bones* . . . "sleepin' in da shade . . ." As the eldest, I was often privy to contentious moments between my parents while my siblings slept. On one such occasion I watched tearfully as Mother wielded a butcher's knife, ended when my father disarmed her in a manly fashion, without

15

a single blow struck. I'll never forget the ways father would goad or tease her with blues lyrics. His favorite for this purpose was *The Blues in the Night*.

What, I wondered, did this "nigger music" *contain* that was so dangerous that Mother did not want it in our home?

> *When ol' man blues taps my shoulder*
> *I gets up to dance (don't matter what shoes I wear).*

When Father finally got the opportunity to play his music, we were treated to Johnny Ace, Hank Ballard, T-Bone Walker, and the like. Among his favorite songs, repeatedly played, were *Baby Don't You Tear My Clothes, The Hucklebuck, I Believe I'll Dust My Broom, Rag Mop,* and *T-99.* Curiously, that solitary day on which Mother allowed him to play his music uncensored, parties excepted, was Christmas Day.

Our home had no chimney, but for years we had a fake log fireplace that nested in the hollow base of the mantelpiece. Its yellow electric bulb flickered behind a plastic façade tinted to create the illusion of flames. Nevertheless, it threw a romantic cast across our living room into which Mother enjoyed snuggling on the couch, in father's arms, before our glittering Christmas tree, as Bing Crosby crooned "I'm dreaming of a white Christmas, just like the ones I used to know," or Nat "King" Cole lilted "Chestnuts roasting on an open fire, Jack Frost nipping at your nose." But Charles Brown's *Merry Christmas, Baby*—"May Christmas bring you happiness"—was Father's blues noël of choice.

Mother's censorship piqued my curiosity to such an extent that Christmas became as memorable for the opportunity it afforded me to hear Dad's race music—boogie-woogie, jazz, and bebop, but especially the blues—as for anything else. Our Christmas Day pleasures included the opening of gifts and the fact that we children were allowed to eat as much of anything we wanted, any hour of that day. But watching the pleasure on my father's face as he cleaned then mounted a stack of 78- or 33⅓-RPM black vinyl disks on the console turntable, was the true meaning of "a joyful noise." (Later, I would wear the grooves off his copies of *Flamingo*, Herb Jeffries' signature song à la Ellington, 1941, and Roy Hamilton's *Unchained Melody*, 1954.) It was a double joy when Father broke through Mother's resistance, grabbed her arm, and showed us the dances of their youth and courtship.

When it came to jazz, Mother enjoyed Dixieland via radio, and never hesitated to pop her fingers to the big swinging '40s band sounds of Jimmy and Tommy Dorsey, Benny Goodman, and Glenn Miller. At the colored-folk end-of-the-war-years spectrum were Louis "Satchmo" Armstrong ("my only sin the skin I'm in," à la Andy Razaf's *Black and Blue*), Cab Calloway (*Minnie the Moocher*), Duke Ellington (*Prelude to a Kiss*), and Ella Fitzgerald (*A-Tisket, A-Tasket*). Unfortunately, hearing these songs today usually evokes the onerous racist atmosphere of the times in which they were recorded. To this day, Armstrong's voice instantly brings back memories of Black adults afraid to voice their anger and indignation over their shabby lots in life, even in their own living rooms.

By the mid '50s we were watching the Nat "King" Cole and Dinah Shore shows regularly (the unfounded rumor that Shore was passing for White sparked speculation in our household too). But Mother did not like Billie Holiday. At one time Holiday was played so often on local radio broadcasts that Mother actually complained. I recall one instance when she turned the dial from one station to pick up another, and both were airing the same Holiday song as I listened, ear-stung in the back seat, hanging on to every incredibly haunting note. The other Negro musicians and singers who appeared on our radios and TV made a shortlist prestigious for the era: Marian Anderson, Harry Belafonte, Sammy Davis Jr., Erroll Garner, Earl "Fatha" Hines, Eartha Kitt, Mahalia Jackson, Sarah Vaughan (in her days as an aspiring journalist, Mother interviewed Vaughan), and the groups the Inkspots and the Mills Brothers. Later, Ray Charles, Jackie Gleason, and Mitch Miller. While the whole family watched *The Johnny Otis Show* ("doin' that crazy hand jive") on Channel 13, I had pop-culture shows like Bill Horn's *Bandstand* (soon to become

17

Dick Clark's *American Bandstand*) to myself after school or while finishing homework. As puberty deepened, the new musics took hold of my attention, hawked by regional DJs like Chuck "quiver mah liver" Dyer (victim of the payola scandal), Hunter Hancock (kingpin of the beauty parlors), Magnificent Montague (popular-izer of the ghetto phrase "burn, baby, burn," a reference to the hor-izontal dance "the alligator crawl," which often gave young Black men rug burns), Tom "Master Blaster" Reed (still on local cable TV with *For Members Only*), and the legendary croak-throated Wolfman Jack. I was among the thousands watching *The Big Beat* when Frankie Lyman stepped down from the stage in 1957 and took the hand of a young White teen queen, in a move that would knock rock impresario Alan Freed off ABC-TV and into alcoholism.

My grasp on racism in the entertainment world was a mere child's grasp, yet I wondered what my parents thought of the absence of Our People on these programs. Rarely did they com-plain, expressing gratitude and relief whenever "one of us" appeared. I usually felt embarrassed and angry at things I sensed but could not lend words to. My two brothers and baby sister seemed too young to notice. But thanks to Christmas, I was beginning to regard certain kinds of music as tepid if not tortur-ous. Mother tried but could not keep out the world. On outings, she was unable to control what was accessible. The airways of Black Los Angeles left the country-and-western, border-Mexican, and gospel sounds she preferred out of range. Not to mention the afterschool sock-hops or dances staged for teenagers where the 45s were spun over the PA system. Transistor radios were intro-duced in 1959 and within a few years all the well-heeled teens were carrying the portables to and from school, annoying bus drivers and teachers alike.

(In my junior-high-school days, young ladies—a.k.a. bobby-soxers—were not yet allowed to wear nylons except for special events. The bobbysox fad was a holdover from the '40s when swooning over crooners was epidemic and the traditional Oxfords were in the process of displacement by plimsolls or sneakers. At the height of our local sock-hop era, two-toned socks—that is, differing pairs of socks cuffed to show two colors—were as big a fad as switchblades, tattoos, gang insignias, and smoking in the bathroom. The rebels wore nylons under their bobbysox.)

Rhythm and blues, rock 'n' roll, and the street-corner serenades of doo-wop (that splendid harmonic answer to barbershop-quartet a cappella) were soon dominating my listening hours, supplemented by the classical and popular tunes Mother allowed at home.

> *When ol' man blues taps me, darlin',*
> *I hit the floor (smelly bare feet will do).*

In the mid-to-late '60s, long gone from home, I would trail my first husband, an itinerant folksinger and civil rights worker, through the coffeehouses and music dens of Hollywood and Echo Park. Jazz, rhythm and blues (soul), and rock 'n' roll (psychedelic soul) were my musics of choice; nevertheless, he would introduce me to the world of folk and blues musicians, from Woody Guthrie and Hank Williams to Robert Johnson and Son House. I would learn the difference between playing with a pick, a slide, and fingernails —more about the dialogue that took place between the words, and the workings of the music. Ed Pearl's Ash Grove, a club on Melrose Avenue in Hollywood, would be our main stomping ground. There I would witness the artistry of blues and folk men from Gatemouth Brown to John Lee Hooker, Lightnin' Hopkins to Pete Seeger and Josh White. I even saw the Ash Grove debut of Taj Mahal (and still have the LP). At another venue, we witnessed the dramatic reunion of Sonny Terry and Brownie McGhee, which brought everyone in the crowded room to their feet.

In 1969, I was reintroduced to Ma Rainey and Bessie Smith by a songwriter-musician friend. She also reminded me of how great Billie Holiday remained, whether singing jazz or blues, nearly a decade after death. Through her, I would rediscover the indisputable power of a cappella, hosted one night by Jimmy Witherspoon at Howard Rumsey's club, the Lighthouse, in Hermosa

Beach. There I would witness the single most electrifying performance—of any kind outside the call to worship—I ever expect
to see as the Persuasions proceeded to literally rock the rafters.
Five Black men jumped up on the wooden tables and stomped. I
sat wide-eyed and gasping throughout the entire splendid spectacle. What I felt for them was as powerful as it was nameless. I
wondered at my luck that my friend had opened for them, as the
only act in town unafraid of the group's monstrous performance
style, and that I was her transportation for the night. I didn't even
drink wine in those days, but I was so sound-drunk afterwards it
was all I could do to drive her home safely, then get home alone,
to tremble for hours as I relived their greatness. The recording
device has not been invented that could capture what those five
men gave to an audience.

Certainly, while the new blues was rooted in the going contemporary residuals of Slavery, it was, like jazz, finding mainstream acceptance as an original American art form. Others were
adopting it, and I listened, intrigued by what those who did not
necessarily identify as Black, did to our form. How the blues
moved through the Allman Brothers Band, Big Brother & the
Holding Company (Janis Joplin), Cream, the Rolling Stones, Ste-
vie Ray Vaughn, and Led Zeppelin fascinated me. Acculturation
on all sides of the racial/cultural divides was, I noted, an
inevitable part of the blues tradition and—because of the constraints of the fad-driven music business—necessary for its survival. The blues was essentially Black, however. It stained
anything it touched.

The Jimi Hendrix Experience claimed a musical realm of its
own, it seemed to me, and its psychedelic blues-rock found a special chamber in my listening heart. (A blue on black velvet portrait
of Jimi graces my office wall; I visited his grave the fall of Y2K.)

In the '70s, divorced and on my own, I danced at the discos,
dug on Black Sabbath, David Bowie, and Alice Cooper; I interviewed Bob Marley (*Catch a Fire*) on three occasions, and made
the St. Patrick's Day Riots at Elks Hall when New Wave stormed
Los Angeles—the Plugz, Go-Gos, and X on stage; yet, I began

wearing the grooves off my Bobby "Blue" Bland, Taj Mahal, and Otis Redding LPs. On the jazz-hand side, I was a devotee of Herbie Hancock (*Hornets*), thrice catching him crosstown at Doug Weston's Troubadour. I was also rediscovering the merits of Little Esther (Phillips) and Nina Simone alongside Mingus and Monk. While listening, I am able to visualize fingering, particularly piano and guitar, instruments I've studied. Monk's keyboard style would eventually influence my poetic style once a critic pointed out to me that I was writing jazz poetry. (I would eventually discuss Monk's influence in two essays, "On Theloniousism," in *Caliban*, 1988, and "Avant-Garde with Mainstream Tendencies," in *Tripwire* 5, 2001.)

Nevertheless, when it came to private pleasures, the blues held its spot. Several live performances by Etta James in the better clubs across town would make me a forever fan. Yet, it is the unmitigated funk and grit of those ghetto nightspots that still makes my heart pound. That period of my nightlife would be highlighted by the Ike & Tina Turner Revue (featuring the Ikettes) at the California Club; I caught their dazzling act up-close twice. The Hide-Away, Jefty's, the Sportsman's Lounge (particularly open mike on Blue Mondays), the Parisian Room, and Memory Lane were among my haunts. Ironing Board Sam, Swamp Dogg (Little Jerry Williams), Big Mama Thornton, and Big Joe Turner were likewise becoming permanent parts of my (musical) vocabulary.

By the '80s a number of Black women writers emerged who laid claim to Holiday's heady influence (such as Alexis DeVeaux, *Don't Explain*). I was doing likewise; but in recent years, upon looking back, I've come to acknowledge that, thanks to Mother, Patsy Cline is as much a part of my vocabulary as Lady Day. However, after catching Betty Carter twice at the Vine St. Bar & Grill in 1980s Hollywood, I determined that this incredibly gifted improvisator, like Monk, is much more my aesthetic kindred.

Roots *à la symphonie* had become the issue.

> *Come on out here with me, lover. Let's*
> *make romance (do that hoochie-coo)...*

As much as the rhythm and blues enjoyed by my friends and schoolmates, the rock 'n' roll of the '50s was a music rooted in the culture of Americans of Slave Origin. I found my evidence for this in the traditional place, the Negro church. Throughout childhood and into my teens, our family attended the African Methodist Episcopal churches my mother preferred, and often I sang in the youth choirs; but I was repeatedly shocked whenever we attended the Baptist churches my father favored, overwhelmed by the differences in how the music of worship was presented, often the same hymns with radically altered lyrics and arrangements. The third Sunday, during the call to worship, that ritualized form of mass hypnosis was particularly memorable, the minister and choir at its core. The trauma I experienced, centered in the stomach and lower intestinal tract, was akin to the blistering shock and confusion felt when watching James Brown's debut appearance on *The Ed Sullivan Show* (*Please, Please, Please*, in the early '60s). I was disturbed by all of that—a disturbance compounded when I asked Mother why people like the Baptists behaved as Brown did. "Because they are happy," came her answer, which puzzled me.

Happy?

Father's explanations of "speaking in tongues," "being touched," and "feeling The Spirit" were significantly better. Once my stomach settled, I decided that when it came to musical expression, I preferred the Baptists' way. (The Holy Rollers', too, tambourines included. What impressed me most about the music was its undeniable power to move.) But I dwelled on Mother's one-word expression for this phenomenon, eventually discovering others used that word as well. (Might it be akin to the bliss of Zen? I later wondered.) Within my limited knowledge and exposure, White entertainers of the period, with the exceptions of Johnnie Ray and Elvis Presley, simply did not behave in that manner, nor did those within my sphere of observation. The 1960 film *Elmer Gantry* would suggest otherwise, but I was still nearly a decade away from attending my first Pentecostal revival meeting —in a tent.

22

On weekend afternoons, while we listened to the radio as we did chores or played board games, there aired for too brief a period this magical vocal jazz composition that blitzed my nine-year-old ears, making me instantly happy, in the usual sense of the word. Enthralled, I could never grasp enough of its lyrics to fathom its title no matter how hard I listened. Perhaps it was being played too softly, I thought. My parents objected to loud music unless a party was in progress. Mother said turning up the volume wouldn't help me because they were singing in French and she couldn't understand it either. I would become an adult before I rediscovered *Lullaby of Birdland*, by George David Weiss, sung by the Blue Stars of France, 1955.

For a number of years, my father worked as a janitor for RCA Victor records (RCA developed the 45 in 1951), bringing home returns or the undistributed boxes of 78s, 33s, and 45s discarded by management, allowing us to have our pick of whatever we liked. One of my lucky picks was "Mambo King" Perez Prado's 45 of *Cherry Pink and Apple Blossom White* (1955). As the oldest of four children, left in charge whenever my parents were out of the house, I began going through Father's record collection, playing my favorites over and over to my ears' content. This was doubly forbidden, because my father, too, objected to his children playing his 78s, should we scratch, crack, chip, or break the heavy yet delicate disks. Eventually, Mother raised her restrictions and permitted Father to play his records any time he pleased, if he could get past me to get to the hi-fi. My hunger for the Black in music was insatiable. Circa 1960, Father would take me across town to purchase my first 45 singles, *Harlem Nocturne* by the Viscounts and Barrett Strong's *Money (That's What I Want)*. Mother would soon buy me a portable record player to keep the peace.

Over time, with close observation and careful listening, drawing on my musical training, I began to patch together my version of a blues aesthetic, stitching what I had garnered into some semblance of understanding, with added bits and pieces from the friends and mentors to come, and from authors read. At the root of all of this cultural quilting, I surmised, lay the blues, which, like ragtime, was a fusion of the slave musics brought from Africa and the folk music of indentured Scotch-Irish servants. It had emerged after the end of the post–Civil War Reconstruction period before World War I, in the years between 1877 and 1910, and fused with the field hollers, spirituals, and work songs as it evolved.

> *Ol' man blues comin' ta get me,*
> *Gonna take me way up high*

In my mother's refusal to allow my father to play his music in our home, she was, in effect, keeping out of those "dirty low-down" places in Black culture, those that the White world defined (and was largely culpable for). In this music, natural rhythm was wedded to a forbidden and mythified sexuality, and to the notorious streets. Mother was, in her way, being a good Christian (like the reverend father in the movie *St. Louis Blues*, in which Nat "King" Cole plays W. C. Handy), keeping the music of the cotton fields, gin mills, bawdy houses, gut buckets, and various dives of iniquity away from her children.

Around fall of 1989, as one of my husband's poetry students left Los Angeles to return east, he left me a tape of blues songs featuring Otis Rush (*Right Place, Wrong Time*) and Larry Smith (*Funny Stuff*). I played that tape until its ruination by a faulty tape deck. Months later, on one of my first trips to Illinois, I chanced to catch Otis Rush during the Chicago Blues Festival. The remarkable thing about that night was that there were more African Americans on stage than were seated in the packed house. I was, uncomfortably, one of two. The blues, I was reminded, had long crossed over.

In today's Black urban subculture, few young people seem to care about the blues, if they are informed about it at all. It remains associated with the roots of racism, the rural (plantation), and the impoverished. On the flip side, jazz is considered demanding and elitist. The signifyings of Oscar Brown Jr. and Gil Scott-Heron, the scattings of King Pleasure, the autocratic hipness of Lord Buckley, the jazzifications of Jack Kerouac and Ken Nordine, the rhythm-rap of the Last Poets and the Watts Prophets, to name the few, have merged and caught fire as hiphop (diminutive of hippity-hoppity) and as rap in all its incarnations, especially the gangster rap inspired by the toasts of "mackdaddy" Robert Beck (a.k.a. Iceberg Slim) and his hustler's novel tour de force, *Pimp*, a cultural dynamic that would bring forth the Sugar Hill Gang in 1977 and Grandmaster Flash & the Furious Five in the '80s— and eventually spawn such rhythm-rap extremes as Cameo (*Word Up*, 1996) and Niggaz With Attitude (NWA, *Straight Outta Compton*, 1988).

Yet, the blues persists despite fad and fashion.

Music folklorist Alan Lomax once described Negro music as having the greens, the reds, and the yellows as well as the blues, each color having a specific social context, lost to me as of this writing. However, it's my contention that those other kinds of Negro folk song have been recast or transmogrified into vaudeville/ musical theatre, like the cakewalks and minstrel shows, or else they have been absorbed into their sibling, the blues. Granted, during Slavery, as is now known, there were freed men and women, an infinitesimal landed Black gentry, and Blacks who, as some say, "came over on the Mayflower." However, encapsulated in our blues is the path walked by that majority of us who were denigrated by involuntary servitude in America's past. Our blues also contains the bigger mechanism designed to set off the resulting bitternesses, hurts, rages, and sadnesses that must be suppressed by the individual in order to ensure collective day-to-day survival. Thus, the inherent danger of intraracial violence (or, rarer, violence outside the barrier of race) is the organic consequence of the oft ill-examined residuals of Slavery still manifest in present-day American society.

Them blues were also fight songs.

In this new millennium, my love affair with music continues— at this stage, oldies, retro, jazz (acid jazz), and new music. Also, listening to music remains a family affair. My son has become an authority on rock from the '70s forward, my daughter is a Golden

Oldies maven, and I often enjoy discussing the merits of one classical composer over another with my husband of twenty-odd years. But when it comes to rhythm and blues, I'm usually on my own.

When I'm feeling down in those dumps, instead of seeking the head shrinker's couch or pharmaceuticals, I hit the stereo to get my music fix. There's an unobtrusive pasteboard box kept atop one bookshelf in the master bedroom where the scratchy 45s sleep. I recently purchased a teenager's old record player for three dollars at a yard sale, exclusively for those precious excursions into my youth. I might warm up with Muddy Waters' *Still a Fool*, or Funkadelic's equally turgid *Qualify & Satisfy*. Freddie King's *Going Down* or Fugi's *Mary Don't Take Me on No Bad Trip* will get into my hips. O. V. Wright's *Love the Way You Love* or Dyke and the Blazers' *Let a Woman Be a Woman—Let a Man Be a Man* usually brings on my feet. By the time I get to Syl Johnson's *I Only Have Love* and the Watts 103rd Street Band's *Your Love (Means Everything to Me)*, I'm full tilt in good motion and mood. Should I be in a dreamy, nostalgic state, I'm more apt to groove to Chairmen of the Board's *Try on My Love for Size*, Gene Chandler's *Rainbow*, the Delphonics' *Tell Me This Is a Dream*, Sam Russell's *Play It by Ear*, or the Soul Generation's cover of *Tell Me This Is a Dream*. By the end of each musical journey I'm myself again and feel like dealing with the world.

Or—while working about the house, doing chores, I'm apt to turn off the digital stuff, dust off the turntable, and start spinning those old LPs, from Bootsy to Grover Washington. Between long spells at the computer I often jump up from the monitor, run into the playroom, and dance the Duck, Four Corners, or Pony to the likes of James Brown (*Baby Don't You Weep*), Al Green (*Drivin' Wheel*), and Curtis Mayfield (*Ain't Got Time*), or cry to Smokey Robinson & the Miracles (*When Sundown Comes*) or Otis Redding (*These Arms of Mine*). Without fail, whatever ails me passes almost instantly. It may not be what most call happiness, but it probably is as close as I will ever come.

When that ol' blues come to get you
Ya bettah bolt the door 'n' run . . .
When ol' man blues come to get you
Ya bettah bolt that door 'n' join the fun
When ol' blues done gone and got you
Your soul be singing sun to sun

Love-Ins with Nietzsche

There are preachers of death: and the earth is full of those to whom desistance from life must be preached.
—Nietzsche

"I hung with Charles Manson—for a niggah minute."

Chuck stares at me with disbelief.

I'm behind the wheel of his red hardtop 1965 Mustang. It is Saturday night, December 13, 1969. We're tearing down the road toward home after a rowdy weekend's fun up Fresno way. Minutes before, hitting the rise that marks our descent into the Los Angeles basin, we had caught a late-evening radio newscast. Charles Manson, the notorious cult leader, had been arrested. Chuck and I shared a déjà vu. We had also been on the road the night of August 10 when it was announced that the authorities were stopping and arresting anything Black in their search for perpetrators of the bizarre killings soon to become infamous as the Tate-LaBianca murders.

That was unsettling enough. We had never heard tell of any of our people committing a mass killing in recent history, and certainly not in such ritzy parts of town as the Hollywood Hills and Los Feliz. ("Naw, naw—that cain't be it!" Chuck protested. "That's

28

not Black folks' style.") Besides, gauging by our experience, it was nearly impossible for a Black man or woman, even domestics and servicemen, to enter such areas without being stopped and questioned, if not frisked, by the notoriously overzealous officers of the Los Angeles Police Department, who religiously rousted people of color—guilty and innocent alike.

That was four months ago. Now Chuck says "Is this dude White or Black?"

"Manson? He's White. And he's a *shrimp*!" I cry. "That's *got* to be a mistake."

Chuck drops his jaw pockmarked with razor bumps and Jinn-eyes me sideways, wide high forehead collecting sweat under his stingy brim. "Honey bunch, you didn't have anything to do with killin' those people, did you?"

"Uh—I—uh—well, no. Nothing like that."

I remember well enough, but am not quite certain how to relate the story to my new "Loosiana" macho boyfriend. Chuck does not consider himself a bigot, yet largely hates and fears Whites. He clowns and smiles in their faces, then curses them when their backs are turned. Unlike Chuck, I was raised in Southern California and consider myself every bit the fearless equal of anyone. In our explorations of one another, I've made it clear to my lover that I am eager to succeed as a writer. But there is nothing I can do in the White world that makes a dent in Chuck's blue-collar thickheadedness. "He's the kind of man you want on your side in a fight," one friend said, "a true member of the lumpen." All it took to make Chuck happy was a fifth of V.O., a late-model GM, and hot poontang.

Throughout the rest of our trip toward our ghetto digs, I curtail my impulse to speed to the rhythm and blues. Instead, I drive to the posted limit, ears on the radio, hoping for updates. It's difficult to envision Charles Manson as the evil mastermind of anything.

"My husband and me—we hung out with the dude, a year or so back." This casual summary easily defuses any issue of involvement with rabid hippies. As long as it means we won't be arrested, Chuck doesn't care.

Nor has Chuck, the auto mechanic and detailer, any use for the budding intellectual I think I am. Feminism is silly. I am "a babymaker"—an about-to-be-single mother of two. He wants to make it three. He humors my ambitions as poet and playwright and dismisses my Black militancy. He regards my desire to complete my education as foolhardy. Chuck is quick to disdain any middle-class pretension he suspects I harbor. He also lets me know that he has nothing but contempt for my five-year marriage to a White man.

> *In the world even the best things are worthless without those who represent them: those representers, the people call great men.* —Nietzsche

Charlie Coleman was not only White but a Southerner, and wore the Stars and Bars tattooed on one forearm. He often jokingly described himself as a "peckerwood"—a nasty expression for White southerners I had seldom heard. He also called himself a redneck and a Georgia cracker and did so with cavalier daring. He fancied himself a "troubadour" at a time when TV's *Route 66* had inspired a new generation of vagabonds (another word he called himself). Youths were traveling the country, going from happening to happening, experiencing America with empty pockets and guitars or cameras slung across their backs. He played the mouth harp or harmonica, the acoustic and twelve-string guitars, and carried a banjo. He never missed the opportunity to lead the group-sing on *Oh Freedom, If You Miss Me from the Back of the Bus*, and *Kumbaya*. He idolized Woody Guthrie, Hank Williams, Pete Seeger, and Phil Ochs (we would meet Ochs at a MacArthur Park love-in). He also idolized many Black musicians, particularly Josh White, John Lee Hooker, and Richie Havens. He could groove with any sound from Memphis to Chicago to Texarkana. He believed Robert Johnson had sold his soul to the Devil, and he would have sold his too if it meant he could play like that. (Left-handed, a "southpaw," he played his instruments "upside down.") A pacifist and teetotaler, his favorite pastime was arguing politics and religion. He disdained drugs except the occasional toke around the campfire—the metaphorical "passing of the peace pipe."

On the day we met, Charlie was carrying a banjo slung across one shoulder and a biography of Marcus Garvey. The folksinger and factotum claimed status as one of the original Freedom Riders —cum civil rights worker—and had "fled a good lynching" in the company of Andrew Goodman, Michael Schwerner, and James Chaney. (I still remember the hunted look in his eyes when he described being chased by the Ku Klux Klan. We were in bed together when the phone rang and he was told of their deaths. He was grief-stricken.) He had befriended the journalist Viola Liuzzo just before she was slain. He had been one of the few Whites in Martin Luther King's inner circle, trusted enough by Martin and Coretta to babysit their children. When he came to Los Angeles in 1964, he traveled in the company of Vernon Jordan, Stokely Carmichael, and Jesse Jackson—then troubleshooters for SNCC (Student Nonviolent Coordinating Committee). The president of the local chapter of the Friends of SNCC owned the beauty shop where my mother went, and occasionally pressed my hair.

One evening, Mother returned from the Fifty-fourth Street parlor in a rare state of excitement. She had done a special shop for supper. As we put groceries away, she told us about the civil rights workers, and how thrilling it was to meet such adventuresome young men. She liked them all. She had been particularly charmed by the only White member of the quartet—a spunky folksinger "with lots of personality." She had been tickled by his attempt to pass as Black, or high-yellow, and was impressed by the fact that he had almost convinced her. When she laughed at his lie about his racial origins, he caved in and confessed his secrets: he was on the lam, with warrants for his arrest in two states related to various movement activities—the marches, hunger strikes, and sit-ins. He had been jailed, beaten (with a bad back as the result), jolted by cattle prods, and bitten by police dogs. He was from a poor family and didn't own a thing except a lamb's wool cap (after his hero, Malcolm X), a seaman's coat, the boots on his feet, and the belongings in his duffel bag—the banjo and a six-string guitar. Then Mama announced that she had invited him over to earn a few dollars mowing our lawn, and to join us for supper. After that evening, Charlie began to court me, as he called it. By late fall, we had married.

> *Bitterness is in the cup even of the best love; thus doth it cause longing . . . thus doth it cause thirst in thee, the creating one.* —Nietzsche

Fancying ourselves activists, we plunged into the political and cultural fray of the mid to late '60s. We straddled two youth sub-cultures—one White, the other Black. We were denizens of the coffeehouse scene—the Scorpio Rising, the Bridge, the Ash Grove, the Queen Jane—the twenty-two-year-old folksinger lugging his instruments and pregnant eighteen-year-old wife across town. Whenever he got up courage, and was given the nod, he'd sit in with the likes of Taj Mahal and play the end of a set. Charlie always went over well. He had a pronounced lisp, but it didn't stop his winning over a crowd. We partied incessantly, around the clock on weekends, sometimes on our own, sometimes by the grace of friends. Charlie was a gifted charmer, a natural con. People liked him. He had a knack for going straight to the top of an organization. In his compulsive drive to assist the Lord in creating a perfect world, we cruised L.A.'s underground, group to group, event to event.

On the White-hand-side of life, we crashed concerts when tickets were unaffordable. We partied at extremes: with The Mothers of Invention, at the homes of artist Steven Oshatz and actor Will Geer, once stomping the floor of actor Eddie (*Green Acres*) Albert's digs twelve hours straight. We chatted with Ornette Coleman (in L.A. while negotiating a festival date), danced on stage with Janis Joplin and Time, and double dated with Jayne Cortez and jazz pianist Horace Tapscott. We made the Topanga Canyon scenes with local personalities like Captain Hershey Bar and General Wastemoreland. We frequented the raves held in politico Levi Kingston's low-ceilinged attic in an old corner office building, near L.A. City College. As the '60s boomed, headshops and counterculture hangs sprang up along Melrose Avenue, Sunset and Hollywood Boulevards, up and down side streets like Hoover, site of the new Haymarket. The heart of the scene throbbed in trendy Echo Park, Silver Lake, and the Mount Washington area. Blighted neighborhoods on "the other end" of Hollywood were prospering. We attempted to move into Echo Park, but no one would rent to the White Southerner and his Black wife.

We lived near South Park—the only mixed couple in our part of the ghetto. To avoid conflicts, Charlie began to pass as a Negro. Unlike the troubled John Griffin of *Black Like Me*, who risked death from cancer by taking a drug that blackened his skin, Charlie didn't have to do much beyond being himself. As a Georgian, he loved soul food. I had never heard of it. (My mother had been a domestic in the homes of wealthy Whites—including the Doheny mansion of Ronald Reagan and Jane Wyman—and insisted we were good enough to eat what they ate. Mom's specialty was "cheese pudding," or macaroni and cheese, a legendary dish at family gatherings; Reagan, who often consumed a whole casserole dish of it, loved it more than anything else "Lewana" made. The secret to this simple recipe—basically a custard of cheese, butter, *al dente* elbow macaroni, eggs, evaporated milk, and salt to taste—was two to two-and-a-half pounds of grated Tillamook medium cheddar. [*Preheat oven to 325°. Butter bottom and sides of casserole dish. Sprinkle layer of grated cheese on bottom of dish, then add layer of macaroni; continue alternating layers of cheese and macaroni, ending with cheese layer. Pour mixture of eggs, milk, and salt over cheese and macaroni and top with pats of soft butter. Bake till custard is set and top is golden brown.*] This, too, was my groom's favorite of those recipes I brought from home, but to adjust our diet to suit his cravings, Charlie taught me how to cook grits and make hoe cakes, and in lieu of peanut butter and jelly, insisted on peanut butter and banana sandwiches with mayonnaise.)

No matter how hard Charlie worked, his salary as a common laborer, janitor, or handyman barely supported us. When extra money came in, what wasn't spent on a new instrument, or re-stringing an old one, was splurged on a night out in one of the better parts of Los Angeles.

One evening, while Charlie and I negotiated the extremely rare luxury of steak dinners at an upscale restaurant, a tall well-dressed Black man in his forties, pimped out in a fur-trimmed leather jacket, crossed the room and my line of vision at a lope. As he passed our table he glanced at Charlie, went bug-eyed, dropped his jaw, dug in his heels, and skidded to a stop. He switched around and came back to our table. With a shriek that startled the other diners, he declaimed, "*Mannnnn*, do you know Who-in-Hell you *look* like?"

Charlie blanched, gulped, and knife and fork in hands, braced his wrists against the table. Reluctantly he looked up and nodded.

"Goddamn, Sucka! You're a dead ringer for Lee Harvey Oswald!"

"Yeah. So it's been said before."

The man squinted with suspicion and anger, breathed heavily, and removed his black leather gloves as if priming for a fight. "Are you sure you ain't The Real Him?"

"Oswald was killed by Jack Ruby before millions of people on television. So I couldn't be him, now could I?"

"Maybe that wasn't Oswald that they assassinated on TV. Maybe *that* was all to fool John Q. Public. You *know* how it is with all that Spy-versus-Spy shit. And Oswald *was* a spy!"

Charlie kept his gaze steady. "No, I'm not Oswald."

"Well *who* are you? Can you prove it?"

The whole room was listening. We had already sustained sufficient stares from the fact that we were a mixed couple, but this was turning ugly. The man grabbed an empty chair from an adjacent table, turned its backside to our table and straddled it. "Well go ahead, Sucka. Prove it—to ME!"

"I don't have to prove anything." Charlie braced, knife and fork still in hand. "To you or anybody else."

"Please, Sir—be a *gentleman*," the beefy headwaiter intervened, laying a heavy hand on the man's shoulder. "You're disturbing

34

our other customers." He rose reluctantly as the waiter returned the chair to its place with one hand and ushered him off with the other. We sat quietly as the diners retracted their stares. Charlie was revolted and nauseated, eyes on his plate.

"Please accept our apologies, Sir." The waiter returned, leaned over Charlie, and spoke softly. "The gentleman is extremely *high*. Please go on with your meal," he said and sped away.

"High? What does that mean?" It was the first time I had heard the expression.

"That guy was drunk or on dope."

Still a teetotaler at nineteen, I could not tolerate wine, had never smoked anything except one disgusting menthol cigarette, and could not appreciate or understand the man's paranoid behavior.

"Never mind, Wifey-Wifey. I'll explain later."

It would be the first of many similar incidents to come. Charlie's admiration for John Fitzgerald and Robert F. Kennedy was surpassed only by his love for Martin Luther King Jr., Mahatma Gandhi, and Jesus Christ. To be mistaken for JFK's assassin simultaneously demoralized and enraged him to tears. While I did not share my husband's feelings for JFK (because of his soft position on the racial issues of the day), I empathized with him. Charlie went back to staring at his plate. Unable to continue eating, he asked the headwaiter for a doggie bag and we ended our evening.

Toward the end of May 1968, just days after his twenty-sixth birthday, Charlie and I and our toddlers (fourteen-month-old Luanda and thirty-four-month-old Anthony), together with my high-school classmate Kenneth Postel, drove into town, parked our car, and made the hike up Vermont Avenue into the Greek Theatre at Griffith Park. Pushing a stroller, carrying a diaper bag and a picnic basket, we were among the hundreds to attend the preprimary political rally for presidential candidate Robert F. Kennedy, who was scheduled to appear. We baked under the sun for nearly an hour before the doors opened and the excited crowd surged forward. We could not afford tickets, but Charlie was confident that he could talk the box-office manager into freebies.

He was expert at using his charm and gab to get into places where others could not follow. We had crashed dozens of private parties, rallies, and rock concerts, often finding ourselves backstage as if we, too, were VIPs. But on this occasion, his hustle was useless. Even the ploy of a sweat-soaked baby in the papoose cradleboard on his back failed to elicit sympathy from armed-and-alert security. MLK had been assassinated that April.

Discouraged, we wilted in the marginal shade of saplings, on the grassy oval island outside the box office, among three-hundred like stragglers, television camera crews, newshounds, and paparazzi awaiting RFK's motorcade. Charlie schemed, and when it clicked in, he snapped his fingers and grabbed my shoulders.

"It's up to you, Wanda. If you don't mind waitin' for us here, Kenny and I can scale the wall. I know I can get us behind stage. I know it isn't fair to leave you standing out here with the kids, for however long it will take, but we'll be back as soon as we introduce ourselves to Robert." He was already calling the man by his first name. Postel was giving me his you-goddamned-right look. I agreed, not wanting to make the trek downhill to the old black Dodge coupe alone. Postel held Luanda while Charlie helped me into the cradleboard. Miffed, I watched as they scampered across the wide lane and, aided by viny overgrowth and a willing volunteer, they allez-ooped the high wall, unnoticed by the guards and agents. Then I stood there fuming, Luanda on my back, Anthony napping in the stroller, awkwardly reading snatches from Will and Ariel Durant's *Story of Philosophy*.

Within ten minutes, a motorcade rolled onto the grounds. A cheer peppered by screams broke skyward. I watched in mild consternation as the crowd ran a quarter of a mile toward the chauffeur-driven convertible in which RFK stood, trailed by suit-heavy vehicles and mobile broadcast units. By the time the throng reached the motorcade, it was moving too rapidly to slow and overshot the sea of waving arms, microphones, and autograph books.

In seconds, the motorcade rounded the outside lane of the oval and stopped before me. My hair was half-hidden plantation-style under a scarf, and I had yet to shed the weight I had gained with my last pregnancy. I looked as if I had just stepped away from the kitchen stove, out of the nursery, or off a pancake box. Embarrassed, I laid my book on the diaper bag, and stared at the pale, exhausted R F K. A male staffer clutched each armpit, his right arm cradled on a cloth-covered wooden brace, sun- and clasp-reddened hand extended for the onslaught of well-wishers. I stood staring into R F K's flushed, pasty-white face, the strain visible beneath his fixed welcoming smile, eyes so deeply shadowed and sad they looked more charcoal than blue.

"For God's sake, shake his hand."

I stepped forward and did as commanded in a blaze of flashing camera lights, not knowing who spoke. The hand of Robert F. Kennedy felt clammy and pulpy. When I stepped back, the motorcade pulled curbside, and R F K was escorted inside, surrounded by agents, security, and the press corps. Seconds later, the throng of spectators caught up and, disappointed, quickly dispersed. I was briefly besieged with questions from several onlookers.

My few seconds of fame sustained me in a glow until a disgruntled Charlie and a red-faced Postel reappeared. They complained that though they'd made it backstage, they could not get to R F K and were tackled by security and thrown out by the scruffs. With delicious spite, I described what had just happened to me. They were this close to calling me a liar when a platinum-haired man ran over, grabbed my hand, and shook it vigorously. "I want to shake the hand that shook the hand of Senator Robert Francis, next President of these United States," he said, and then ran off—leaving Charlie and Kenny speechless.

Determined to meet R F K, Charlie canvassed the local politicos, looking to score an invitation to the June 5, 1968, victory gala at the Ambassador Hotel, celebrating R F K's anticipated win in the California primary. He also attempted to hire on as kitchen staff, but backed off, fearing any background check would turn up his warrants. That night, I stayed home while Charlie drove down to the Ambassador with friends in a final effort to crash the event. He woke me from sleep at three the next morning with the news that RFK had been shot. We would spend the next two days in bed in front of the TV set watching newscasts of the tragedy and the burial between retrospectives on the assassinations of JFK and MLK. This time, Charlie was grateful that he bore no resemblance to Sirhan Sirhan. Passing for Black was one thing, being mistaken for a Palestinian Arab or for Oswald was another.

Charlie's complexion was sallow, and his naturally curly hair was frizzy up top where it had begun to thin. He knew all the handshakes. He played dominoes and checkers. He could hold his own with any community leader when it came to Black history and culture. He was a believer, born again, and could sit around the table with the elders and quote the King James Version chapter and verse. He usually knew more blues and spirituals than anybody in the house and never hesitated to demonstrate. When doubts surfaced, he used the one-drop-of-blood method of racial identification to his advantage. Other than my mother, no one ever blew his cover. He enjoyed being a Black man. What had begun as a simple ploy soon became an elaborate deception.

On the Black-hand-side of life, we frequented the paranoiac gatherings of political and cultural activists, and even donned dress clothes to attend the mosques—Orthodox *and* Black Muslim. Whenever his authenticity was questioned, Charlie reveled in proving he had forgotten more about being Black than his challengers had ever known. During one nasty showdown, he mollified the majority of the skeptics, but the atmosphere remained threatening. Someone put James Brown on the stereo as the ultimate test. Charlie could not only bop, camel walk, and Madison, he could do the dog, the funky butt, and the alligator crawl. His dance performance dispelled all remaining doubts. Whenever challenged to unzip his fly, he did so with pride. Once, three hardcore bruthas escorted him to the john. They returned in consternation, embarrassed. Quick to drop his drawers, Charlie would never remove his shirt, mindful to keep cuffed sleeves just above the elbow, hiding that Johnny Reb tattoo.

I never betrayed him. No one ever demanded I do so.

✿ ✿ ✿

Love-Ins with Nietzsche

O my friend, man is something that hath to be sur-
passed.   —Nietzsche

A native Angelena, I had married Charlie right out of the local high school I hated. My years in the racist Los Angeles school system had been horrific and I felt lucky to have survived them with spirit intact. My salvation had been one astute English teacher— my debate and public speaking coach, Mr. Robert Bruce Newsom. I had joined his Forensics Club in my freshman year, and had become one of his A students. Mr. Newsom ran on the periphery of the Hollywood underground captured in the movie *Ed Wood*. He knew Criswell of *Criswell Predicts*, which, after *Queen for a Day*, was my mother's favorite TV show. When he overheard me and a girlfriend waxing gaga over Bela Lugosi, he confided he was close to Lillian Arch, Lugosi's widow, and destroyed our romantic notions by telling us that Lugosi, dead eight years, had been a heroin addict.

Even more important to me than Mr. Newsom was the pleasure, knowledge, and escape I found in reading. In my hunger, I devoured every good book I could get my hands on, but almost none of it was Black literature save my parents' stash of novels by Richard Wright and James Baldwin. As a closet bookworm, I had long found a way to shield myself from the ugliness I encountered in world literature, particularly that of American authors and European philosophers: Raymond Chandler, Ayn Rand, Mark Twain—bring 'em all on, Nietzsche and Heidegger, too. I understood that these writers could not imagine the existence of one such as myself. They were of their times. I was genius enough to extract and extrapolate and keep moving. Alas, my choice of reading materials coupled with my rebellious teenage posturing soon had me in trouble—dropping out or flunking out.

I wanted to transfer to another school, but needed my parents' permission. My mother refused. The eldest of four, I was her helpmate. She wanted me close to home. I was under threat of expulsion my senior year. Mr. Newsom became my warder or supervisor, seeing to it that I behaved in classes and did my

39

homework. I had long retreated to the library during breaks. Now I spent recess, lunch hours, and free periods in his classroom, up to my eyeballs in books. As a graduation gift, Mr. Newsom presented me with three fat volumes published by the Modern Library. I would read half of *War and Peace* and put it aside to devour William Shirer's *Rise and Fall of the Third Reich*. But *The Philosophy of Nietzsche* enthralled me. I read it cover to cover, then reread it, then studied it, focusing on my favorite section, *Thus Spake Zarathustra*, underlining and memorizing the passages true to my experience.

When the Nietzsche in me met the Mohandas K. in Charlie, we began "to debate," as he called it. Pity the poor Jehovah's Witnesses who came to our door—Charlie's delight in tormenting them was absolutely sadistic—but between us, our debates were sweetly intense and interesting fun. I was starved to test my mettle, and he was a willing sounding board. I argued vigorously against his cornpone pacifism—a muddle of Quaker homilies and Gandhian strategies filtered through hours of "meetin's" with MLK and, according to Charlie, the real brains of the SCLC (Southern Christian Leadership Congress), the Reverend Ralph David Abernathy. (Charlie was proud that MLK's "Letter from Birmingham Jail" was a collaborative effort, to which he claimed to have contributed. Martin Luther was not a writer.) But as months passed, I was able to absorb everything he could muster. As my powers grew, his seemed to diminish. If I managed superior logic, my position became his, which he in turn argued with others. Nietzsche was bedside reading, as we argued questions of social parity and race. Still a teenager, I was relentless and morose about everything. Charlie was serious only when matters were personal; otherwise, he argued for the pleasure of the sport. I steadfastly held that violence would be a factor in the equation of true equality for my people. In time, Charlie began to agree. The groups we joined became more and more radical. Yet, when King was assassinated in Memphis on April 4, 1968, Charlie was inconsolable.

❀ ❀ ❀

And often with our love we want merely to overleap envy. And often we attack and make ourselves enemies, to conceal that we are vulnerable. —Nietzsche

Reports about the gatherings of "the beautiful people" in local parks were on the grapevine—feeding the poor and sharing songs at be-ins and love-ins. Eagerly, we joined the throng, acutely aware that our double lives had doubled again. (We had two children.) Often we packed a lunch and Thermos to spend mornings and afternoons among the flower children, picnicking, dancing to conga drum music, ogling trinkets for sale, collecting leaflets—basking in a sandalwood-scented atmosphere of unbridled peace, love, and sexual freedom. The evening and night of the same day, we might find ourselves in the backroom of a community center, abandoned building, or church debating the merits of sit-ins, boycotts, and armed struggle, wondering who among those gathered was the counterintelligence snitch. Charlie loved the excitement and the danger. I sat owl-eyed and silent, keeping my cynicism—on both extremes—to myself. Nearly four years would pass before our two disparate worlds merged during the Griffith Park love-ins of summer 1968.

Charlie had promised to help a peace charity set up their tables to hand out free food. We packed up our babies, double stroller, and diaper bag, and went into our larder for a jar of Skippy peanut butter and strawberry preserves to donate. It was early when we arrived, the area nearly deserted. My habit was to anchor myself to our blanket with my book, playing with the children while they crawled and toddled, keeping one eye on the oversized guitar case. Charlie had added a twelve-string to his collection. His habit was to roam, strapped with the lighter acoustic guitar, mouth harp in a pocket or a neck brace.

The park filled with a vast assortment of people, but Charlie gravitated to musicians, spending most of his time jamming with the conga drummers. If he liked someone, he brought that party to meet me, or moved us to their spot. This particular Saturday morning, only the families were there, tents up, homemade standards flying. There were ten to a dozen of them. We had seen them several times before. Some of the peace-love revelers complained about them. He rarely visited the families. They struck him as strange. But once the tables had been set up, Charlie found nothing to do. The conga drummers hadn't arrived, and the crowd was disappointingly sparse.

"Curiosity ain't killed this cat," he'd say as he kissed me good-bye before wandering the park. "I got nine lives and always land on my feet."

He returned a couple of hours later, ecstatic, urging me to hurry, pack up the babies and the twelve-string. He had discovered a kindred spirit. The man led a family that was virtually all female. He was also a songwriter and was trying to learn how to play the guitar well enough to perform his own music. He was looking for someone tolerant enough to jam with him. Not only that, he liked to "debate politics," enjoying talk hard and fast. They had liked one another instantly. The man was short, White, and "a righteous brother." Best of all, they were both named Charlie. Blushing, he confessed they had shared the peace pipe.

We walked to the tent. My Charlie introduced us. Manson's eyes glittered when he looked up at me. I was not what he had expected. I was darker than assumed, a full head taller and outweighed him by eighty pounds. Charles was not the type Charlie was usually drawn to. His angular face and sable shoulder-length hair gave him the look of a shrunken, wily-eyed Christ. We shook hands, his bony grip firm. We went outside and Charles helped set out our belongings near the tent. The girls were "off and around," and the two Charlies wasted no time resuming their talk. I was not about to sit idly by and listen. I joined in, keeping one eye on the children, breaking from the conversation only to feed them and change diapers. We chewed over such issues as the Warren Commission report on the death of JFK, voters' rights, Mao, Castro, and Che. When the talk turned to music, I excused myself while the two Charlies studied lead sheets.

As our afternoon wound to a close, Charles noticed I was carrying my volume of Nietzsche and asked to see it. He thumbed through it and asked if he could borrow it. I made him swear an oath to give it back. He kept his word. But when he returned it two weekends later, he had questions. Didn't I realize that what Nietzsche wrote wasn't intended for the likes of me? Especially the part about a race of supermen? As a Negro, wasn't I offended by Nietzsche? My Charlie chimed in. And it wasn't long before we got around to one of the two Charlies' favorite topics, if for different reasons—race war.

I eloquently parroted the going militant rhetoric. This amused Charles. He asserted he wasn't a racist but a realist, and bluntly dismissed my arguments for Black revolution as ludicrous. Charlie idolized John Brown, the song and the man. His contribution to the argument centered around Brown's attack on Harpers Ferry—that Whites could and would one day lead Blacks into armed struggle, that the struggle would be integrated. Charles Manson turned his illustration around as evidence for his assertion that legions of Blacks did not rise up to join Brown because they couldn't. Negroes had been whipped, co-opted, and cowed by slavery. Blacks would never rise against Whites, if history were any witness. They loved Whites too much. Denmark Vesey was the exception, not the rule. Manson maintained that if any cultural revolution—or revolution of any kind—was to take place in the U.S., only Whites could defeat Whites because Blacks, if Martin Luther King was any example, did not have the guts or the intelligence to lead either an armed or organized resistance. Whites would have to do it for them.

I immediately dropped my third of the argument, took my Nietzsche, and retired to the blanket with the babies. Early in our encounter, Charles had suggested that I check out his women. Two of the dazed-eyed naiads took me by the arm and led me to the women's quarters. Curious, I made an attempt. They liked playing with our kids. But I could not connect. We had nothing in common. Their sole interest was their reverence for their Charlie. They spent hours discussing his needs, wants, and lessons.

Otherwise, they always seemed spaced-out, or high—flitting about without ambition or purpose. I had no experience with the drug culture and no way of understanding who they were.

Once he and the girls settled into real digs, Charles repeatedly invited us to visit them. We just couldn't spare the gasoline. Things were extremely tough for us, life was love-filled but terrible. Charlie couldn't get a decent job to keep one and I couldn't get work because of my inexperience, pregnancies, and color. We lived on public assistance, between any odd job he could get. We drove old clunkers for as long as we could keep them running. We always needed money, and Manson was eager to involve Charlie in a couple of schemes. One Saturday morning, Charlie accepted Manson's offer and went out to the Spahn Movie Ranch, in Chatsworth. I stayed with the children, fingers crossed.

Charlie was gone the entire day and returned after sunset without a dime. I had been worried. When he came in, he looked haggard, hands in pockets. He stood in the doorway, in his denim jacket and jeans, lamb's wool cap tilted slightly forward on his forehead. I was eager to hear the news. What kind of job was it?

"Sweetheart," he said, solemnly. "Those are some *baaad* people." The "job" had involved auto theft.

Charlie was proud of his outlaw status as a renegade civil rights worker. But he was not a criminal. He had walked away from Charles Manson without looking back. He was twenty-six going on twenty-seven, and I was twenty-two. Within the year, our relationship, too, would end.

> There are the terrible ones who carry about in them-
> selves the beast of prey, and have no choice except
> lusts or self-laceration. And even their lusts are self-
> lacerations.   —Nietzsche

But now, in December 1969, Charlie Coleman and I are separated. Chuck is my first new boyfriend, and I have no intention of spoiling our chances by talking excessively about my recent past. "I only knew Manson briefly. I wasn't a part of his family—

they called 'em families—I met him at a love-in in Griffith Park."

"That musta been some crazy fucked-up shit."

"Yeah. Well, at least now we know they aren't looking for any of us." I let my voice drop to indicate there is nothing more to say. We ride on between spates of rhythm and blues and news updates, Chuck periodically turning up the pint of V.O. snug in its brown paper bag as I monitor the rearview mirror for the gendarmes. By the time we arrive home in South Central, I am in the throes of a nostalgia attack. While Chuck unloads his kidneys in the john, I put Jefferson Airplane's *Surrealistic Pillow* on the turntable and start dancing solo—the way Charlie and I once danced at the be-ins, love-ins, at all the happenings, not so long ago—the Black and the White.

"Take that shit off!" Chuck barks. If it isn't on the order of Wilson Pickett, Garland Green, or Bobby "Blue" Bland, he doesn't want to hear it.

"But—"

He slams his fist onto the turntable and splits the LP in half.

"I don't give a good goddamn 'bout all that hippy-dippy shit!"

I hold my tears, trash the broken vinyl, and fish out the 45s. His favorite of the day is on top, Wilson Pickett's *Mustang Sally*. I lower the player arm. Chuck snatches me to his bulky chest, slaps my behind, rolls his hips, and sings along coarsely—the odors of menthol, sweat, and sadness sting my face.

"All you got to do is ride around, Sally—ride, Sally, ride!"

NOTE

The Reverend Charlie J. Coleman died at the age of sixty-one in June 2003, in Salt Lake City, Utah, leaving behind a second wife, four children, and four grandchildren. He was preceded in death by his mother, Lois Coleman, and by his son, Anthony.

Angela's Big Night

Inspired by Lois Lane—one of my favorite comic-book characters—I longed to become a journalist. Divorced from my first husband, I was, in the early 1970s, still trying to complete my college education, attend writers' workshops, maintain a full-time day job, and raise two school-age children. I was poor but determined, and I believed that I could and would overcome the adversity that attended being "young, gifted, and Black." Therefore, I was thrilled when Art Kunkin, publisher-editor of the *Los Angeles Free Press*, L.A.'s controversial '60s underground newspaper, gave me my first official freelance reporting assignment: covering a legal-defense fund-raiser for the then-incarcerated Black Power Movement heroine Angela Davis.

I was twenty-six years old and eager to do my best. I desperately needed the extra money but was even more anxious to do a good job, one professional enough to start me on my way toward a salaried newspaper gig. First order of business was contacting the PR people who were organizing the event. My calls were not returned. When I at last got through to a Davis representative, she called me "a nobody" before I could finish my pitch. This woman said she was disappointed that Kunkin hadn't handed the assignment to one of his star reporters, and then she slammed down the receiver. I have never forgotten that shocking instant. I had naïvely assumed that the last person to put down a "for-real sistuh" from the ghetto would be another "for-real sistuh."

I swallowed the insult and bravely went on to do what I thought was my job, unaware that I was about to cause a tumult of outrage that would shake the left coast. As a result of my report, I would be secretly boycotted from journalism for the next ten years. Looking back on the piece, it seems my punishment—whatever it was—far outweighed any so-called transgression. My report reflects my surface at that time—a brash young woman trying too hard to be hip.

Here, then, is the document, a strange little chapter of personal and cultural history. Except for standing ovations, I was, as the cliché goes, *glued* to seat 30, row 12, in tunnel C of the Shrine Auditorium on Saturday evening, March 4, 1972.

Wooweeeee, Baby!

It was a stone trip wading through the multitude of Black faces and every now and then, the few White faces of folks high steppin' it down Jefferson Boulevard toward the doors of the Shrine Auditorium. Everywhere my eyes turned they were staggered by all the visible symbols of American wealth—or, rather, Black America's attempt to mimic White America's wealth. There were Cadillac limousines—and, a first for my poor unemployed eyes, a Mercedes limousine. I didn't even know they made those.

Hallelujah! It was Nigger Night at the Shrine Au-di-to-ri-um! Black folks from all over L.A. were gettin' it on in the revolutionary name of Sistuh Angela Davis. Dudes slicked out cleaner than a bone were pimpin' it down the avenues in fine fine threads on the arms of show-stoppin' eye-poppin' sistuhs. I recall a

47

quote from Sammy Davis Jr. as he strutted across the stage in his outlandish tux: "I got clothes for days!"

If Black people had a "show of the season," this was emphatically it. The enthusiastic crowd filled the Shrine in what was probably one of its first sellouts in some time. There may have been ten empty seats in the house, if there were that many.

I saw old friends I hadn't seen since high school and many recent ones. Black community celebrities were there and Black stars, local and national, turned out. My eyes weren't big enough to take it all in and if I'd had a camera I wouldn't have known where to aim it.

There were cameras there. And guards. And men with walkie-talkies. I'm sure there were cops there too—and agents—had to be —but I didn't see any—frankly, why spoil such a fun evening with gruesome realities?

After a few long minutes the people in the audience got tired of lookin' to see who and what they could see and settled down to watch the show, which was s'pose to start at eight-thirty but, like a true colored performance, began late as usual, at eight-fifty—go head on!

Opening the Black star-studded concert was Quincy Jones, whose music—if not the man— is well known to TV watchers from Eugene, Oregon, to Baton Rouge to Attica. He opened with a little mellow number, *What's Goin' On*. The impatient audience immediately snapped to it and began to settle down. He did two other numbers, among which was his new blacker version of the *Ironsides* theme. His backup was a well-stocked band of some of the finest Black, White, and Chicano musicians in the business—ex big band men and a few excellent newcomers like David T. Walker. Accompanying the band for this set were four beautiful sistuhs.

Teee-da!

What we saw, we definitely got as Sammy Davis Jr., fresh in from Vietnam, stepped out on stage in what looked like a black felt jacket with bold black and yellow plaid slacks, white shirt and black bow tie. He was a visual crack-up. Through him we learned: 1. All the bread was going to Sistuh Angela. 2. The event was being broadcast on KPFK to Radio Free Ghetto. He did a brief monologue, which said in effect, "even Beverly Hills Black folks got soul." Then he anointed the audience with *I Gotta Be Me*.

Whew!

Next, we heard from Yaphet Kotto. Introduced by Sammy Davis Jr., the gruff young Black hero-star came out on stage without pretension in denims and white shirt and a no-nonsense manner. He laid a reading on us dedicated to Sistuh Angela.

Drum roll.

The lights darkened.

"Ladies and gentlemen—the President of the United States!"

There was a sharp sucking sound from the audience for a brief second as the dark figure parted the curtain. It was as if the audience was shocked to think that *He* would really show up. But it turned out to be the beginning of a routine by actor Donald Sutherland and his partner (who was never introduced, and

I'm sorry to say I didn't recognize him). They did a cute satire on President Nixon.

Mr. M.C., Sammy Davis Jr., scooted back on stage to do a medley of old Blood, Sweat and Tears hits. During his reign on stage it was impossible not to applaud his unique showmanship. After years of seeing the shadow on TV, it was fantastic to see the man—a man of super energy. It was impossible not to laugh as he strutted across the stage, showing us that the red lining in his coat matched the red band around his waist. He did *Mr. Bojangles*, giving the audience only a taste of his legendary dancing talent. It's a gas how a man no bigger than a minute is such a giant of a performer.

Too much, Baby! Too much!

Sammy brought Jimmy Witherspoon out onto the stage for several soul-stomping moments. The fine bluesman brought it up front and down home with some blue blue funk.

Now comes the part where I must step down off my pedestal of praise for a while and rap a serious line—because here came the part of the show that turned me completely off: the offering—the call to worship.

I'm sure there are bruthas and sistuhs everywhere who'd—if they could afford to—give their last dime to see Sistuh Angela *and* Ruchell Magee and the hundreds of other political prisoners all set free. It just chilled me that Mr. Kolonski (I am probably not spelling it right) and his co-workers had the crude audacity to interrupt the show and—in the cliché fashion of a Baptist preacher—pass the plate. I freaked as the wizened White man underlined his heavy revolutionary sermon with the phrase "we need that money!"

The audience, stirred up by several rabble-rousing introductions of such notables as the family of Sistuh Angela and the McAfees who went her bail, reluctantly got off some spare bread behind the heavy heavy heavy speechifying of this boisterous man who Sammy had introduced as "the hub" of the event, the man who got it together.

There was clear resentment expressed in low tones by people in the audience for whom just the price of a ticket ($4.50–$7.50) was already a big enough sacrifice—and, of course, those like me who still maintained, despite all assurances, a heavy doubt that little, if any, of those thousands of dollars was ever going to reach Angela Davis. Truthfully, I'd have to hear it from Angela's lips myself before believing it.

The "movement" was a shameful but clear history of money collected in the name of others, like Magee, Cleaver, George Jackson, etc., being ripped off by scheming fakers who weasel their way to the top and manage to rake off the cream cash. I can't help but raise a sticky stinky question of disbelief. Yeah, I liked the show so far, but! Yeah, I'd give money for Sistuh Angela, but! Yeah, I can dig all the heavy things you sayin', but I cannot completely accept the validity of a typically capitalistic evening of entertainment laced in what came off as pseudo revolutionaryisms—a gross attempt to get reactionary Blacks to pay conscience money. Some sistuh behind me summed it up, "I'm gonna start the Doretha Owens collection."

Merciful shit—intermission arrived and gave us time to recover, cop some water to swallow that pseudo-revolutionary pill, then hurry back to see the main reason why most folks bothered to show up in the first place.

As the curtain hung a split, Quincy Jones sent out more mellow vibes, then explained how, wiped out from his Vietnam gig, Sammy had left for the evening. He then introduced actor Greg Morris, who read a poem by Bernie Casey. The Black man looked so much like the *Mission Impossible* caricature of a Black man as "human being" that I was shocked. He didn't look real. But I guess he was as he read on about Black womanhood . . . "dark and dusky . . ." Yeah.

Donald Sutherland reappeared, this time reading a telegram sent in support of Angela Davis and all Black people. The audience cheered when he said "from . . . Shirley Chisholm."

Teee-da!

The curtains parted. Three voluptuous sistuhs were rockin' as the band sounded out. The audience shrieked as Lady Soul, Aretha Franklin, stepped on stage. She dazzled in a white pantsuit aglisten with silver sequins, bracelets, and earrings, and a pink head rag, belting out *A Rose in Spanish Harlem*. With professional slickness, she slipped into a medley of her hits: *Respect, I'll Say a Little Prayer for You*, and *Call Me*, almost too fast—we only got a good itchin' taste. Then, Lady Soul grooved on into *Rock Steady*, rocking on a while, lookin' good! On to "Me, oh my . . . I'm a fool for you, Baby!"

Electric soul! She tore up the audience and put 'em back together.

A touch of *For Once in My Life* and *I've Got to Be Me* was a comedown, but was still all right as much of the audience stood in tribute to the Beautiful Brown Sistuh.

She went to the piano. The first bars of *Spirit in the Dark* shot a cheer and a thrill through the audience, which became one massive clap and on time, can you dig that?

Aretha burned the ivories a bit, then got up to style a while in root gospel feeling. She got a standing ovation, no less. She introduced the Supremes and one of the Four Tops, for bows, then went into an intense rendition of *Take a Look at Yourself*, requested by Angela's family.

When she finished, nobody had to be told the show was over.

The spirit might have been with Angela Davis, but the soul was with Aretha.

Within hours of this item's appearance, a copy of the paper was shown to Davis. Soon thereafter, I was told about the controversy it had aroused in the Davis camp. Speculations circulated as to whether the *Free Press* would be sued and I would be named co-defendant. I explained to one of the editors what had happened in my phone call to the Davis people. After several days of consternation and tension, I was informed that Davis had instructed her people to "leave the poor child alone." There would be no lawsuit.

Eleven years later, in 1983, I would share a podium with infantryman-turned-journalist Ron Ridenour (1947–1999, known for his March 1968 exposé of the My Lai massacre). We were reading together at an L.A. college, and one of the poems I read described the plight of a Black Vietnam veteran. Moved by the poem, Ridenour approached me after the session. As we stood alone at the back of the auditorium, he surprised me by bringing up the long-forgotten "Angela's Big Night." He asked me how someone as politically savvy as I seemed to be could write something that so misrepresented the spirit of the event and demeaned the hard work of the people involved. I told him how inexperienced I had been and how rudely I had been treated by the Davis camp. He said that while formal legalities had not been pursued against the *Free Press*, I had been "placed under boycott for ten years." He did not detail what that boycott entailed, admitted it had been unfair, and confessed that he had been one of those responsible. He apologized. Amazed, I accepted his statements at face value, and told him that if the boycott had been effective, I knew nothing about it and had never heard of it. We shook hands and went our ways, with his promise to buy my book.

NOTE

Shirley Chisholm (1924–2005) was the first Black woman to win a seat in Congress and to run for the presidency of the United States. Ruchell Cinque Magee, now in prison for more than forty-five years, was wounded in a shootout following an escape attempt and hostage-taking at the Marin County Courthouse in August 1970. His fellow hostage-takers included William Christmas and Jonathan Jackson (brother of George), both of whom were killed during the incident. A shotgun used by Magee-Christmas-Jackson was purportedly smuggled into the courthouse by Angela Davis. Davis was a Marxist-Leninist, a graduate of Brandeis, and a former assistant professor of philosophy at UCLA; she was also co-chair of the Soledad Brothers Defense Committee. After the Marin Courthouse incident, she went underground to evade arrest for "attempted kidnapping" and was busted two months later. After seventeen months in jail, she was released on bail and finally acquitted. Davis resumed teaching and wrote several books; today she lectures internationally on contemporary political issues.

Primal Orb Density

"A pimp is really a whore who has reversed the game on whores ... Be as sweet as the scratch, no sweeter ... always get your money in front just like a whore."
—Iceberg Slim

Here I am. I prize myself greatly. I want the world to enjoy me and my art, but something's undeniably wrong. I've come to regard myself as a living, breathing statistic governed not by my individual will but by forces outside myself. Where do I end and the stats begin? My struggle with this question compels me to the podium, though I much prefer sitting curbside and watching the traffic pass. Who am I but a certain weight, a mass of blood and bone that breaks when dashed to stone? Am I my people's keeper/griot who sings and in song passes truth along? Could it be my kinkiness/ my grade of hair has affected my brain?

I have become adept at articulating pain through seeing clearly and unapologetically. I am unreconciled in my strivings to overcome the war within and the war without my body; the war between the me that I am and the me that other eyes see; the war in which I measure myself by "the tape of a world that looks on in amused contempt and pity."

In an attempt to determine my place in this unspeakably brutal reality, I turned to the bookshelf. The author who has shed the most light onto my darkness is the one I've just quoted, W. E. B. Du Bois.

Implicit in Du Bois's *The Souls of Black Folk* was the hope that once the Negro joined the broken halves of his "double self," his strife would cease and White America and Black America would become one greater America. His great hope was that American society would recognize the inner strength of the "whole" Negro, and that this unique form of internal fortitude would, almost superhumanly, bolster the Negro against any further physical or emotional onslaught. Du Bois's emphasis was on faith—the belief that the obvious wrongs done to the Black Race would be rectified over time and that the Negro, by somehow forging his dual identities into one truly American identity, would at last assume his rightful place at the table of plenty.

At the beginning of this century, Du Bois could not foresee that the shape of the table itself would change; that, perhaps, by the time the Negro found his place at it, the sumptuous meal would already be devoured; that the souls of Black Folk might be beset with an altogether new crop of hungers grown on the plantations of a sophisticated technology and an accelerating swiftness in the alternating currents of global affairs.

Du Bois's vision could very well encompass the extermination of one or two races from the face of the earth—a matter of great interest to a few anthropologists, perhaps, but of no great concern to humanity at large. He could not, however, imagine the coming of the computer chip or the arrival of Armageddon at Hiroshima and Nagasaki. He could not imagine the probable annihilation of the Earth itself; or how knowledge of that probability would affect the souls of all humanity. He could not imagine how these complexities might eclipse the Negro in his struggle, and might exacerbate that struggle. Nevertheless, Du Bois's vision would become seed to and inspiration for a new generation of "seers."

Today Du Bois's "double-souled" Negro faces renewed struggle.

On the part of White Folk there is no longer pity for the plight of Black Folk. The amused contempt resonates. The troubled State of the Race has become the product of a deeper, more calculated condition, one endemic to domestic political apathy and social denial. And I must see through to this.

And so I have grown another eye, a primal orb density that provides me constant double view. With it I observe with such intense focus that I become emotionally cockeyed, my vision so skewed I can't witness any racial incident without relating it to my personal circumstance. It's impossible to read a book or newspaper, watch television or a movie, or listen to music without perceiving the racist ramifications. I even see racism under my bed.

although he was not a suspect two officers fired multiple rounds from their weapons striking him in the upper torso clad only in his underwear he was pronounced dead at the scene no weapon found

BLACK AMERICA IS UNDER SIEGE

Whose jobs earn the lowest pay?
Black female domestic and health-care workers.

What was begun in the 1920s, and restructured in 1958, was completed with the nullification of the gold standard by President Richard M. Nixon in August 1971, when America's economy (and the world's) essentially became a gigantic currency pyramid scam as the U.S. ended its commitment to swap gold for dollars in the world money chase.

Domestically, in order for those at the top of the pyramid to remain there, a strong and solid base of the disenfranchised must be maintained. This base consists of the least stable individuals the nation produces: the lower middle and poor working classes.

I am a member of the latter.

The hellish circle I go around and around in is called the effects of the leading stock-market indicators on a poor Black working-class mother born west of the Hudson River, created in Southern California, and raised in the Los Angeles *barrio* of Watts.

During the Angel Dust rage, back in the days before crack, I received googobs of criticism for living in "the boonies." I lived there because it was the only part of L.A. where I could find decent housing at fair rates. Black friends egged, "Return to civilization." White friends never visited. On one occasion I poured out my survival miseries to an old Maoist revolutionary buddy, an expert on Black capitalism. After soundly criticizing my ghetto lifestyle, he suggested I relocate to Jonestown. He had just returned from Guyana and was quite impressed with Jim Jones's little colony and thought it just the cure.

her body was found hanging from a tree in the suburban community she was young and poorly dressed sheriff's spokesmen said there was no obvious indication of suicide

What is Never Never Land?
The place Black applicants go to get home loans
at higher interest rates.

**BLACK STUDENTS, 16% OF THE NATION'S
PUBLIC SCHOOL POPULATION,
ARE TWICE AS LIKELY AS WHITES
TO BE SUSPENDED,
RECEIVE CORPORAL PUNISHMENT
OR BE CLASSIFIED RETARDED**

To further strengthen the pyramid's base and keep it solid (because, remember, if it isn't kept solid the whole structure will become unstable and cave in on itself and virtually everyone will lose, even those on the bottom who've been there all the time and have little hope of climbing up), corporations, businesses, and wealthy individuals must be competitive as they operate their variations of economic scam. In the process the worker/employee/ flunky becomes more and more modular in nature (the name changes but the game's the same) and significantly less important to the workplace, therefore replaced with minimal if any disruption in the cash flow. This increasing devaluation of the worker includes loss of such benefits as medical and dental insurance. Workers are routinely fired as they approach retirement. The age of the full-time wage-earner is passing as America becomes not only a nation of service workers but a nation of part-timers. In this climate of cutbacks and union busting, the so-called traditional work ethic (quality, loyalty, integrity, sincerity, etc.) is invalid if not downright disadvantageous. The worker, whether white-, blue-, or pink-collar, has become devalued or dehumanized. The laws of the streets have become the laws of the boardroom. (Weren't they always? someone asks.)

With each severe shrinkage of the American economic pie, prospects grow dimmer for those who have yet to taste their bite of a slice.

he was shot and killed they believed he had pointed a gun bystanders said he was unarmed and fleeing a beer in his hand when he was shot in the back of his neck no gun was found

SUBPOVERTY JOBS REPLACE MIDDLE-WAGE JOBS WHILE NUMBER OF HIGH-WAGE JOBS FALL

The process of worker dehumanization has been aided by the rapid advance of computer technology. Ultimately every participant in the economy who is not couched in wealth, who must earn money to survive, is increasingly forced to obey the dictates of those at the top while having fewer and fewer opportunities of acquiring wealth by their own honest sweat. This is the world according to Las Vegas, where society is a casino, luck is a matter of fixed calculation, and the odds are with the house.

The economic effectiveness of the earnings of those on the bottom of the pyramid are minimized by taxing, in one form or another, the necessities: food, shelter, family, medical care, and the grave. The ability of those at the bottom to transcend their circumstances is minimized by limited access to education, information, and the media. It is impossible to pull oneself up by one's own bootstraps if one has no boots.

Now factor in race.

FAILURE OF GOVERNMENT TO TAKE POSITIVE ROLE IN ENDING RACISM

To maintain their rarified places, those at the top of the pyramid, with maximum power, may change the rules of scam with minimum effort (be the motivation class-based, gender-specific, racist, religious, political, or merely selfish). Doing so ensures keeping the bottom the bottom. Because of their powerlessness, those at the base of the pyramid are effective only when able to organize en masse. Their inability to organize is frequently exacerbated by differences in ethnicity, gender, and degree of hunger.

they saw him running it remained unclear whether he actually was the target and police officers involved declined comment the man was not armed and was not a gang member according to witnesses

What is a buppie?
A fictitious demographic created to substantiate
the illusion of "overall betterment" for the equally
fictitious "Black mainstream."

I must censor myself to obtain what I need to liberate myself from poverty. This psychological Möbius is numbing in the traversing. In order to establish communication with a sensibility unlike mine I have to gauge the points of potential cultural collisions and then navigate accordingly. Like a periscope, my primal orb density enables me to pierce the layers of social prejudice and steer an intelligent course through its terror-infested waters, a sea of assumptions based on ignorance.

In my eye, and in my frantic scramblings to become substantial, I imagine myself functionally insane, operating within the constraints of a society itself driven mad, made sick by its unresolved history of slavery and the ongoing trauma of racism.

"The enemy is aware of . . . ideological weaknesses, for he analyzes the forces of rebellion and studies more and more carefully the aggregate enemy. . . . He is also aware of the spiritual instability of certain layers of the population. The enemy discovers the existence, side by side with the disciplined and well-organized advance guard . . . a mass . . . whose participation is constantly at the mercy of their being for too long accustomed to physiological wretchedness, humiliation, and irresponsibility. The enemy is ready to pay a high price for the services of this mass."
—Frantz Fanon, *The Wretched of the Earth*

---

as she watched television she was rendered brain dead by a single shot to her head she died hours later police call the incident an apparent drive-by shooting no suspects identified at this time

UNEMPLOYMENT OF BLACKS MORE THAN TWICE THAT OF WHITES

The horrible irony of the federal government passing laws to impose the death penalty on drug dealers is that it, the government, is the granddaddy of all drug dealers; using alcohol to devastate the nation's indigenous population; using the criminal underworld to introduce heroin into the veins of its Black underclass.

The death penalty is not meant to eliminate drug usage and dealing. It simply redefines the context under which usage and dealing occur, especially in the Black community, where drugs have always represented "the devil's work," the most heinous means of escaping stultifying poverty for the circumstantially failed. The death penalty is one more device to keep "certain elements" from rising to the top of the pyramid.

61

THE AIDS DEATH RATE FOR BLACKS IS THREE TIMES GREATER THAN FOR WHITES

"He's a Negro, he has a right to sell drugs 'cause Whitey makes it impossible for a Black to make enough honest bread."
—Charles Mingus, *Beneath the Underdog*

Drugs have historically proved effective tools of creating and oppressing an underclass as long as the designated freebooters control traffic, those designated being members of the dominant culture and allowed to ascend in the pyramidal hierarchy (to schmooze with the pharaohs).

As a result of cultural shift, political developments "south of the border" brought in immigrant drug dealers who went straight into America's ghettos to exploit whoever they found there, mainly us Blacks, according to their own needs. Control unexpectedly fell into the hands of a new breed of gangsters-of-color, young Black and Hispanic males set on "living large."

responding to a complaint of domestic violence they ordered him to place his hands on his head without provocation they clenched him from behind began to drag him backward began to knee him in the groin and strike him in the face though he was unarmed and offered only natural resistance to the blows to his groin the officer drew a revolver and shot him in the back

What is a chokehold?
Asphyxiation due to wallet restraint for abnormal behavior associated with constant copings with racism exacerbated by a hostile and combative attitude.

THE KILLER OF A WHITE PERSON IS MORE LIKELY TO BE SENTENCED TO DEATH THAN THE KILLER OF A BLACK PERSON

62

I play on racist assumptions to facilitate my daily doings. There is the woman of diverse feelings and capabilities. There is the stereotyped angry young Black poet who only gets applause as long as her teeth are bared. It makes life easier on the one hand. On the other, dangers arise if I'm to maintain integrity. How morally strong am I? If I fail, how much of myself will I be able to salvage as I scramble for my spot in the pyramidal hierarchy?

Poetry has little monetary value in society and being Black compounds the issue.

To paraphrase Justice Thurgood Marshall: A child born to the most ignorant, poorest Black mother in these United States, by act of breath, has exactly the same value, worth, and rights as a White child born to the wealthiest, most intelligent White woman.

With the establishment of direct links to the drug source, dominant-culture freebooters, despised for their raw, unconcealed bigotry, were suddenly unemployed insofar as the dope business was concerned. This was an unexpected circumstance, one which allowed enterprising Black and Hispanic males to claw their way into the pyramid elite, if over the backs of their peers. Therefore it was incumbent upon those freebooters who hadn't cemented their positions on top to get out of the dope business.

Once the dominant culture perceived dealers were no longer predominantly ethnically White, it was permissible to impose the death penalty since the lives of Blacks, Hispanics, and poor Whites traditionally remain devalued.

he was wandering in the middle of the street acting bizarre he received three jolts from the taser gun but they had no effect officers employed a swarm technique and brought him to the ground he died as a result of the altercation while being treated the spokesman said no cause of death had been determined pending outcome of toxicological tests

URBAN BLACK MALES ARE LESS LIKELY TO REACH AGE 65 THAN MEN IN BANGLADESH

What is workfare?
Unskilled welfare mothers forced to leave preschool
children to go to work yet expected to provide
adequate childcare on lower than average wages.

Delicious irony is that the political vision of Americans of color
is so largely clouded the majority fail to see how this death penalty
is leveled specifically at their own males. Most of our law-abiding
voters would, predictably, favor the penalty, failing to understand
the sophisticated economic dynamics behind it, and would be
rightly unsympathetic to those who feed so destructively on their
own kind.

My poet-consciousness shattered, I nevertheless armor myself
for battle with the secondary me defined by the American
conspiracy of circumstance. It is this second self who poses problems and is a barrier I must break through in order to effectively
communicate. This barrier self resides in the eyes of those with
whom I conduct my daily doings: my attorney, a bank teller, my
lover, a child, a grocery-store clerk. For example, if I want a job,
I have to carry myself in a way that is non-threatening or seen as
safe by my White employer. The energy I exert in this barrier
busting exhausts me. My opinions and values must be suppressed. The only place I experience liberty is on the page (within the limits of what's salable imposed by the White publishing
establishment). I cannot afford to do otherwise in the course of
daily commerce without dooming my primary self. The means by
which I protect myself have come as gifts from mentors who've
taken time to "school" me or "give me game."

*the 25-year-old man was hospitalized bruised and comatose after
his arrest he never regained consciousness officials maintained he
was drunk and died while violently resisting arrest*

THE AVERAGE BLACK FAMILY EARNS HALF
AS MUCH AS THE AVERAGE WHITE FAMILY

There's a lot of serious moola in hate: White men experience un-favorable treatment in 27 percent of their job searches while Black applicants are treated unfavorably in 50 percent of theirs. White applicants are three times more likely to receive job offers and almost three times more likely to advance in the hiring process over Blacks. Fifteen percent of White applicants receive job offers compared with only 5 percent of Blacks.

It's all about value: the value of life vis-à-vis money. You are only worth your weight in dollars inherited or earned. When the dollar is devalued so are you. Now what do you do when your skin cripples your earning capacity?

For the U.S. economy to be transmuted into a pyramid scam, additional phenomena had to take place: An erosion (or politiciz-ing) of the illusive moral underpinnings of the nation, namely the Constitution and the Bill of Rights. The ideals embodied in these documents, fodder for political careers, have to be controlled and the national waters muddied if the financial infrastructure of the pyramid is to be maintained.

These ideals never existed in reality, especially for the slave underclass. Yet these ideals became dangerous once Black demands for equality and first-class citizenship gained enough leadership momentum to become the Civil Rights Movement with its battle cry of "one man, one vote." They had to be neutralized by devaluating worker status as well. The era of the blue-collar wealthy was short-lived. *Without full realization on the part of the worker, his/her prostitution was legalized.*

EROSION OF PAST GAINS

My delicious dilemma is language. How I structure it. How the fic-tion of history structures me. And as I've become more and more shattered, my tongue has become tangled. I find conventional forms and dialogues stifling, draining; I am glassed in by language as well as by the barriers of my dark skin and financial embarrass-ment. Under these constraints I cannot reconcile myself with such dualities: Black/White, male/female, mother/daughter, child/adult, friend/lover, worker/artist, street/university, hard/soft, as they kaleidoscopically affect a whole.

"The race problem is not a problem of the facts of biology, of scientific data thoroughly analyzed and systematically taught. It is first and foremost a social problem, which can be satisfactorily dealt with by social means of a kind that will require important revisions of some of our present ideas. For until the psychological disturbances which are created in the person by our processes of socialization are modified, the race problem will continue to plague us. Hence, the importance of inquiring into the nature of these processes and the effects which they produce upon behavior."   —Ashley Montagu, *Race, Science, and Humanity*

---

he played with his prized toy gun all the time he waved it around and would point it at anything residents tried to look out for the 6-foot-tall 180 pound retarded 13-year-old police officers mistook his plastic pistol for a real weapon drew their guns and fired four shots from their .357 magnum service revolvers

BLACKS ARE MORE LIKELY THAN WHITES TO BE VICTIMS OF MAJOR VIOLENT CRIMES AND BURGLARIES

There are moments when I doubt the clarity with which I see the world, when I say to myself "this can't be" or dismiss what I've seen as madness. My vision, my second sight, allows me to distinguish between matters of racial prejudice and matters of taste. It also allows me to cope with that strange post-'60s phenomenon in which anyone non-Black who personally knows someone Black fancies himself an expert on the Black condition.

If Black Americans of slave origin successfully obtained the social parity that we have rightly demanded, and did so by per-

66

sistently appealing to the so-called morals of a nation (as did the Southern Christian Leadership Conference and Martin Luther King), we would effectively share economic power and would be able to alter the cultural dynamics of the pyramid. The danger of Black social parity was foreseen by the pyramid's elite and has been successfully aborted.

But where is the sanity in appealing to the morality of a nation whose economic wealth is rooted in the immorality of slavery and whose growth is predicated on the ongoing, sophisticated process of dehumanization?

she answered a knock at her door was shot as the two men opened fire she died at a nearby hospital her youngest son standing behind her was killed on the spot a 16-year-old who wanted to become an actor the two gunmen retaliated for a weekend slaying they believed committed by the older son

NEGATIVE TO ZERO NET PERSONAL WEALTH

If I make an assertion about my particular Black experience invariably it will be countered by the experience of another not-always Black individual. I have no authority and to use myself as a standard proves valueless in marketing myself to the White literary establishment. No matter how many prizes I win I am still "just another niggah." (A Nobel Prize winner—Black—once confided that the only thing that seemed to matter was the next book.) This stereotyping diminishes the significance of Black thought when any and all Blacks are considered experts on themselves at a man-in-the-street level. Should the word of a nineteen-year-old gangbanger carry the same weight as a fifty-year-old university professor? Are we talking Uzis or Ulalume? Other ethnic groups are granted their intellectuals but (our) Black spokesmen/women seem forever held suspect, ever having to substantiate themselves; one can never have too many credentials or pay too many dues.

If Black individuals were allowed to pursue their notion of the American Dream it would mean full Black participation in the shaping of America's future, its language (which is already long in process), its eco-political terrain. Ramifications would be world-wide (as in the rap/hip-hop phenomenon), the assumption being that Black influence would be so great it would cause familiar terrain to become unrecognizable if not infertile for ethnic others on every level (witness certain contact sports, where team make-up has gone from all White in the 1950s to virtually all Black today). The game and the name would irrevocably change.

his body was found hanging from a fig tree along with a suicide note testimony from a handwriting analyst claimed the note was not written by him it was determined the hanging death of this young Black homosexual was unrelated to the same-night assault on two Black men by men in KKK robes

Five easy steps toward the eradication of poverty (token solution designed to counter criticism that all Black intellectuals must pro-vide solutions if to merit serious consideration):
   1) Minimum-wage increases tied to cost-of-living index.
   2) Government-subsidized childcare programs.
   3) Nationalized medicine and health care.
   4) Mandatory education through four years of college.
   5) Rigid enforcement of anti-discrimination laws.

NATIONAL CLIMATE OF SELFISHNESS

They come to these shores with psyches intact. They know who they are despite oppressive governments and strife. They've never been subjected to the immense cultural negative feedback American Blacks suffer. These immigrants, including those of similar coloration, willingly buy into the All-American Lie and isolate themselves from Blacks only to the extent they can use our backs to strengthen their own positions economically.

I mean, what do I say when my son's first experience of being called "nigger" is provided by the son of a Nicaraguan émigré?

We Blacks remain the lowest, least integrated underclass in a

68

"nation of immigrants," albeit ours was the forced-immigration of slavery. It was apparent that once we achieved full citizenship (ceasing to be wards of the federal government and second-class citizens) then (automatically) what was true for Black Americans, of slave origin, would automatically be true for every other oppressed group within society. This recognition gave rebirth to the White women's movement, the American Indian movement, Gay Liberation, the Brown Berets, the anti-Vietnam War movement, etc. ad nauseam. The only problem being that racism as it manifested itself on America's political left caused these second-level social "movements" to evolve apart from the thrust of the Civil Rights and Black Power movements instead of in tandem with them, borrowing their strategies, rhetoric, and style.

the 15-year-old girl was shot by the foreign-born owner of a liquor store in dispute over a bottle of orange juice the girl gave it back and tried to walk away the store owner shot the Black teenager in the back of the head killing her

COLOR-BLIND SOCIETY

What is a Black farmer?
A species it is predicted will be extinct by mid-century
as they are losing their land 2 ½ times faster
than their White counterparts.

Lyndon Baines Johnson's misguided "War on Poverty" bureaucracy reinforced the social evil it arrogantly presumed to eliminate. It failed because the extent to which racism permeates every aspect of the American psyche and terrain was underestimated. At the close of the '70s many Blacks felt abused by Jews, White women, gays, and anybody else who stood to gain from the passage of the Fourteenth Amendment (and affirmative action, for that matter) precisely because skin color per se was never a major issue for these factions. Thanks to advances in medical science one can alter one's facial features, sex organs, and hair;

69

skin-color change, however, has yet to be perfected. Plus there was an unexpected outcrop of trendy, safe, and sometimes frivolous movements, some rooted in Christian fundamentalism, which allowed many dominant-culture causeniks to get their protest kicks without exposing themselves to the kind of violence suffered by those at Kent State. These movements served the double purpose of luring the attention of the media, keeping focus off the deeper, more urgent issues of race.

the despondent mother who had been evicted from her apartment fatally stabbed her children then leapt to her death from a 13-story building

TWO-THIRDS OF CHILDREN IN BLACK FEMALE-HEADED HOUSEHOLDS LIVE IN POVERTY

The pathology associated with skin color and how it affects one's ability to survive and to move from one socioeconomic class to another, was and still is of major significance for those like me who identify as Black Americans. Once we began to flex new-found political clout with cries of Black Power, Whites who embraced us during the Civil Rights phase of the struggle could not understand a fledgling, almost adolescent, expression of a people who wanted long-denied social parity on their own terms. This naïve nationalistic rush would not be supported by their philanthropic dollars.

someone in a passing car swung through the quiet neighborhood fired two shots at random toward the muted light filtering through kitchen curtains the 45-year-old school teacher was struck once in the head she was pronounced dead several hours later

INADEQUATE WELFARE BENEFITS CONTRIBUTE TO HOMELESSNESS

Not all members of the pyramid elite are unsympathetic to those at the bottom. During the Civil Rights Movement some channeled money to various groups and causes or underwrote Black leaders. Wealthy individuals, businesses, and corporations could afford to sponsor their cause-of-choice and still get a break from the government through certain tax loopholes and deductions. A second step in "muddying" the moral waters of the nation was in altering the tax structure to close those loopholes and impose new limits on deductions, making certain pursuits less profitable as tax shelters. This effectively cut off major cash flow to the Black subculture. The recession and oil crisis of the early '70s polished off the rest.

Once monies, and so-called guilt funds, were dried up, the movements they supported collapsed.

As the seer beyond the veil, as the gifted possessor of a primal orb, I am compelled to explain and explain, to join a chorus of explainers articulating the Black/Afro-American experience, to constantly provide the context in which I will be more clearly understood and perhaps appreciated. Success at this brings on euphoria, failure despair.

a 21-year-old Black man died under mysterious circumstances after his arrest for reckless driving the coroner's special team reported unanimously he burned himself out suffering a sudden cardio-respiratory collapse the result of stress and exhaustion

AMERICAN APARTHEID

The pyramid scam underscoring America's truly "voodoo" economics is maintained by actual human sacrifice, the lives of those at the bottom of that pyramid; those most vulnerable to changes in the stock-market indicators; those most likely to be devastated by social ills from drugs to acquired immune deficiency syndrome (AIDS). Whenever the garden-variety all-American Negro accentuates the positive, eliminates the negative, and latches onto the affirmative in transcending cultural bias, a countermove is made to mess up any and all progress (failure to enforce legislation, use of immigration to fuel the underclass while simultaneously setting back Black advancements, deregulation, etc.).

Socioeconomic factors coupled with the persistence of White prejudice and the layering on of new immigrants compounds contemporary Black segregation.

the 34-year-old bus driver was shot seven times in front of his home police officers said they thought they heard a sliding gun bolt and fired after he failed to raise his hands as ordered

THERE IS NO CHANCE OF BLACKS CATCHING UP WITH WHITES BEFORE THE MIDDLE OF THE 22ND CENTURY

Does the process of making the invisible visible transform the seer as well as the seen? When does the victim become the perpetrator? A panel of experts says, a Ph.D. study addresses, a recent poll says, a committee report states, a government report issued says, a national study determines, a crime survey indicates, and a federal study finds . . .

Some reversal of these oppressive social circumstances must be found if one is to effectively "pimp the system."

The diabolical beauty of the American pyramid scam is that Blacks, like any other segment of society, must buy into the lie of White racial superiority if they are to succeed within the structure. And to buy into one's (and one's race's) ultimate destruction is pathological.

It is this devastating knowing that develops my other eye, strengthens my dual seeing. If I am to do more than merely survive it is imperative that I see clearly. I must not allow the fact that I'm born a statistic, a living comment on the hypocrisy of my America, to cloud my vision. Yet I am compelled to wonder where the statistics end and I begin. And if I persist as a statistic, have I the terrible fate of dying as one?

II

TEA LEAVES & JEREMIADS

Looking for It

An Interview with
Wanda Coleman—1991

by Andrea Juno and V. Vale

Thirteen years after the fact, I am no longer clear about where this interview took place. It may have happened on the road, while I was in San Francisco or Oakland for a performance/poetry reading, or in my home at the time, an apartment on Van Ness Avenue in the Hollywood-Larchmont area of mid-city Los Angeles. However, I clearly remember my inner responses to the questions (and where my responses are now different, I say so in square brackets). I had answered similar questions before, mainly from the podium during post-reading Q&A sessions, and have answered them again many times since. Woven into the text are further pertinent comments taken from an unpublished interview conducted on January 12, 1995, by Kate Pearcy, a University of Sydney student who was completing her dissertation on Black American women poets known for performance. Some of my answers below inspired poems or were fodder for my third of the "Three on the Town" column in the Los Angeles Times Magazine, *which I shared with journalists Jonathan Gold and Patt Morrison from 1993 to 1995, but some of my clearest, purest, most off-the-cuff*

75

responses were captured on this occasion. The Juno-Vale interview was one of the most enjoyable I had done to that date. I was skeptical at the time that it would see print—so many previous interviews hadn't—and was pleased to discover my interviewers, the editor and publisher of Re/Search Books, San Francisco, had really done their homework on me and my oeuvre, considering . . .

JUNO: You grew up in L.A.?

COLEMAN: Yes. I was born and raised in Watts. Then *all* of South Central L.A. became Watts after the riots in August '65. Until fifteen years ago I lived in that area.

I have some college, but college and I did not get along too well, so I dropped out. I had a hard time—I was taking workshops, and I was usually working two or three jobs, including waitressing on weekends. I had two babies by the time I was twenty, and they were being shuttled from one babysitter to another.

All of the problems that are "trendy" now, like childcare— see, I was *avant-garde* even for *that.* How do you deal with childcare? How do you build a survival unit? To survive, I was networking with girlfriends in everybody-eats-when-you-have-money kinds of situations. When I divorced my first husband at the end of the '60s, I was still thinking, "There's so much liberation going on—*of course* I'll be able to get a good job." Little did I know! I discovered I would really have a hard time getting a job, especially since I wore my hair in a natural—

VALE: White people were getting naturals, then—

COLEMAN: Oh no they weren't! I applied for a job with a Black employer who told me, "You're a very striking woman . . . but you've gotta do something about that hair! My White clients won't do business with me, if they see you looking like that." [*Laughs.*] I never went back! And because I was working two or three jobs, my hair was too hard to maintain, so I started wearing a wig. People will accept a wig before they'll accept

76

your natural hair—even a *natural* wig, because the real thing, *authenticity*, is a threat.

VALE: What were your parents like?

COLEMAN: My parents were petit bourgeoisie. My mother was a domestic—she came to California from Oklahoma when World War II started and jobs opened up for Blacks here. She worked in movie stars' homes, and in fact worked a year for Ronald Reagan when he was married to Jane Wyman—she quit when he wouldn't give her a raise! [*Laughs.*]

VALE: "Inflation—what's that?" [*Going along with the joke.*]

COLEMAN: *Even then!* [*Laughs.*] My father moved to Southern California from Little Rock, Arkansas, in 1931 after a young black man was lynched from the church steeple. They just left the body hanging there ... Some people with California license plates were passing through town; he offered them fifteen dollars for a ride, and they brought him to Los Angeles.

VALE: And he got a job—

COLEMAN: Well, his aunt was a domestic who also worked for Ronnie Baby as the washerwoman who did the laundry. She invited my mother to church and that's how my parents met.

JUNO: I think people don't realize how recently Black people were getting lynched—

COLEMAN: Well, it's still happening! Just like the drug problem —no one tells you that the drug problem was the creation of the federal government from the start. Blacks were targeted and drugs were put into the Black community by the federal government of these United States, and the drug problem didn't become important until it spilled over to the dominant culture. Then suddenly it became a problem, just as with LSD. And where did LSD come from? The *government*. [These "party lines" minus specifics are held over from my underground days. Vis-à-vis heroin, speculation goes that after the

77

riots in Harlem, federal officials, anxious to prevent future violence, allowed Lucky Luciano—among others—to introduce
the use and sale of the drug into Black communities via the
Negro entertainers who worked in Mob-owned clubs. A similar
tale that circulated, and still circulates, was that Thelonious
Monk was introduced to LSD stolen from a government experimental laboratory.]

VALE: I saw a photo of a Black man who had been lynched in
San Jose in the '40s—not that long ago. I thought that only
happened in the Deep South.

COLEMAN: Well, in downtown Los Angeles they lynched nine
Chinese gentlemen in the '30s. Ah—America the Beautiful!

VALE: There's a lot of hidden history—

COLEMAN: And you won't get it if you don't look for it—you're
certainly not going to be taught it in *school*. [*Laughs.*] I
remember being in high school in '64, taking World History
and reading, "The Negro race has made no major contribution
to the history of the world." Uh—*right!* There's a whole lost
history, and as a writer, I constantly think about the fact that
no one's ever written, say, the history of Black Los Angeles . . .
I've written six books and feel it might have been sixteen books
if I'd had the quality time to do just *that*.

A cult figure? Some consider me such or have said as much to
me. And I say, "Oh, really? Where's the cult?" [*Laughs.*] Point me
to the cult! It's unfortunate, the problems we artists have because
we aren't invited to help shape our own images.

—Kate Pearcy interview, 1995

JUNO: That's how they keep you from having a voice—

COLEMAN: You're spread so thin trying to survive or make ends meet that you have no voice. This is true of women in this society, and particularly women with kids—I think it takes a genius to be able to write in the middle of this! Yet there are more of us than you think—have you seen the *Breaking Ice* anthology? There's fifty-two writers in there, most of whom I've never heard of, and most of them have five or six books out. And they range in age from twenty-five to seventy. But it was, initially, hard for us to get in the mainstream of literature because our books were seldom reviewed, and we're seldom interviewed. This society has what I call the "Nigger of the Minute syndrome"—also known as HNIC, or Head Nigger In Charge. Only one token nigger is allowed at any given time, regardless of regionality or differences in style.

It's strange, but in recent years there's been quite an increase in "artificial opportunities." All of a sudden you're in demand, but this demand is really tokenistic: "Hey, it's Negro History Month!" So the only time you'll get work will be during Negro History Month, or on the anniversary of a riot—the rest of the year you'll be ignored.

JUNO: As if you don't have something to say about the human condition in general—

COLEMAN: Well, according to the gentlemen who put together the Great Books of the Western World—we don't. Whatever literary prizes may be available to us are doled out tokenistically: you have to fit a certain mold, you have to be *safe*.

VALE: How did you start writing?

COLEMAN: Even as a kid I tried to keep diaries, but I was so full of hate and rage that when I go back and look at them, they're nothing but bursts of *anger*—very little else. But my parents encouraged me; I had my first poems published when I was thirteen in the local "fishwrap," throwaway newspaper.

I was the kid who always got an "A" on the Father's Day poem—I was sort of an egghead, but a dumb egghead! [*Laughs.*] I was always daydreaming and reading literature other than what was given me in school. At that time books were segregated—you had boys' literature and girls' literature. When I went to the library (Ascot and Downtown branches), I could read *Cheryl Crane, Nurse*, books by the Brontë sisters, and Nancy Drew mysteries—yes, those horrible things! But I wasn't allowed to read Sir Arthur Conan Doyle or H. P. Lovecraft —the boys' books. So I would have my father go to the library with me. I would pick out what I wanted and he would check the books out.

Then I could read to my heart's content! And I was reading way beyond my years: when I was ten I read the complete works of Shakespeare. I read Sir Richard Burton's *Unexpurgated Arabian Nights*—in fact I had a gorgeous leather-bound copy of the *Arabian Nights*, but left it in the trunk of the car one night, then came down with encephalitis for two months —there was an epidemic going around—and while I was sick my father sold the car! It was *beautiful*—it had all these colored plates in it. And it was gone . . .

In high school I began reading the heavyweights: Nietzsche, Sartre, Heidegger. And my teachers started getting upset. One of them actually told my parents that these books were bad for me; that they were making me rebellious, and that my parents should forbid me to read them. By then I knew I wasn't getting a good education, because I had done all this reading. Also, I was on the debate team. So I would go from Black inner-city schools to White schools in Beverly Hills and look at other kids' books and compare them to what I was reading —and I knew they were getting a better education!

This was when the "White flight" was beginning—when Whites were fleeing the inner city of Los Angeles and moving elsewhere. When we first moved to our house, the neighborhood was White, but by the time I had graduated from high school only two White families were left on my block—and they were old people. So the classes became 80 percent Black and 20 percent "other"—Latino, Filipino, etc.—with maybe one or two poor, lower-class Whites left.

In class there were so many ugly situations. I remember one time the kids called our White male teacher a homosexual —you didn't do that in those days—and he went berserk and proceeded to tell us how superior he was! I remember teachers getting beaten up by kids or parents or uncles because of some racial incident or slur—they would wait for the teachers after class and beat the shit out of them, or destroy their cars. These were mostly White teachers.

VALE: After high school, you had two kids by the age of twenty?

COLEMAN: Blame it on the Civil Rights Movement! [*Laughs.*] My first husband, Charlie Coleman, was a trouble-shooter for SNCC who came to Southern California with Jesse Jackson, Vernon Jordan, and Stokely Carmichael. He was a White guy who was part of Martin Luther King's inner circle; he had been in several early protest marches. He was from Georgia—and called himself a redneck—but he was a very unusual person, unique for that time. He came out here for a fund-raiser and stayed.

JUNO: So you were getting politicized then?

COLEMAN: I would say that he politicized me. Interestingly enough, his politicizing brought our marriage to an end— because I began to *outgrow* our relationship. I still wanted to be a writer for the "revolution," but I knew I was being treated patronizingly—the men didn't take me seriously. Because if you don't have something to offer—either sex or money— you're of no value for the most part ... *still!* [*Laughs.*] The roots of this haven't changed.

Also, my father had given me a lot of ideas, even though he didn't have a college education—he had dropped out of school when he was eight years old. He taught me a lot about graphics, advertising, and the media—I know how to dummy a newspaper, for example. He tried for years to get a Black men's magazine going in the '50s, but Johnson Publications— *Ebony, Jet,* etc.—stonewalled any competition.

81

VALE: The Black media establishment. How did they react to the emergence of the Black Panthers? Did they even cover it?

COLEMAN: Well, those publications had a policy: unless it's sanctioned by the White media—unless it's recognized or sanctioned by the pop culture—it's not going to appear in their pages. Because they're not about exploring or finding out about anything.

VALE: So for them the '60s never happened? The Black Panthers and SNCC were never covered in their pages?

COLEMAN: Only after they became big names and received national attention. My first husband and I were involved in the organization "US" when Ron Karenga, the founder of Kwanzaa, and his group [of Black nationalists] were photographed for the cover of *Life*. I still have that issue. [We left "US" to join the Malcolm X Organization for Afro-American Unity or MOAAU, then others.] It's funny—my husband was so in tune with the movement that he was able to sit among people like Ron Karenga and Huey P. Newton—and he was White.

JUNO: Those were exciting times—

COLEMAN: Very exciting, because I was living in two worlds. We were living in the world of the Black militants, but we were also living in the world of the hippies. So we would go from love-ins to underground meetings plotting the overthrow of the government! My first husband and I were on our way to becoming members of the Weather Underground when we split up. At the time we belonged to a paramilitary organization. We went from group to group, starting with the NAACP Youth Council, just getting steadily more and more militant. We had heard about the Symbionese Liberation Army, but decided to join the Weather Underground. Then I decided I wanted to become an artist—that was more important to me. So we split up—I decided I'd had enough of being married, anyway . . .

VALE: You'd begun to see inequities in the "revolutionary" underground?

COLEMAN: Definitely! Plus, there was a strong anti-intellectual climate—if you saw through somebody's game, you had to keep your mouth shut. You couldn't call them on it. There was a subtle group pressure to conform to the party line. You didn't ask questions—you didn't question your leadership, so to speak. And there was a lot of intimidation . . .

If you really looked at some of these people . . . if you were bright enough to see through their "mack" [con game or rap] and say, "Well, I don't necessarily feel like doing that; that doesn't make sense to me," well—! I'd always thought the Panthers were wonderful *theater*, but I didn't think they were *revolutionary*. But when they'd come into a room dressed in black leather and carrying those rifles on their shoulders—if there was any grumbling in the room, it would *cease* [*snaps her fingers*]—everyone would just snap to attention! So it was an exciting period. There was this feeling that, "Wow—we really are going to make a difference!" Little did we know . . .

We also spent a lot of time in Griffith Park at the love-ins. That was the other thing—the music was such a part of the excitement! We were always crashing concerts and doing things like jumping up on the stage. I remember when Big Brother & the Holding Company came to L.A. and did a concert in Montebello Park, and I jumped up onstage with Janis Joplin and was dancing—me and my brother and a guy with a banana in his crotch—I'll never forget it! And they [security] wouldn't push you off the stage. They would let you dance. You can't do that now. Back then you could get up onstage and then go backstage and get high with the band, or whatever. And when you went to Griffith Park, the families—there were several "families" there, including the Manson family—they would pitch tents, and you could go inside and sit and talk with them or share their food. It was great! Everyone was young and beautiful, and drugs were free, and it was a fabulous time.

83

We went to San Francisco during the Summer of Love. We had a '58 Studebaker convertible and one day we jumped in it and headed north to the Haight-Ashbury, in and out of crash pads and head shops—we just did the whole trip. It was a wonderful experience—like an endless series of parties and meetings—it was really something to go through!

It's funny, because I was going through all of this with one eye open and one eye wary—I was cynical even *then*. I felt that people were underestimating the enemy—and I was right. I thought a lot of the leadership was extremely naïve, if not downright stupid. During the Poverty Program, they were handing out all this money, and it was like the program was designed to fail. These old "churchified" preachers who didn't know what they were doing were getting paid to "train" young people—on obsolete equipment. Money was being stolen right and left by young hotshot accountants, Black or otherwise, who spent what they stole on gold Mercedes while poor Blacks and Hispanics weren't getting anything.

JUNO: But now things are so much worse.

COLEMAN: Of course! When you talk to a lot of Blacks, they reminisce about how wonderful the March on Washington was, when Martin Luther King gave his famous "I Have a Dream" speech. Well, that march was supposed to be angry—not a giant love-in! What happened was this: when the government found out that Blacks were going to be furious, they got on the horn and contacted Black leaders and told them to get the militants outta there. [Disappointed, we backed out when word of this reached us via the underground grapevine.] They got all these old "biscuits" like King to turn the march into a giant love-in. And that's one of the reasons things are the way they are now.

VALE: You called King a "biscuit"?

COLEMAN: I was never in his camp. [I was in Malcolm X's camp. Contrary to recent myth, the groups were in opposition long after their leaders were assassinated. Reconsidering Martin Luther King Jr. later, I realized there was more to what I expressed than I could discuss with my interviewers. My attitude had as much to do with my upbringing as it did with MLK; also, beneath it was the residual of stories related by my first husband about MLK. I had long known about MLK's purported infidelities *before* they became public record vis-à-vis former FBI chief J. Edgar Hoover, and, therefore, I had long regarded MLK's "content of character" posture as hypocritical. I also believed MLK's own words would be used against his own people, when opportune, holding Blacks to an unrealistic moral standard suspended for others in a culture that celebrates and romanticizes its white- and blue-collar criminals, sexual outlaws, and serial killers and allows bigots and mediocrities to run for national office and be appointed Supreme Court justices. Finally, I hold with John Henrik Clarke's assessment of MLK and the marches on Washington as "ceremony without substance," expressed in the 1996 film *John Henrik Clarke: A Great & Mighty Walk,* directed by Saint Clair Bourne. As for MLK's birthday, I appreciate the sentiment, but I would've preferred a national holiday that celebrated all great men of color—including Malcolm X and W. E. B. Du Bois.] I always felt that what happened in the South was fine, but that it didn't have universal application to all the problems that Blacks face in America, that you had to use different strategies in other parts of the country, particularly in the Northern cities, and out West where racism wears a smiling face and is much more sophisticated . . . where people kill you with kindness—saying "Oh, yes, Brutha!" while they're stabbing you in the back. But who was going to listen to a nineteen-year-old female? I had no influence. Usually people would just look at me and tell me to shut up.

JUNO: Now things are so bad that there's no hope of mobilization. Do you think rap music will—

COLEMAN: As long as we're dancin', we ain't fightin'! When

85

Blacks were rioting, a song by Martha and the Vandellas came on the radio: *Dancing in the Streets!* I think [recalling the rumor] that the song was deliberately promoted by the government, after that long, hot summer of 1965, to distract Blacks from taking care of serious business.

Me do hip-hop? I stay away from it as much as possible. Music is not about language, so much, as it is about sound. If you have a good drivin' rhythm and beat, it virtually doesn't matter what you throw in the mix in terms of language. I think rap music is terrific. I like it, listen to it, and put my money behind it. If I were ten years younger, I might be making money too, instead of sitting here in this hell-hole trying to write a grant proposal. [*Laughs.*]

—Kate Pearcy interview, 1995

Do you know we have never had a major Black actor? Sidney Poitier and Harry Belafonte are not American Black men —they're islanders. [*Laughs.*] And [until the '80s] the ones we've *had* have been comedians or comics [with the exception of New Yorker Ivan Dixon in Michael Roemer's *Nothing But a Man* (1964) and Texan Al Freeman Jr. in Anthony Harvey's *Dutchman* (1967). But these serious native-born actors never achieved the stardom of Poitier and Belafonte, as would no Black actor until *Soldier's Story* (1984) and Spike Lee's *She's Gotta Have It* (1986) introduced a new generation]. See, the clowns and the gangsters always have work. In the Black community, those are the people who make the money—the clowns and the gangsters/sharks. Everybody else suffers.

VALE: What do you mean by gangsters?

COLEMAN: I mean just that. And you can make those appellations as broad as you want. By "clowns"—and I don't want to demean some of these people, but I'm talking about how

86

they're viewed by the dominant culture: Michael Jackson would be a clown, Oprah Winfrey would be a clown, Bill Cosby would be a clown, Eddie Murphy would be one. These people are allowed to make money in the system and in the society because they're no threat, no danger.

JUNO: And very rarely do you ever have a Black male sexual, romantic figure.

COLEMAN: Exactly. Here we are on the verge of the '90s, and they're censoring Whoopi Goldberg kissing a white man on-camera [*Fatal Beauty*, 1987]—give me a break! But you have to remember this is *Hollywood*, the en-ter-tain-ment kapital o' da world. Women have made inroads in science, in politics, but they haven't made many inroads in Hollywood. It's the same old *same old*.

VALE: Women are sometimes film editors, but rarely directors—

COLEMAN: You have a few . . . And the men are hip to the game —if feminism becomes trendy, all of a sudden they're writing feminist scripts, too! [*Laughs.*] Blacks also have been tied into this "artificial liberation"—this illusion that Blacks have achieved all of their goals—and women too! That's right. Therefore, whenever you have a spokesman for the so-called "Black point of view"—and there may be five different attitudes within the Black community—they'll pick a conservative Black.

Perhaps I'm particularly sensitive; maybe you could talk to somebody else Black and they'd say, "*I've* never experienced racism." Recently I went to hear a friend read at a punk-rock place called the Anti-Club in L.A. and there were these jigaboo pictures on the wall. I don't know who put them up—a Black artist could have painted them, for all I know, but I found them insulting.

The paintings were recent—they weren't old. I didn't need to see this shit, so I tried to ignore it. My present [and third] husband is Jewish; he's from Brooklyn. I was trying to pretend

I didn't see them, but finally he said, "Wanda, look at those jigaboo pictures on the wall!" I saw the owner, a French Jew, sitting by the counter, and I said to my husband, "Austin, if you want to file a complaint, go talk to the owner over there." He went over, and all of a sudden she couldn't understand English—kind of convenient, you know? [*Laughs.*] I was listening to him trying to explain, and finally I went over and said, "Yes! As a Black person, I can testify to the fact that these paintings are offensive. In fact, they make me feel like getting an ax and putting it in the head of the first White person I see—*you!*" [*Laughs.*] The owner went into shock ... then started snatching pictures off the wall! I mean—if I had put swastikas upon her walls, I'm sure she would have understood that. For her not to have understood—give me a break. Let's get *real*. [A shouting match ensued, after which we were thrown out of the club and missed our friend's performance.]

When I was a kid my first experience of being called a "nigger" involved a White kid. My oldest son was called that by his White grandmother. My youngest son's first experience involved a *Nicaraguan* kid—see what I'm saying? There's a real lack of understanding about this: when you go to another country, you buy into whatever the lie is if you're going to survive there economically. Foreigners who come to live in America buy into the lie of American racism, which means keeping Blacks at the bottom of the society. These immigrants haven't been oppressed on that same deeply racist level. So when they come here, they don't understand Black Americans—who we are or where we're coming from. And they're not going to get enlightened by our history books, psychology books, newspapers or TV. These people have no way of understanding us when they get here. So you end up with conflicts between communities: the Blacks and the Koreans, or the Blacks and the Vietnamese, or the Blacks and the Cubans ... as an outgrowth of this lack of information and understanding.

JUNO: And of course the White establishment—

COLEMAN: —feeds off that and encourages it. In the '60s I would encounter people from Nigeria or Kenya or wherever, and the first thing they would say is, "We have been told by your government that we're not supposed to associate with you; otherwise they will cancel our visas."

VALE: Did they also feel superior because they were Africans?

COLEMAN: Yes—and rightly so, because they're coming here the same way a European would—they're immigrating into the country. They have been subjected to colonialism, but even colonialism did not erase their culture. Even South Africans have their identity as a tribal people—they didn't have their language taken away; they weren't forced to intermarry the way Aborigines were, or the way Blacks were in the breeding plantations in the United States.

   The victims are constantly blamed for being victims in this society. Historians will tell you, "Well, you Black people sold each other into slavery." But actually that wasn't what happened: one tribe might have sold an enemy tribe into slavery, but that isn't the same thing—that's tribalism, whereas racism is a uniquely American product. Throughout the history of the world you always had one tribe, regardless of what race they were, fighting another. There was warfare, and one culture would absorb or cannibalize or be parasitic upon the other. To the victor went the spoils—that was the way of the world. But Black Americans are a whole new animal. We are unique in the history of the world. Our situation is not comparable to what happened in the West Indies, in Africa or in South Africa.

JUNO: Your writing is giving voice to a stifled culture—

COLEMAN: If I had left L.A. for New York in 1969, I might be nationally well known. But I had two kids so I had to stay here and make a living. I was invited to be a member of the first Black delegation that went to China, when China opened up to United States citizens, but I couldn't go—I had to work.

89

Juno: So how did you manage to raise three kids and survive?

Coleman: I went without sleep! [*Laughs.*] I would go two or three days without sleep and without the assistance of drugs, and I didn't drink coffee in those days, so it was really hard. And most of the time I wasn't eating. I would sleep on my break; I carried an alarm clock in my car and would put it on the dashboard and sleep in the car until the alarm went off.

Vale: But you managed to keep your writing spirit alive—

Coleman: When I was a child I was reading all these tomes by these so-called great writers, and every now and then I would stub my metaphorical toe on the word "nigger" or "negress." And the hunger was always there to present my worldview, because my worldview didn't exist—it didn't even exist when Simone de Beauvoir wrote *The Second Sex*. She wrote about women all right, but what she wrote didn't apply to *me*.

Juno: You felt that the Feminist movement omitted Black culture?

Coleman: Well, I thought that it mainly belonged to rich White women who were not interested in my concerns—I saw that right off. What did I need to do—trade one oppressor for another? And they were using tactics that Blacks had pioneered in the Civil Rights Movement . . . that people from the left had pioneered when there was a strong Labor Union movement in the United States.

Juno: So . . . what are some of your goals in your writing?

Coleman: For a while I was writing for television, but finally I decided to leave the world of popular culture. I was on the staff of *Days of Our Lives*, and they got an Emmy award; then the writers got the ax, and I never went back—nor was I invited back—I disappeared and didn't keep in touch. And what did I want to do? I decided I wanted to be a "literary" person, because I felt that's where the changes originate—the popular or "low" culture always cannibalizes the "high" culture. Also, working in television I tired of being told what I could and couldn't say—so I went to books.

JUNO: Do you feel hopeless or enraged?

COLEMAN: My anger knows no bounds—it's unlimited. I'm a big lady, I can stand up in front of almost any man and cuss him out and have no fear—you know what I'm sayin'? Because I will go to blows. But when I get older, I'm not going to be able to do that, and with my temper—I'm going to have to start carrying a gun! And if I'm going to carry one, somebody's ass is going to be shot! Because at the rate things are going . . . I won't tolerate this bullshit. Some of my colleagues have mellowed with age; I'm not among them yet. Maybe I have to go through some kind of biochemical change or menopause—I do not know! [I will later discover that I have hypertension related to stress and diet.] I'm tryin' to come to terms with this, because I'm tired of dealing with racial incidents on a daily basis. Why can't I just leave the house, go shopping, do my thing and come home? Why do I always have to deal with some bullshit?

JUNO: What do you think the future will hold?

COLEMAN: I don't know.

VALE: Don't you think things are getting worse?

COLEMAN: Well—times are tough. If you ask a young person today, "What do you want to be when you grow up?" the assumption is that you're going to live long enough to grow up; someone's not going to drop a bomb on you. You're not going to be shot by a cop. I have a twelve year old, and what is his future going to be as a Black male in society when a third of the Black men in the state of California have records, have served time, or are serving time in jail? Unemployment for Black males is in excess of 60 percent. So what's the future? I don't know. All I can do is try to arm him—give him psychological emotional armament, so he will be ready for what they throw at him!

JUNO: You've got the warrior mentality—

COLEMAN: Because it's a war! Certainly we're being warred against. In my book of short stories *A War of Eyes*, all the stories are about this constant self-conscious confrontation that happens the minute you meet a Black person. Because in order to have any kind of constructive dialogue, there has to be a proper context. And often that context is music, like jazz or rap music—which gets to be a drag!

When I go somewhere like Atlanta, I get really excited because I am not used to seeing so many Black people—I start staring! I go into a restaurant and it's amazing! I go into the street and the police are Black. You don't have that experience in Southern California. So for me, when I go to D.C. or Philadelphia or even Chicago, I get really excited—

JUNO: Because here you can never forget you're Black.

COLEMAN: And it gets to be a chore. Every time you go to a party, you're an *issue* just because you're there; I don't have to say a word. It's hard to have a good time! Even socializing on a minimal level gets to be a pain—why can't it just be a party?! But somebody always opens their mouth and says something wrong, like, "Well, Wanda, your people have sure made a lot of progress, haven't they?" And then I have to say, "Wait a minute . . ."

JUNO: They say that *now*?

COLEMAN: Oh yes—in fact, that happened a month ago, baby— here in the 1990s! Ignorance yet abounds . . . And the other side of the coin is: I get tired of being "Wanda the Explainer." I get tired of giving people an education on racism—having my brain picked for free. I feel like saying, "Motherfucker, if you can't handle it—tough!" [*Laughs.*]

A synthesis has taken place ... that wrenching separation defined as the Middle Passage, as a physical fact, has made its way into language ... over these hundreds of years, and has made its way into the cultural structure through music, sports and the penal system. It has had significant economic impact ... that resonance that began when slaves were taken from Africa. Like the existence of racism itself, it morphs ... it isn't going to go away. Our legacy is feeding a lot of people, not just Blacks.

—Kate Pearcy interview, 1995

VALE: "Read my books!"

JUNO: Do you get hassled for being sexually explicit?

COLEMAN: [*Laughs.*] So far I haven't. If anybody's denied me anything, I don't know about it. I've gotten my share of grant money, because not everything is a diatribe, and not everything has four-letter words. I like communicating with mature minds, and you need a certain life experience to really appreciate the bulk of my work. So I don't talk to a junior-high-school audience without giving them a certain context. And I have enough work to select from—I've written a couple thousand poems and a hundred short stories—so we can come to a real good understanding without my having to blow their lids! I don't need to do that, nor am I interested in doing that, because I'm about *communicating.* I'm not about shock; if any shock is present it's the shock of *recognition* ... or the shock of *understanding,* which might just go with the turf. But I'm not deliberately out to just shock people. I'm not about being sensationalistic.

I want *freedom* when I write, I want the freedom to use any kind of language—whatever I feel is appropriate to get the point across. There's a piece in *African Sleeping Sickness* where I use very pornographic images, blatantly sexual imagery—I'm just downright *nasty* ... but I choose that language deliberately, because I'm talking about a downright nasty situation,

93

namely my experience in literary workshops, how I was treated. I start out using the metaphor of a circle jerk, and it gets nastier from there. So I'm deliberately using sexual imagery, but I'm talking about writing poetry and my workshop experience as a poet. The subject matter is not really sexual at all —the imagery is!

When I moved to Hollywood, little did I know that it's now a hardcore ghetto! When I was working in the entertainment business, my associates were afraid to come there. I live right on the borderline between Hancock Park—wealthy homes with real mahogany and crystal and beautifully kept grounds —and a lot of drug activity; there's a heroin dealer down the street, and gangs. There are eighty different languages spoken here. To the northeast is the Armenian population; the Korean population is just south; the Chinese and Japanese are further south; and there are a lot of Thai and Vietnamese.

The ghettos have changed a lot. In South Central L.A. people are dying—sitting in their living rooms watching TV and catching stray bullets. So there's no haven, no sanctity—I worry about my mother living there. Because the new-school gangsters are sociopaths—they don't respect anybody. They don't care who you are: "Oh, you a great poet?" They don't give a fuck. If they want your car and they've got an Uzi and a bicycle, they're gonna make you get out of your car and give it up. If they think you have some money and you don't, they might shoot you because they're mad 'cuz they took their time to hold you up and you ain't got nothin'—so you're dead either way! There's no respect for anything.

JUNO: Did there used to be?

COLEMAN: Yes, when I was growing up, gangs had their turf and they respected "civilians." They wouldn't shoot a woman unless she did something, stepped on somebody's toes—she would have to do something to a gangster to be the victim of gang activity. Now you don't have to do anything—just be in the wrong place at the wrong time and you're in trouble!

JUNO: How did that develop?

COLEMAN: These young kids know that if they work at McDonald's—they know the American dream is a lie ("If you work hard in this country, you'll succeed!") because they saw their parents do that, and look what happened to *them*! They know that you cannot count on a job being there for twenty-five years, and if you decide to retire, you cannot count on your retirement funds being available, because they may have all been lost on Wall Street, or turned into junk bonds, or embezzled.

JUNO: But that's been happening in the Black community forever—

COLEMAN: It's happening to the whole culture now! And it hadn't been in the Black community all the time, because before integration there was this big hope: that once the doors opened, we would be allowed in! Now that hope is gone—Black people know their lives are of no value. Twelve-year-old Black boys know that our government wants to fry them—boys my son's age. They want to put them in the electric chair or gas chamber or in prison for life.

You see, Black people were believers back then—they're not anymore. They know the American dream is a crock of shit, because they saw what happened to their parents who were believers, who can't get insurance coverage—or when they do get it, they're charged unfair rates because they live in a certain community. Now they know it's all jive and bullshit; they know their lives have no value. And if their lives have no value, why should they value anyone else's lives? No matter what age they are—whether they're five or a hundred and five, whether they're a preacher or a pauper, if their lives have no value, no one else's does either!

The generation before them believed that the White boy would let them play the game. Now we all know that the White boy has no intention of letting us play the game. And you cannot afford to wear gold chains around your neck if

95

you're working at McDonald's twelve hours a day. You know you will never make enough money to be driving a Maserati or an Excalibur or live in the Hollywood Hills. And you will never be sitting in the front row at Trump Tower watching the Mike Tyson fight if you're working at McDonald's. And these young guys know it.

They also know that not everybody has the smarts to get a Ph.D. or the money to buy that education. And education is being undermined left and right; the advances made in the '60s are being reversed: Blacks have a higher dropout rate across the board. So on every level you look, where do you go? You can't even go to church anymore—church used to be strong in the Black community. The preacher could actually protect a young man and keep him out of jail—he can't do that no more. There's no more dialogue; the preacher can't protect your ass anymore—his ass is being shot up, too! He doesn't get the respect from the community he used to get.

There's only NOW. Our society has created that kind of psychosis. Where there is only now, there's no such thing as consequences. If there are no consequences then you don't have to be concerned about paying them. There's no way to punish anybody who doesn't have a future. If they've never had anything, you can't deprive them of anything. If they're in jail inside the society —if they're in jail outside the society—what's the difference?

—Kate Pearcy interview, 1995

JUNO: Were you part of a church when you were growing up?

COLEMAN: Yes. But these young people don't respect the church —they'll shoot it up just as soon as they'd shoot up a liquor store!

VALE: There's a literary tradition of celebrating (if that's the right word) Black criminals or Black underworld activity, by writers such as Melvin Tolson in the '30s, up to Donald Goines. How do you feel about the Iceberg Slim books?

COLEMAN: I got an autographed copy! I've got about four auto-graphed books by Robert Beck. [This is too long and complex a truth to tell well in an interview. There isn't enough time to travel back through my days as a magazine editor, during which I had a brief friendship with Donald Goines before his violent death, and during which I met Robert Beck. I was working for their publisher at Holloway House. To answer the interviewer fully would be to tell tales I still hope to spin else-where, should Fate be kind. I do my awkward best, and what may come off below as coyness is actually pure reluctance and evasiveness.] I knew the real "T"—which we will not discuss today! [*Laughs.*] As far as myself—well, I consider myself in the tradition of Western Literature! [*Cackles evilly.*] W. E. B. Du Bois is My Man—he wrote *The Souls of Black Folk*. [I want to stay out of the streets.] And even though his language is a little stiff and archaic, he's important because he identified our context: that we live in two worlds simultaneously. Every-thing in the dominant culture is ours also; there's this two-way mirror effect: you can see their world, but somehow they can't see yours! So you have your world as source material, but you also have access to theirs. And they refuse to see *your* world because they consider their world to be the only one of value.

So you're bicultural—and if you're smart enough, you're bilingual. Because there's definitely a difference between writing with a Black sensibility and what I call writing White. If you want to succeed in this culture you learn how to write "White"—I mean I've written ad copy and done other kinds of writing; I can write about another poet's work without neces-sarily having to be "Afrocentric" or "Afrocultural." I'm able to do that, but I doubt that a White writer could read my work and divorce himself from his culture—that would be an im-possibility! Because he wouldn't be bicultural. [I no longer fully agree with this fast talk—which is an oversimplification of an extremely complex dynamic—particularly since some of the best writing about my oeuvre has been by White males. I am also forgetting the non-Black male who is acculturated.

97

Furthermore, a new generation was emerging as I spoke, the product of Black/African American/Africana studies programs in colleges and universities.]

I can criticize a movie or piece of fiction because I belong to both traditions. I'm affected by the literature I grew up with, which includes Edgar Allan Poe, Nathaniel Hawthorne, Evelyn Waugh, Nathanael West, Somerset Maugham, Albert Camus, André Malraux, Chekhov . . . these are all people I read, they're all my influences. I was privy to that literature as a teenager; I read Plato, Aristotle, Kant, Emerson, all of them. But I also listened to the blues; I also know who my culture is. I read Richard Wright, James Baldwin . . . although I came late to most Black literature—Jones/Baraka, Petry, Toomer, *et al.*—because I didn't have access to it until I became a young adult.

If you ever want to read my biography, read *The Street* by Ann Petry—my biography's already been written. Do you know what it's like to discover that your biography was written the year you were born?

VALE: Still, she got her message across—

COLEMAN: I don't know—you'd have to ask her! [*Laughs.*] I came across that book in my early twenties and it had a very profound effect on me—as profound as listening to Billie Holiday or Nina Simone or Etta James or John Coltrane or Jimi Hendrix.

VALE: How would you context Iceberg Slim?

COLEMAN: [I suppose my interviewers were expecting me to label Iceberg Slim a clown and a gangster. I might have, but their question again sent me reeling back nineteen years to my days as an editor at Holloway House.] Well, he does not give up as much game as you think he's giving up! He doesn't really give you the full "T" in his books. I used to go to young Black guys' houses and that's the first thing I saw on the coffee table: a copy of *Pimp*. Well, I read *Pimp*, and if you've had experience with pimps you know he ain't telling all the game. If you follow that book you might end up dead somewhere rather than as a successful pimp, because there's different kinds of pimp "macks" . . . and he lays down one, but that's not necessarily the style you might use if you were going to go that way.

VALE: But you do respect him?

COLEMAN: I like the man; I met him. And I know some things about him that are not public knowledge, so—what can I say? I understand who he is—I have the proper *context* for him [but this would require a sociology thesis on race and sex in America]. Other people who read him wouldn't necessarily respect him. *Okay?* So because of that, I like him [actually, "empathize with" is the phrase, but I can't get my tongue around it]. But I wouldn't consider him an influence on my work. And on my Top Ten List of Black writers he would not appear—neither would Chester Himes, whom I don't like because of all of his shame, all his bootlicking, all his catering to racist conceptions about Blacks. *Cotton Comes to Harlem, Crazy Kill*—awful stuff! [I had just plucked *Pink Toes* off a friend's bookshelf, the reading still fresh. To date, my opinion of Himes's work is unchanged.] Even though the language and some of the descriptions may be interesting, nevertheless all that self-hatred is there and it's sick—from my point of view it's very unhealthy. And he was not a great writer by anyone's standards—Black, White, or otherwise. He was a mediocre writer; he did his job—probably the best he could. I never met the man so I couldn't assess that, but what he has left behind —with the exception of an autobiography—is awful.

VALE: But you don't feel that way about Iceberg Slim?

COLEMAN: Well, I can see how some people could evaluate him that way, but I've had personal contact with the man so . . .

VALE: How did you discipline yourself to produce a couple thousand poems and a hundred short stories?

COLEMAN: Just by *sheer force of will*. It's harder now than it ever was; I've never been able to have the luxury of a routine. There was a time when I could get up at four in the morning and my kids were little, but I've never had a lot of "golden" or peaceful time—it's always been catch-as-catch-can. When you're poor you spend a lot of time standing in line and waiting for service—and it's usually not *good* service, either. Like getting your car fixed—you're sitting in the shop *cooling your ass*. So I use that time constructively—I always have a book to read, or a book to write in. If I'm in the bank standing in line, I have a notebook to write in. That's how I do it.

VALE: How do you regard your sense of humor?

COLEMAN: My humor is a weapon. And as far as my taste goes —I went to see *Goodfellas* [Scorcese's 1991 ultraviolent gangster film] and I roared! To me that was one fucking funny movie—I thought it was hysterical. I was laughing; I was trying to control myself because I knew I was probably interfering with other people's experience—the audience was being horrified [*gasps*] while I was going, "Hee hee hee!" You know what I'm sayin'?

So as far as my sense of humor goes—for a long time people told me I didn't have one, or that I was too serious . . . I think they just didn't appreciate or understand where I was coming from, or how my sense of humor operated.

I love irony—that's my favorite. I love satire. And when I laugh, I laugh loud, and long, and hard . . . and mean! Sometimes I can be a little sadistic: "Oh—did that hurt? Want some more?" I can sometimes be cruel, but then again—I haven't been spared. So if I can dish it out, I can take it—and I don't dish out anything I can't take . . .

The pop culture in America romanticizes every bloody thing—when you live in a culture that can romanticize an ax murderer—what can one say? Give me a break! [This, too, would require a thesis.] To me those are the true obscenities: movies like *Halloween*. Because to me that's part of the dehumanization process; to me that's an extension of what racism does. Because you're dehumanizing these people so you can just kill one after the other: these are not human beings who are falling, they're props in a movie! So you can hack them up, you can butcher them, you can have all this disgusting shit happening on the screen, and it *inures*. So that when you really see someone killed, it's not as exciting as it was in the movies. And usually not as gory, either. A girlfriend of mine killed her old man—she served about three years in jail. I remember talking to her at the time, and she was absolutely amazed that what little she did could actually kill a person—there was no loud music playing when he was shot! Whereas the movies build up all this sound and drama.

JUNO: Do you think you're angry?

COLEMAN: If you're sane and you're perceptive, you have no choice! Maybe the word "perceptive" has to be wedded to the concept of anger, because you have to be perceptive to see what's *really* going on—there are people who have blinders on, and who don't see it.

JUNO: Have you ever seen anyone die?

COLEMAN: I have seen people in the process of dying, but I haven't actually been present at the moment of death. I haven't seen anyone killed, and I've yet to kill anyone. I have exhibited great restraint.

Bobbi Sykes

An Interview

A letter from, and a talk with, the Black Australian political activist, journalist, and poet Roberta Sykes, from a KPFK/Pacifica Radio broadcast of *The Poetry Connexion*, Austin Straus and Wanda Coleman, co-hosts.

Alice Springs

Dear Wanda,

I am sitting out here in the Central Desert having a great time. I was first here in 1972. At that time there were no Black organizations here; in fact, there were very few anywhere in the country, as we had only got "citizenship" some five years earlier. Blacks mainly camped in the dry creekbed of the Todd River, huddled in dirty blankets to protect against cold. Abuse by police was widespread—rape, murder, and exploitation were constant. Now there are more than a dozen Black organizations. We are formulating land claims based on traditional ownership, operating health and legal services, etc. Of course everything is under-funded, so nothing is glamourous.

It is winter here. Days are warm. We sit outside in the dirt for

102

sunshine to warm us. The nights are zero temperatures here and inside it is bitter cold. We build small fires and huddle around them, often wrapped in old tatty blankets—if we can find any— for the additional warmth. We watch anxiously as the supply of wood dwindles. No one owns more than they can carry—a blanket, a small pot, whatever. Books, of course, are too much of a luxury. Even if one can read them, one can't carry them as the living circumstance is too temporary.

Some of us went to a disco—well, what passes as a disco out here—because some folks wanted to show me a good time. Many couldn't come because they had no shoes. The White management had put boards over the hole that Blacks had used to pass their shoes out to others so that everyone could get in.

Last night a White woman had a housewarming and some of us went there and enjoyed the warmth of the free fire. Unfortunately, the food consisted of things mostly foreign to the palate of Blacks here—imported cheeses, pâté, and stuff; but we had our own space and got into talking, joking, laughing and clowning, and had such a lovely time in our own company that the Whites left their space to come over and find out what was happening, and try and join in. They couldn't understand it all, but a couple of Whites around here are learning and speaking some languages, so it didn't go too badly. The trouble is that "in" Black humour is more than language, and this mob around here is big into mimic, so maybe you wouldn't have understood much of it, but you would have loved it all. There is a peace for me here . . .

STRAUS: Isn't the situation of aborigines/Black Australians one of the best-kept secrets in the world?

SYKES: We're one of the globe's best-kept secrets. Until 1967, which is the year in which the Australian government allegedly gave Black Australians citizenship, we had virtually no access to the press and we were unable to get passports for travel— which still remains difficult. Last year, for instance, there were only three of us here in the United States. We had no legal access to education. We had to have permits to go on and off

103

the reserves, and still do in some places. Any image cast of us was always tribal. People around the world who thought about Blacks in Australia saw us standing naked on rocks, holding spears and mumbling in "mumbo-jumbo." It's only recently that we've been able to project our own images.

COLEMAN: Why poetry in the midst of Australia, where the "finer things of life" are inaccessible to Blacks?

SYKES: My poetry and that of other Black Australians is not "fine art." It verbalizes the agony in which we live. Given how many we are, and how few writers there are, it is surprising how many of our writers are poets. Kevin Gilbert spent most of his adult life in prison, where he taught himself to be literate and published when he came out. Kath Walker is another well-known poet. Most of the women poets don't have a prison background, but most of the men do. That's similar to the Black situation here in America.

COLEMAN: How did you come to poetry?

SYKES: I had no other way to cope with my emotions other than put them on paper. I'd write things furtively in the middle of the night and shove them into drawers. At the same time I was a political analyst, writing for newspapers all around the world. For almost ten years I'd been known as a militant activist writer, critical of the way institutions in our society operate. I published my book *Love Poems and Other Revolutionary Actions* in 1979. The newspapers that covered my book party wrote: "Activist turned poet."

STRAUS: How did it come about that you are at Harvard?

SYKES: A Black American professor came to Australia, noticed me, went back and arranged for Harvard to invite me into the postgraduate program. When I received communication from Harvard University, I didn't know where it was. I thought it was a not-very-good joke. It wasn't. The significance floored me. I don't have a formal education. The idea that I would go anywhere like that without background education over-whelmed me. It took me three years to go—to get ready emo-tionally. I got there because I was pressed into it by members of the community. Initially the government said they would be pleased to fund me. About six to seven weeks before I was due to leave, they suddenly said they didn't have the money. The Black community became outraged. They felt that it wasn't just me who was being stopped, it was the Black community being stopped from reaching out to opportunities overseas. Amongst themselves they gathered money and held fund-raising events. It was amazing. For many years I worked at the Health Com-mission as a crisis counselor. I've never been in a position where I've felt so humble—to have people on welfare walk up to me and press a dollar into my hand and say, "Go to Boston, dear," having no clue as to where they were sending me. And they said, "How do you feel about going?" And I said, "I read in this book that it's very cold there." And I'd come the next week and they'd have knitted me socks. People lent me coats —and of course, nothing was coordinated. You can't say no. I turned up at the school with the most motley collection of clothes you ever saw.

STRAUS: Was this feeling rising up, *she* is going to speak for us?

SYKES: *We* were going! So we had to get ourselves warm. Har-vard doesn't attract a lot of poor Blacks even from America. Suddenly I'm there with Blacks driving Mercedes and wearing three-piece, $400 and $500 suits and I'm wandering around in raggedy clothes. It was a difficult period—the gap between Black Americans and myself, although we look the same, the gap between Indians and myself because we don't look the same. I'd be sitting in the cafeteria and I'd speak in my strange accent and Black Americans would stop dead and look around immediately for a White person.

STRAUS: What did Harvard expect you to do?

SYKES: They were very flexible. I didn't have a clue what I

wanted to do because I had no idea what went on there. I've almost completed the doctoral program. I'm in the middle of my thesis, an analysis of education in the Black community in Australia.

STRAUS: When you go back to Australia, will having a doctorate from Harvard give you more credibility in the White community?

SYKES: I have no idea. I'd hate to think my credibility depends upon a piece of paper from Harvard.

STRAUS: Are there Black Australians who make it through the system to university level and get Ph.D.s?

SYKES: I'll be the first Black to have a doctorate.

STRAUS: Wow—my goodness—isn't that something! The first Black Australian to get a Ph.D. anywhere, including Australia. Amazing!

>
> *AMBROSE*
>
> They say you took your life/
>   with your
>   own hand.
> But I been looking
>   at your life
>   these past
>   four years
> and I see other
>   hands
> in the taking
>   of your life.
>
> Your mother was
>   helping
>   you
>   to die

since
your first breath.

You showed me
        her picture
        once
        taken with you
        as a babe.
You lay, pretty boy,
        on a table.
Behind you she stood
        your bottle in one hand
her bottle in the other/
symbol of your childhood.

Your father helped
        by the hole
        he left in your life
when he split
                &
        you
only seven months in
        foetaldom.

Teachers had a hand:
        laying hands
        upon you
        (not in love)
        in punishment
for your dirty clothes
        & later
        for your lies
        (your survival kit, haha—
        you told me later).

Incorrigible:
you lived more

a uniformed life
contained
by uniformed men
than in the free air
of which you
often spoke.
I don't like to talk
about
how the 'helpers'
helped—
moving you closer
& closer
to your inevitable fall
(or were you pushed?).

Helpers who
let you know so soon
that your best
wasn't good enough/
for them.

'There is no place
for me here'
you told me/
already 17
and floating now
in the only space
you could see open.

There were handmarks
& fingerprints
all over you
when they found you;
but you died
by your own hand
they said.

Yesterday, I was interviewed at the Black radio station. It operates out of a shed. Microphones had to be held together with tape. Girls with no shoes sat in the dust and organized their daily program sheets, then leapt up to the mikes and translated the news into three tribal languages. The Yirpinya Council of Elders traveled many miles to meet with me and inform me. My explanation that I'm writing my thesis on the information that they are giving me is flattering to them and they are going to great lengths to cooperate. It is more than cooperation. They have adopted my task for me. My work was blessed by the Elders and I was embraced by them and stroked for energy to continue.

As all these spiritually rich things were happening, from another part of my eye I saw what other people must see: scrappy Blacks in broken down cars, traveling to meetings in broken down sheds, carrying fragments of food in grey cloths tucked into pockets because of lack of money and inability to get served in most shops. A number of people pool their money to buy already worn-out cars. Everybody drives them and transports everybody else, so they don't last long. There aren't many of these cars, it just feels like there must be a lot because you keep seeing the same over-loaded car everywhere.

People have been great, welcoming me with open arms and skitting of my accomplishments. They are, of course, "our" accomplishments. Each new word I drop into the vocabulary is savoured and repeated many times, such as "Harvard," "degree," etc. They wish to be able to properly explain to Whites exactly what I'm doing with no mistakes and no chance that a White will be able to correct them.

STRAUS: What's the critical response to Black Australian poetry? Is it read by Whites? Are Blacks so invisible?

SYKES: We don't get a big response in general. In America you frequently find White people who have read Black books and can name at least a dozen Blacks in the country. Most White people in Australia would be flat out naming two Blacks; one would be an entertainer and the other a tennis star. We are in a transition period. Whites have been in Australia less than two hundred years. White people rode through the country- side slaying tribes and poisoning waterholes. They wiped out the largest portion of the population—particularly in the south- ern states. They gathered up the remnants of the tribes and kept them on reserves. Thousands of people were killed. All the tribes of Tasmania were wiped out in one of the most com- plete genocide attempts in the world. Whaling boats came by and kidnapped some Black women from the island of Tasma- nia and took them to offshore islands where they were "held prisoner" for nearly a hundred and fifty years. Their descen- dants have returned to reclaim Tasmania.

STRAUS: Land rights is the basic question in Australia?

SYKES: Land rights have been recognized nationally but not in every state. Up until 1967 the states had control of all Blacks within their borders. Only state legislation applied to Blacks. States had the power to define who, in fact, was Black. Each state defined Blacks differently, some for the purpose of main- taining a group that would satisfy anthropologists and others to keep large numbers of Blacks "down." In 1967, for the first time, there was federal legislation that applied to Blacks, so some things could be done politically by approaching the fed- eral government—for instance, land rights.

STRAUS: You had to achieve legal status as a person before such questions could be dealt with?

SYKES: We weren't in a position to instigate court action. Being a noncitizen you don't have access to the courts and you can't claim welfare because these are privileges reserved for citi- zens. We were never asked whether or not we wanted citizen- ship. We accepted this change in our political access readily —without it we would still be "going down the slopes." At the same time, citizenship denies us sovereignty—the right to rule ourselves. This question is being discussed in the Black community. It is not being discussed in the White community. Federal legislation is so recent that some of the states don't acknowledge it. The largest land mass does not acknowledge land rights for aboriginal people—that is Queensland in Northern Australia.

COLEMAN: And you're from . . .?

SYKES: Queensland.

STRAUS: You do have your "champions," people trying to help Black Australians?

SYKES: There are groups of Whites around the country trying to help. Sometimes the direction in which they are trying to help us is a direction we haven't chosen. There is a lot of conflict, but it would be unusual if that weren't the case, given the fact that we've been segregated for so long. One wonders about the influences that create change. The United Nations chastised Australia on its race-relations question and following that we got citizenship. It's certainly not because we were so militant. The Black community here in America, in their demonstrations and protests through the '60s, played a significant part in changing the attitudes of White Australians. Until that time we were on reserves, out of sight. People from outside of Australia said, "We're starting action against South Africa and Australia is next." Australia started to make changes.

STRAUS: Isn't Australia a Mecca—a haven—for Whites?

SYKES: Up until 1973 we had legislation called the "White Australia Policy" that stopped Blacks and Asians from immigrating to Australia. The only migration taking place was large numbers of Whites coming generally from Western Europe. Here people say, "We didn't know there were any Blacks in Australia." Australia has quite a lot of White South Africans who have fled South Africa. We've got White Rhodesians who've fled Rhodesia. They call themselves Rhodesians, which is why I call them Rhodesians. You never find a White Rhodesian who calls himself a Zimbabwean.

COLEMAN: What about the gap between the Black American and the Black Australian?

SYKES: There is little understanding of the Black Australian in the Black community, particularly on the East Coast. Black Americans say, "We don't hear you're very active in an equal-rights struggle." We're not after equal rights. We're after land rights. They say, "You have more in common with the American Indian." In Australia we're both the Black and the Indian. We have problems common to both groups. In Australia we have the question of land rights—it was our country—provoking the guilt of those who obliterated an indigenous people. We also have the situation of extreme visibility in urban areas, evoking fear in the White community.

COLEMAN: You have another book, *MumShirl* (Sydney: Heinemann, 1981). It's the life story of a woman you admire "as told to Bobbi Sykes," correct?

SYKES: Yes. In every community I've ever been in there are strong Black women, figures in the community you go to when you're in trouble and need advice. We have such a woman, MumShirl. She is illiterate, very poor, and wouldn't, under "normal" circumstances, be a person who'd spring to mind as a "heavy." From her background position she has projected such force for such a long period that she's also become well known in the White community. She has been honored by the Queen of England and several government administrations. When I say honored, I mean she's been given a medal or piece of paper. She often says "I wish I could eat medals," because she's won so many.

COLEMAN: How old a woman is she?

SYKES: She doesn't know. She was born at a time when Black

births weren't recorded. She guesses she is somewhere in her fifties.

COLEMAN: Is it so recent that records of Black births were not kept?

SYKES: Politically and educationally we are only sixteen years old. Most adults my age are illiterate.

STRAUS: How did you get involved with MumShirl?

SYKES: I fled the northern states—we call it the "deep north." As soon as I got to Sydney, I started to hear her name: "Has that been approved by MumShirl?" As I traveled, I kept hearing her name, and became tremendously concerned that she might not approve. We finally met at the Aboriginal Medical Service. She is a big woman, unafraid. I've seen her separate two drunks fighting, both bigger than she, just by grabbing them by the scruffs. We started to work together. I had access to resources, like a vehicle. She doesn't drive and I used to drive her from place to place. She is called to prisons during riots. When she appears on the scene, Black prisoners stop and listen. She might not stop the riot, but she certainly begins negotiations. I kept saying, "We've got to be careful about MumShirl. The things we accomplish will slip away if we don't write them down; [that] we did them ourselves and not Whites." I talked her into doing the book, which was passed over to me to write. I wrote it in the first person and she went over it to make sure it was in fact *her* book. I'm proud that people who know her well feel she wrote it and that I sat there with a pencil and notebook and wrote it out for her.

RACISM/MANY FACES

A woman said to me
   t'other day,

"I read one of your poems
   about women,

I thought it very good
but
it didn't say that you
    were *Black!*
Now I meet you and
    see that you
    are *Black.*
I wonder
why you wrote the poem?"

Do they think
    we spend
        our whole lives
            being *Black*
                for them?

STRAUS: Are there outside organizations pressuring the Australian government to do something about your situation?

SYKES: There are organizations that weren't set up to be of assistance but that have changed direction, particularly the anti-uranium lobbies. These groups have been very supportive. Uranium mining occurs on aboriginal land. We are competing for the same areas of land with international mining companies, particularly those in Western Europe, like Switzerland. I went to Switzerland and addressed people who are against Swiss involvement in Australian mining.

STRAUS: Isn't there an assumption that if you get your land back you will not do any mining?

SYKES: There has been that assumption. We are impotent in stopping uranium mining on aboriginal land and some Blacks are receiving royalties. It's like having a few dollars pressed into your hand after you've been raped. Whether or not we would support mining in the future is a question we're in no position to address.

STRAUS: Are there any other human rights organizations working to protect Black Australians from genocide?

SYKES: We've had contact with anthropologists—certainly some of the indigenous peoples' worst enemies. Anthropology groups are the main support one can point to globally.

STRAUS: Why are anthropologists so bad for indigenous groups they're supposed to be helping?

SYKES: I'm sure you could talk to any Indian and they'd tell you.

Wanda, when I'm in America I feel I have a foot in two worlds. When I'm here I feel I have lifted my other foot up and that other world has ceased to exist. I have difficulty remembering Boston or bringing it into focus. There is no "time" here, just daylight and dark. The shadows are getting very long and the cold is creeping around inside my sheepskin boots, so I'd best wander around and see if I can find some wood to contribute to tonight's fire. I've tried to think what I feel it is about this life here that you would so appreciate. I think it is the very basic things, such as the tremendous feeling one gets to find a piece of wood to share in the fire, or having a piece of food in a grey rag to pull out and put down and, having had many opportunities to be very hungry yourself, to be very pleased when someone else pulls out their piece of food for you to share. Locating somebody with a house and a hot shower who is willing to let you use it is also a good find—and even being the seventh person to use the by-then sopping towel is not the same as in other circumstances. The comradeship and sharing, the absence of one-upsmanship—yes, you would be very happy to be here.

Stay well and know that your spirit was summoned up here to partake of the peacefulness—of which only a little is left in this world.

In friendship and struggle . . .

Bobbi Sykes

NOTE

MumShirl Smith (1921–1998) was also known as Colleen Shirley Perry. Poet Kath Walker's birth name was Oodgeroo Noouccal

(1920–1993). Since this article, Dr. Roberta Sykes has published the autobiographical trilogy Snake Dreaming *(Sydney: Allen & Unwin), winner of the 1997 Age Book of the Year Award. During one of our discussions, she expressed her displeasure at the refusal of the media to capitalize the modifiers black, red, white, and yellow when referring to human beings. She viewed this as psychologically demeaning. In agreement, I now capitalize these words whenever I have the editorial option.*

Remembering Latasha: Get Out of Dodge!

Blacks, Immigrants & America

I am terrorized by the murder of a child. Intermittently, dramatic images of her death unreel. It's been two years, but I'm still enraged, upset, unable to sleep. I'm haunted by her murder and by the thousands of murders of Black youths since 1955, when a brutally bludgeoned Emmett Till rose from the autumn waters of Mississippi's Tallahatchie River. Each afternoon, as I wait for my fourteen-year-old son to return from school, I pray. I'm not a religious woman. But when I hear him coming through that door, I'm overjoyed. How long, I wonder, will America allow him to live?

It allowed Latasha Harlins only a decade and a half. In March and April 1991, a year before South Central L.A. erupted, local residents repeatedly witnessed news broadcasts of the video-taped killing of the fifteen-year-old Latasha by the fifty-one-year-old shopkeeper Soon Ja Du. Though central to Black–Korean tensions that fueled the riots, this incident was scarcely a footnote in national media coverage of the riots.

The video, filmed by an in-store camera at the Empire Liquor Market, was painfully graphic. We saw Latasha approach Du, alone behind the counter, with money in her hand. We watched Du accuse her of stealing a $1.79 bottle of orange juice. We saw

117

Latasha turn to show Du the juice in her knapsack, then wave two one-dollar bills. There was a heated verbal exchange, and Latasha threw the orange juice down on the counter. We watched the angry Du grab for Latasha's pack, then catch the flap of her jacket. We saw Latasha slap the shit out of Du, who immediately let go. We saw Latasha turn and walk away. We watched Du fumble for the .38 caliber, firing once. We saw Latasha pitch forward and drop to the floor as the bullet struck the back of her head.

I took Latasha's death personally. Looking at a photo of myself at fourteen, I saw little resemblance, yet I *identifed* with Latasha. I saw in her the truncated future of another self. Why? Soon Ja Du probably did not realize Latasha was a child. The teenager dwarfed the Korean woman. When Latasha slapped Du, her blow staggered the diminutive grocer. This speculation evoked my past as "Big Girl"—my father's nickname for me. Darker and larger than my schoolmates, I quickly learned the advantage (when it comes to intimidation) of being a big-boned, heavyset "mama." Aggression was a vital part of my survival strategy.

The price Black girls pay for not conforming to White standards of physical beauty is extracted in monumental amounts, breath to death. We bend our personalities, and sometimes mutilate our bodies, in defense. Sometimes that bent is "bad attitude," perhaps accompanied by a hair-trigger temper, ready to go off at the mildest slight: neck-wobbling, hands to hips, we exhibit boisterous, hostile, "niggerish" behavior. Latasha, insulted by Du's mistaken assumption that she was a thief, went into her attitude. Then Du unwittingly violated a code of street conduct: You do not put your hands on me without a fight—win, lose, or draw.

Latasha lost.

Initial newspaper accounts of the incident were careful to describe Latasha as "studious and self-assured." But the slant of so-called objective coverage betrayed tacit sympathy for Du. She had lived every bigot's fantasy. She had shot *one of them*.

The fear that motivated Soon Ja Du was couched in statistics designed to justify her killing of Latasha: "In the surrounding 32 blocks, 936 felonies reported last year . . . 5 murders . . . 9 rapes

... 184 robberies and 254 assaults." The fact that Du's son was the victim in one of those assaults was subtly emphasized. The nasties of ghetto life were responsible, not the "feeble and over- whelmed" grocer forced to work fourteen-hour days, ever at the mercy of shoplifters, street hoodlums, and chronic migraines, but never at the mercy of White society.

Incredibly, in one article Latasha's mother, Crystal Harlins, was posthumously indicted, because of her "boisterous behavior," for Latasha's death—and for her own, which had come six years ear- lier, during an argument at an after-hours bar. The chilling impli- cation? Like mother, like daughter.

This troubling reportage was eerily reminiscent of the open support expressed by Whites for acquitted New York City subway vigilante Bernhard Goetz, who gunned down four Black youths in 1984 because he thought they *might* attack. The Goetz case is a notorious demonstration of White loathing of anyone big and Black. To parents like me, it was clear that open war had been declared against our children.

In underreporting these incidents (Michael Donald, beaten and strangled by Klansmen in Mobile, Alabama; Melvin Eugene Hair, asphyxiated by chokehold during an altercation with Tampa police; Loyal Garner Jr., who was beaten and died while in police custody in Hemphill, Texas), the media serve themselves and soci- ety by ignoring, distorting, and/or understating acts of violence against Blacks, as in the November 1992 Bay Area slaying of Jer- rold Hall. Hall, nineteen, was killed by a BART transit cop's shot- gun blast to the back of his head. He was "under suspicion" for stealing a Walkman. Fred Crabtree, the White officer involved, was a seventeen-year veteran. The only detailed account of this fantastic tragedy was reported by Tim Redmond in the *San Fran- cisco Bay Guardian*. No mainstream California newspaper has, as of this writing, touched the Hall story, nor has it hit the inter- national wire services (*60 Minutes* filmed a segment on Hall that never aired).

Like Harlins's, Hall's story initially appeared in a tiny column barely two paragraphs long. The Hall case received the similar treatment of guilt by insinuation. Blame/responsibility for the incident is placed on the victim (as with Emmett Till, for whistling and looking). She or he had to be doing *something*. This "doing" justifies any violent means or ends. Just being Black and being there automatically constitutes grounds for frontier justice. The victim, in effect, becomes the victimizer. And all the news that was news was told.

Redmond surmises that Hall's story is being deliberately ignored for fear it may cause Blacks to riot. Five days before L.A. burned, a young White male asked me if Blacks would riot should Rodney King's assailants walk. I hesitated, thought of Harlins, then stammered that we probably wouldn't but that I wished we would. "Will y'all riot?" was the tiresome question posed after every incident involving Blacks, from Jonestown to the death of Harold Washington. The smug implication was that Blacks were so impotent, all we could do was tear up our own surroundings. It angers me that the assumption is stingingly correct.

Furthermore, I contend that if such lynchings received even minimally fair media coverage, we would witness a numbing tableau of violence and bloodshed. Our national psyche, always in denial about race, would collapse under the onslaught. By relegating stories like Hall's to the back-page boonies, the media help to perpetuate the illusion of a "kinder, gentler America." Loudly voiced community outrage is necessary to dispel this illusion, and to command the media's attention.

Local protests over the Harlins shooting were swift and raucous, the culmination of complaints by Black community leaders about "the Korean invasion" and lack of dialogue between the two groups. For nearly a decade the local media, alternative and mainstream, had refused to investigate the problem initially brought to their attention by a handful of concerned Black writers, including myself. During that period, I had had three especially infuriating run-ins with Korean merchants. One was a fight at a hamburger stand, when the Koreans across the counter refused to accept my newly minted twenty-dollar bill. They'd been burned before, and they thought the bill was bogus. I was guilty of the crime someone else, also Black, had committed. Using my own stubby fuse and lofty blood pressure as a gauge seemed unfair. But when even my demure sixty-year-old mother complained of abuse by "some Koreans because I'm Black," I saw that violence was inevitable in my community.

Black protest over the Harlins–Du incident increased, but was unexpectedly dissipated when attorney Charles Lloyd was hired for Du's defense. Lloyd is Black. As with the Hill-versus-Thomas fiasco, many were reluctant to go against one of our own. A "wait and see" attitude was adopted toward the previously hotly disputed case. When Soon Ja Du's bail was set at $250,000 and her release made imminent, the courtroom, crowded with Korean-Americans, broke into applause. The Black community was virtually silent. It would remain so until after the verdict in the Rodney King beating trial.

The socioeconomic reversals and unchecked discrimination of the Nixon/Ford/Reagan/Bush years stymied progress for most African Americans. And the high expectations many had for President Carter were gradually deflated. One year into the Carter administration, NAACP executive director Benjamin Hooks told three thousand Urban League delegates, "Nearly 80 percent of the White people in America feel that enough has been done for Black people." Since then, study after study has documented his gloomy insight: Blacks still disproportionately live in substandard and segregated housing; attend inferior public schools staffed by underpaid, under-encouraged teachers; confront corporate America's glass ceiling; make do with lower wages as skilled labor devolves into low-paid service jobs; populate worsening neighborhoods plagued by unfettered drug traffic, increased violent crimes, overflowing prisons; battle homelessness. Factor in the unacceptably high rate of premature death due to hypertension and stroke, murder, and AIDS. While the richest 20 percent of America got richer, the largely disfranchised fifteenth-generation African Americans struggled to "keep hope alive."

During the riots, my husband, son, and I braved the violence and walked our little section of Hollywood. We saw no one looting but Latinos, predominantly new arrivals from Central and South America. While Latinos and young Whites later justified their riotous motives as economic, that justification seemed significantly stronger when it came from Blacks. Most of us are being pushed out of L.A. by the lack of jobs and housing, and by the redlining of major lending institutions and insurance companies. (The relentless heat generated by the L.A.P.D. under ex-chief Daryl Gates and his predecessors didn't help.) On April 29, 1992, L.A. became the flashpoint of suppressed nationwide unrest.

Blacks squeezed out of the local economy in L.A. were likewise being squeezed out nationally. Economic statistics repeatedly illuminated the concurrence of events that have conspired to marginalize struggling Blacks. The increasing influx of immigrants exacerbated our crisis. (This does not imply complicity on the part of the average immigrant, but on government bureaucracy, and echoes the complaint of African American leadership made since the days of post–Civil War Reconstruction.) While Blacks were being pushed out of the marketplace by recession and widespread apathy, that same American marketplace was accommodating a groundswell of immigrants, privileged and underprivileged, from as far away as the former Soviet Union, the Middle East, Vietnam, and Korea. Their presence pushed Blacks out of the marketplace altogether. Only lucky exceptions remained.

In his October 1992 *Atlantic* article "Blacks vs. Browns," Jack Miles sidesteps Black–Korean conflicts to trace Black–Latino clashes underscoring "Watts II." (A June 1983 issue of *Time* estimated that 90 percent of illegals come from Mexico. The 1986 Census reported a 16 percent increase in America's Latino population since 1981, making one out of fourteen Americans Latino.) Miles observes that Latinos, even when foreign, seem native and safe while Blacks, who are native, seem foreign and dangerous. Miles implies that Blacks are so "nihilistic, so utterly alienated," that White Americans cannot "make a connection" with us. It's "just easier with the Mexicans." But the point is that the prejudice of White America has promoted the very attitude among Blacks that Whites like Miles find so discomforting. No matter how many immigrants White America puts between itself and Blacks, this national dilemma will persist.

Furthermore, as a price of entry, the majority of immigrants buy into the lie of American apartheid: Black people are inferior. To fail to accept this tenet of American life is to jeopardize what is already a tenuous existence for the newly arrived. When merchants like Soon Ja Du mimic Whites' fear of Blacks, their behavior is condoned, if not rewarded, by our society. Alliances between Blacks and immigrants are troubled because the two groups profoundly misunderstand each other: while the immigrant populations (Koreans, Latinos, *et al.*) expect rational behavior from Blacks driven mad by poverty and racism, Blacks expect immigrants to empathize with our plight the minute they set foot on our turf—when too many of us don't grasp it ourselves. Newly arrived immigrants often do not understand that what may be interpreted as a mere inconvenience or slight by Whites may be interpreted as disrespectful, even life-threatening, by Blacks. "Objectivity" is impossible because racism prevents it.

Like most groups, African Americans are not homogeneous. Long-festering feuds have been waged among Blacks of slave origin and Blacks of freedman status, Black islanders and Black immigrants from Africa. Despite the posturing of cultural nationalists and hip-hop culture militants, differences in skin tone and physical features still matter to many of us. Some still duck at invisible cracks of the whip. Some have internalized the whip and crack it at other Blacks. And many African Americans who have successfully made it into the mainstream have not felt obligated to reach back and help their brothers and sisters.

By the mid-1970s most vestiges of Black pride had disappeared. Our recent embrace of all things "African" (celebrating Kwanzaa, sporting kente cloth, wearing braids) is mostly compensatory; asserting our ties to Africa is largely an act of self-defense. Our psyches have been shattered by the infighting and self-hatred that is the by-product of internalized racism. Our great shame is that we have too rarely been able to unify ourselves long enough to neutralize the forces detrimental to us all. One of those rare periods of unity followed the death of Emmett Till, which was a major impetus for the civil rights movement initiated nearly a half century before by W. E. B. Du Bois's Niagara Movement. Such a moment may follow in the wake of the circumstances surrounding Rodney King.

Why violence after the verdict in the King beating case, and not after the verdict in the Harlins case? Was it because Soon Ja Du was represented by Lloyd, a skilled Black professional adept at squelching any mischaracterizations of himself as Uncle Tom or traitor to his race? Or was it, perhaps, because the racism that operated in the Harlins case was considerably less apparent?

The videotape of the King beating received instant national and international distribution, while circulation of the Harlins video was largely local. The whupping of a Black man by racist Whites went straight to the core of Black experience. Our abuse at the hands of vigilantes, law enforcement, and the criminal-justice system runs generations deep. For the first time, irrevocably we thought, the White man was caught dead to rights—by his own technology and media. Any fool could see. But no one, outside the savvy few, anticipated the blow the Simi Valley jury would deliver.

Our very eyes had lied. Not our eyes alone—those of the nation, the world. Whites who couldn't embrace Blacks could embrace their own ideal, could recognize the failure of an institution they believed in: benevolent American democracy, grounded in the Constitution. The King verdict angered and disillusioned *all* subscribers to this faith because it rendered American justice the figment of a collective imagination, Black and White.

No longer a front-page story, the highly touted recovery of L.A. remains mired in rhetoric and posturing. Beneath the noise, Black L.A. seethes. The city grapples for solutions. The happy face that city fathers have superimposed via the media cracks and drops away under the slightest scrutiny. Even before the curfew was lifted, "A.C.M.D." (all cops must die) became the battle cry on the streets. "For Sale" signs proliferate in the city's remaining White neighborhoods. "No one [White] drives into the city anymore" is the quietly kept secret. And the businesses that relied on their commerce are dying. The Black–Korean Community Relations Committee, an organization of business people and community leaders formed in mid-1987, disbanded this past December. Residual tensions from the Harlins case and an organized boycott of John's Liquor Store, where Arthur Mitchell, an alleged Black robber, was shot and killed on June 4, 1991, were cited as the causes of the breakdown of this experiment.

The Black population also continues to erode, down to half a million. More than seventy-five thousand Blacks have been pushed out of the city since 1975 (among them, my daughter and her family); many of those who remain feel trapped. Gang activity continues: more than eight hundred gang-related deaths took place in the county last year. Local TV news broadcasts report gang incidents at the top of the news, superseding less significant events such as the bombing of Iraq or natural disasters.

Cooked under the pressures of the penal system, Latino–Black conflicts have steadily worsened and are emphasized by the media. Violence on local campuses makes the front pages. Two Black families in the Boyle Heights *barrio* of Ramona Gardens were firebombed last September. Just weeks ago, I got my taste of these tensions when I parked my car across the street from a liquor store and dashed in to play the lottery. Pulling up, I noticed about a dozen Latino men in a nearby alley and on the stoop next door, drinking and hanging out. My car is dilapidated and rusty, so I trusted no one would bother it. I left it open, windows down. When I returned the entire interior was wet. Not a Latino in sight. I wiped it down, sniffing to see if it was urine. It was water. And the message was clear: *Get Out of Dodge!* Black-on-Black crime has in no way diminished. My "play" nephew, Brandon Niles, was buried last October, victim of a gangland slaying just shy of his eighteenth birthday.

Last year a five-year-old girl was killed in a drive-by shooting one block from where I grew up. My mother still lives there, behind cast-iron bars and double bolts in a dope-ridden South Central neighborhood—once predominately White, middle-class, and pristine. Mom's afraid to watch TV in her living room at night, should some gang initiation rite be going on out in front of her windows. She'd like to sell her house and move, but with the current decline in real-estate prices, there's no possible way for her to profit from the forty years of labor and life my parents sank into the property. Her neighborhood is still my home and I've resisted the pressures to leave. But if L.A. continues on its present course, that might not be a bad idea. What keeps me here is my lowered expectations of urban life. The problems that plague L.A. can be found, with slight variation, in every major American city. Each has its Latasha Harlins, its Jerrold Hall, its Emmett Till. If it hasn't happened, it's about to.

In November 1991 Soon Ja Du was convicted of voluntary manslaughter. Judge Joyce Karlin sentenced Du to four hundred hours of community service, a five-hundred-dollar fine, reimbursement of funeral costs to the Harlins family, and five years' probation. A stunned Black community's campaign to oust Karlin from office followed but failed. Karlin was overwhelmingly re-elected by the majority of Southern California voters, mostly White. Ironically, her victory came with the June 1992 municipal elections, in the wake of the South Central uprising, the largest civic unrest in the history of the United States. The resounding message to Black America was emphatic: *The lives of your children are less than the lives of ours.*

Under the circumstances of race prejudice, material things—a bottle of orange juice or a Walkman—are worth the same as a Black child's life. To be born Black is to be born guilty. And sooner or later, you will pay for the crime.

NOTE

Reality shows and the resurgence of court trials as TV programming staples owe their popularity to Rodney King and O. J. Simpson. Since the Rodney King beating was caught on videotape, news programs such as 60 Minutes *report a new wave of citizens armed not with guns but with cameras, using them to rid their communities of drugs and prostitution.*

Uncommon Courtesy

I can't count the times I've gotten into an altercation at the checkout counter: clerks refusing to change a twenty during the height of midday sales, their registers bursting with singles, fives, and tens; managers and store detectives swarming me when my security badge from work triggers the shoplifting scanner alarm; waiting countless minutes when there's no other customer present; demanding my correct change to the point of threatening violence. Too often these clerks are recent émigrés of color in hot pursuit of the American Dream. How dare they! White folk are bad enough.

Sensing his reluctance, I ignored one young waiter's bad attitude and placed my order during a recent dinner out. I was too tired to go into my usual confrontation, spewing curses, bristling with wounded dignity, stomping out. Once I got my meal, I enjoyed it. But I waited more than half an hour for the check. So I left the restaurant without paying, just went to my car and drove off. I turned up the rhythm and blues to match the loudness of my thoughts: Is this a one-woman war? Me versus the restaurateurs and shopkeepers of L.A.?

I think I suffer these indignities because of my skin. One girlfriend, also Black, doesn't agree. But she's tiny, under 130 pounds, wears dresses and high heels. Weighing well over 150, I favor pantsuits and boots. Could I unwittingly be tapping into hostilities usually reserved for Black men? Occasionally I've heard, "May I help you, sir?" spoken to my back, then turned and stared down into a rapidly reddening face.

What's missing here is the operative word *big*. I'm nearly as tall as Rodney King and darker in complexion. I am not round, bouncy, or cuddly. Certainly, the ugly adjectives used to describe King apply to me. And I imagine that if I rose suddenly out of a mist, I might be mistaken for a gorilla of either gender.

The nastiness I encounter when shopping within city limits has forced me to spend time and money in neighborhoods where the nature of bigotry is more familiar. Strangely, I'm often nostalgic for the days when all we Blacks had to deal with were Whites and Mexican-Americans. As the saying goes, better the devil you know than the devil you don't.

Yet shopping in the suburbs also has unpleasant consequences. I frequently startle rosy-cheeked children when they come upon me unexpectedly. Some freeze, struck dumb by fear yet fascinated. Others turn tail and run screaming for Mommy and/or Daddy. The rescuing parent eyes me with hostility or embarrassment. In either case, the message is the same: "What are *you* doing here?"

Lately, however, my fear of shopping has abated. Something different is in the air, something besides the residue from the six-hundred-odd fires that ravaged L.A. On a recent stop to score hay-fever meds, I hesitated as I entered the drugstore, recalling an incident there with a clerk who'd refused to bust a twenty. I destroyed several product displays and stormed out. I was lucky I wasn't shot.

This time, when I entered the store, no one noticed. No probing, suspicious eyes were at my back. I ignored the turnstile and took the easier-but-wrong entrance past a dormant checkout counter. No frowning manager appeared. I prowled the aisles. No falsely obsequious stockboy slurped, "May I help you?" When

I stepped to the counter to pay, the cashier did not ignore me while talking on the phone. My change was not slammed onto the counter. Instead, she promptly rang up my purchase, made the correct change, placed it in my upturned palm, smiled, and said thank you. I went into shock.

To what could I attribute this decent behavior? The recession? No, this was fear at work. The fear of something big, Black, and potentially violent; the fear that inspired the Rodney King beating.

Stuffing decongestants into my purse, I left the store high off adrenaline. But the rush won't last. Business will return to its uncouth usual. In the meantime, I'm going to try that waiter in that restaurant again. Just to see how much good service fear inspires.

NOTE

One Friday night in January 2002, while seated in an Oxnard deli-restaurant, my friend Sylvia Rosen and I looked down into our Cobb salads to find them garnished on top with rotten avocados. The moment almost spoiled our visit as I summoned the waiter and told him that in my entire dining life I'd never seen a salad so served. Sylvia plucked hers onto a saucer and put it aside. I demanded my salad be taken back to the kitchen and garnished properly. As he left with my plate and Sylvia's saucer, I was beset with memories—stories told by family members traveling between "down home" and Los Angeles in the 1950s, stories about what White people did to your food if you didn't accept their bigoted demands and bad service. Doubly, I relived an incident at Ed Pearl's Ash Grove, a folk-rock club I frequented until it was fire-bombed, purportedly by Cuban exiles, in the '70s. They had the best grilled-cheese sandwich I have ever tasted, before or since; however, on one occasion, they failed to get my order right and served the sandwich un-grilled. The sandwich returned to my table three times—each time incorrectly prepared. On the fourth go-round, the sandwich looked perfect, but by then I was afraid to eat it. Such memories and moments flashed before me as I looked into Sylvia's frown of distaste. A fresh saucer of avocado was set before her, which she refused to touch; however, I dived into my salad newly garnished with fresh green avocado. Nevertheless, I was beset with an edgy nausea, difficult to dismiss, and could not help myself from suspiciously picking through the iceberg lettuce for globules of spit.

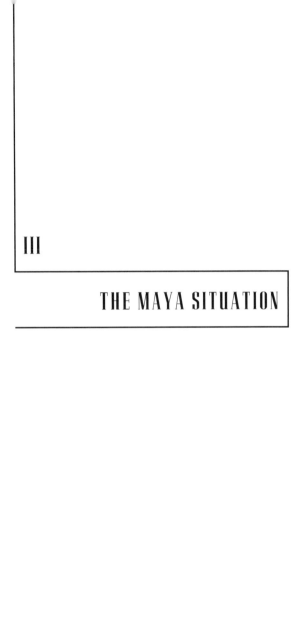

III

THE MAYA SITUATION

Flung into Controversy—Indeed

You must be the change you wish to see in the world.
                                                    —Gandhi

"I *agree*," smiled the African American professor, who leaned toward me with an air of utmost discretion.

It took a couple of seconds for me to absorb the meaning of her phrase, then we both began to titter.

The professor wishes to remain anonymous, as do most of those who likewise let me know, personally, that they *agreed*.

Until I panned Maya Angelou's *A Song Flung Up to Heaven* for the *Los Angeles Times Book Review*, I was just one more poet and writer struggling on the cultural margins of The West, a contender for a spot in a dubious pantheon. Instead of expanding the discourse on African American literary criticism, my review has flung me into the gloppy core of a twenty-first-century literary maelstrom.

In the two years since the review was published, on April 14, 2002, I have heard many confidences from those whom Angelou has trampled in her wake, nearly all such revelations governed by fear of one kind or another. There have been repeated complaints of her high fees, refusals to sign books, slights to faculties and students, etc. One individual, whom I've encountered twice, complains bitterly about being stiffed for a staggering five-figure florist's bill, apparently the result of a misunderstanding over one of the terms in Angelou's contract with that particular campus. After filling in one non-literary friend on what I've come to call The Maya Situation, he laughed, then told me that he had already heard about it from another source.

"I'm surprised," I said. "I didn't know *they* knew who I was."

"They do *now*," said my friend.

Opting to protect my supporters who have not spoken out publicly, I will keep their names to myself as promised. If this makes innuendo and implication unavoidable, so be it.

Unfavorable word has reached me from those who dismiss both Angelou and me as having nothing of value to offer a readership. Some have admonished me for what they consider a transgression. While support on my home turf has run the extremes of hot and cold, my most favorable and consistently effusive support has come from the cities of Chicago, Detroit, and New York, from academics and non-academics alike, and from artists and writers across all other demographics. Favorable word has gotten back to me, but I am reluctant to name my supporters lest I inspire retaliations against them, particularly since learning that one critic of Angelou's received a death threat.

I here reprint the text of my controversial review. The articles and interviews that follow it say all I have to say publicly on the matter, from my theory of *race-defense* to the detailing of my thoughts, from assumptions to certainties, from suspicions to speculations. Keep in mind: no writers' organization spoke out on my behalf, not even those of which I am a dues-paying member. No fundraisers were held for me. No letter campaigns in support of me took place. No symposiums or conferences have been held on the work of Wanda Coleman. I did not make a single list of celebrated banned authors. No one formed a picket line or circulated a petition for me. No one took out a full-page ad in the *New York Times*, rippled with signatures in support of me. No one offered me sanctuary in the upper echelons of literary America. There was no border for me to cross, except that Mason-Dixon line of mendacity that disallowed my point of view, and the right to fulfill my professional obligations without fear of reprisals.

Coulda Shoulda Woulda

"A Song Flung Up to Heaven,"
by Maya Angelou

While many American poets have languished, regardless of race, creed, color, or excellence, the savvy and ever-seductive seventy-three-year-old Marguerite Johnson, a.k.a. Maya Angelou, has parlayed statuesque good looks and modest talents as an actress-dancer-singer into a thirty-year role on the literary stage that is, indeed, phenomenal. In 1993, at the behest of President Clinton, she became the second poet in U.S. history to recite an original poem at an inauguration. Few poets can spark a smidgen of the controversy generated in 2001 by Angelou's undisclosed cut of an estimated fifty million dollars in sales for writing greeting-card verse, a pursuit for which she is superbly suited. Purportedly the final installment of her serial autobiography, *A Song Flung Up to Heaven* (Random House) appears only a few months after the first of her Hallmark card line, and seems calculated to encompass celebrations of Martin Luther King Jr.'s birthday, African American History Month, National Women's Month, as well as her seventy-fourth birthday, which falls in April, National Poetry Month.

It might be assumed that Angelou would take her honorary doctoral degrees, make a graceful bow, and retire from the liter-

136

ary round table with celebrated reputation intact. Alas, a dignified departure is not the trait of the greedy when one more traipse to the trough is offered. Once again, Maya dips into her past to offer up an emotional repast that would starve a skeleton.

I vented my bias against celebrity autobiographies at the outset of a favorable review of Angelou's *All God's Children Need Traveling Shoes* (*Los Angeles Times Book Review*, August 13, 1986), in which I stated that I usually find them "self-aggrandizements and/or flushed-out elaborations of scanty press packets." Relieved, I summarized *Shoes* as "a thoroughly enjoyable segment from the life of a celebrity."

No can do with *Song*.

Song is a sloppily written fake, bloated to 214 pages by large type and widely spaced chapter headings, more than half its thirty-three chapters averaging two to four pages. Powers exhibited in *I Know Why the Caged Bird Sings* (1970) have deserted her in *Song*. Her titillating confessions and coquettish allusions come off as redundant and hollow old tricks. She not only engages in her usual name-dropping but also shockingly makes that the book's content. Shamelessly, she cannibalizes the reputations of three major Black figures—Malcolm X (Al Hajj Malik El-Shabazz), James Baldwin, and Martin Luther King Jr.—using them as lynchpins on which to promote her specious pose as an activist.

Song opens with Angelou's return to the U.S. from Ghana in 1964 looking to plunk herself into the sociopolitical fray. She spends time in San Francisco, on Hawaii's main island, and in L.A. (west of the Harbor Freeway, where Whites were the majority) before moving to New York City, living above the concerns of a new generation of angry young Blacks.

With unflinching piety, she skips her days as a dancer and restyles herself as a militant, fostering the illusion that she was at the core of the Civil Rights and Black Power movements. Rather than substantiate this, Angelou plays the adolescent game of being the first to tattle on others when one is guilty: "The same people who don't give a damn now will lie and say they always supported him [Malcolm X]." Throughout *Song*, Malcolm's name is a mantra as Angelou smokily extols "the importance of his life and of his death" without exposition. Angelou has forgotten the swift reliability of the '60s underground grapevine. Had she joined the Organization of Afro-American Unity (I belonged to the Compton branch), it would have been news coast to coast. The dead (including Malcolm's widow, Betty Shabazz, who died tragically in June 1997) cannot contradict her—which may partly explain the sixteen-year lapse between *Shoes* and *Song*. Meanwhile, Angelou artfully plays the race card, like the muse Euterpe, or Sister Flute, coochie-cooing admirers out of shirts and socks, transforming bigots into simpering ninnies and academic cowardice into five-figure honoraria.

If *Caged Bird* put Angelou at the fore of those braving fiction's devices to enhance their truths, in *Song* she regresses, making it a textbook example of the primary danger inherent in that technique: misinterpretation. For example, taken alone, Chapter 19 might approximate any single woman's search for work on hostile urban turf; but, when wedded to Chapter 25, it becomes a "choose," in street parlance—straight out of Iceberg Slim—making Angelou, in her thirties, seem less the ingenue ward and more the procurer when setting up her benefactor with a lady-friend.

Ever age-conscious, Angelou relies on innuendo and inference to blur time, avoiding dates, locales, and other details, thus muddling events. She did this in *Caged Bird*, too, when recounting the excitement generated by a Joe Louis fight. (She confused Louis's June 25, 1935, bout with Primo Carnera—she was age seven— with his June 22, 1938, championship bout with Max Schmeling.) In Chapter 9 of *Song*, the book's lengthiest, Angelou bizarrely mangles the events of the Watts Riots of August 1965. After exclaiming that, in 1964, "the cry of 'burn baby burn' was loud in the land" (the phrase was the signature of KGFJ disc jockey Magnificent Montague, and was not heard nationwide until *after* the riots), she patronizingly defends residents with whom she is unable to identify, tiptoeing down to Watts to see the devastation.

In writing that is bad to God-awful, *Song* is a tell-all that tells nothing in empty phrases and sweeping generalities. Dead metaphors ("sobbing embrace," "my heart fell in my chest") and clumsy similes ("like the sound of buffaloes running into each other at rutting time") are indulged. Twice-told crises (being molested, her son's auto accident) are milked for residual drama. Extravagant statements come without explication and schmooze substitutes for action. Her most intriguing character, "The African," is underdeveloped. She softly decries racism between snipes at those who marginally offended her during her "rise" (Eldridge Cleaver, a White woman at a party). Tiresomely, she repeats her mother's homilies when not issuing her own. There is too much *coulda shoulda woulda*.

Unfortunately, the Maya Angelou of *A Song Flung Up to Heaven* seems small and inauthentic, without ideas, wisdom, or vision. Something is being flung up to heaven all right, but it isn't a song.

Black on Black

Fear & Reviewing in Los Angeles

To have great poets
There must be great audiences.
                                    —Walt Whitman

The quotation above appears on the business envelope of the Academy of American Poets. During November of 2001, exactly two months after 9/11, I was among twenty fine writers across four disciplines (poetry, young-adult literature, fiction, and nonfiction) gathered in Manhattan for the National Book Awards ceremony, many of us flown in for the event and braving the dread of possibly another skyjacking. Appetizer for the final ceremony was a mid-afternoon book signing at one of the big chain stores. The room was packed. I was impressed to see so many interested readers during working hours. After the welcome and introductions, the audience was invited to buy books and have them autographed by the authors. There was a modest roar as those most eager broke from their seats and strode toward the tables where we authors were poised. Virtually, to a person, they headed for the fiction table (the lion's share queued up for Jonathan Franzen's signature on his novel *The Corrections*, an Oprah's Book Club selection), the nonfiction and young-adult literature table attracting notice-

140

ably smaller numbers. But those who stood before us poets could be counted on one hand.

As I sat there absorbing the embarrassment, I recalled a similar incident at a bookstore in Atlanta, Georgia, a decade earlier. Amiri Baraka, Eugene B. Redmond, and I sat abandoned at a book-signing table, while a block-long, predominantly Black crowd jostled for signatures in front of the solo short-story writer, also Black, whose name I can no longer recall. When a precocious, bespectacled twelve-year-old stopped in front of me, I was relieved. Now, I wondered how many more centuries would have to pass before there was a great American audience for great American poetry—African American or otherwise. Could there ever be such an audience if the books of excellent poets were never reviewed in mainstream publications or carried by the big bookstore chains, and if bad poetry was received in silence or passed off as children's literature? When TV and movie personalities have taken over as arbiters of public literary taste, what kind of cultural wars will have to be fought to bring genuinely great postmodern American literature into its own? How will that happen, and on what ground, given the megabuck nature of the corporate publishing business, the assault on public education for the poor, and the fifteen-year trend of dismantling state and federal arts funding for individual artists, poets, and writers?

The night of the NBA ceremony, it felt strange to hear my name (I was a poetry finalist) called out from the podium by Steve Martin—a Hollywood celebrity, a comic actor. How ironic. (I did not win.) I had devoted my best writing life to the financial wasteland of poetry, working pink-collar jobs to feed my children, partly because there was no place in the Hollywood of the last thirty years of the twentieth century for me—a dark-skinned African American scriptwriter with absolutely no interest in comedy writing.

My post-WWII baby-boom generation had produced barely a dozen active Black writers steadily available in Los Angeles. Most of us who persisted in staying were hemmed in by the machinations of race as it operated in Southern California. What money

I had earned at writing was insignificant, having come at sporadic and difficult moments. By the '90s, I had managed modest earnings as a lifestyle columnist for the *Los Angeles Times* and was doing the occasional book review for *Black Issues* and *L.A. Weekly* at less than twenty-five cents per word. As Black Studies and MFA programs bore fruit, the number of books by African American authors increased and so did the number of Black writers available to review them. By the year 2000, I had to painfully compete for what was being made to seem like a privilege. So be it. Despite chasing down book editors with my résumé, by spring 2002 I had written more blurbs for books than reviews, receiving fewer than six assignments—the last of those being my negative review of Maya Angelou's memoir *A Song Flung Up to Heaven.*

According to one *L.A. Times* editor, the paper was immediately besieged with letters and e-mails. These ran fifty-fifty, pro and con; also, it was confided, a number of readers were simply confused, and an angry minority cancelled subscriptions. Even an old girlfriend from my hard-core South Central ghetto days weighed in: "I told 'em I know you personally," she said, "and that Wanda always tells it like it is!"

Three months later, the e-mails, letters, and phone calls continue. At a literary salon, one poet echoed the majority when she thanked me under her breath and said, "I never liked her work either." At a round-table fundraiser, yet another poet tilted his head and smacked his lips during general discussion of my review. "Well, I think you Blacks are as entitled to your mediocrities as we Whites are to ours."

The majority of the communications I've received to date have likewise been supportive. One postcard from the Bay Area chastised, "Can't you keep out of trouble?"

When I was a columnist for the *Los Angeles Times Magazine* (1992–95), I was rarely offered the chance to respond publicly to letters to the editor criticizing my point of view. I had suspected this was for a complex number of reasons, which I narrowed down to two: (1) to prevent deeper discussion of serious issues related to race, and (2) to prevent me from exploiting any editorial situation for celebrity. (Upon stating this to yet another book-review editor, months after the original appearance of my review of *Song*, he diplomatically suggested that there may not have been enough space, and that given the lack of financial support book reviews receive, my editors may have had little choice but to drop the matter.) Usually, favorable letters were used to speak for me, thereby ruling out my direct reply. Therefore, I never complained. In the first instance, I was satisfied that the deeper discussion was more properly taking place in my creative work, the essays, poetry, and fiction, as I wrote them—and, as a poet, I was willing to pay the price for whatever freedom I had to say anything I desired. In the second instance, my ego didn't crave celebrity, which is shallow by definition. Like most literary writers, I was concerned with what I call "a presumed immortality," that is, the assumption that one's words will live forever provided planet Earth isn't blown to mesons first.

I was also well versed in the forces governing the literary world —its cabals, gamesters, grant gangsters, *machers*, and snipers— and the fear. I had become uncomfortably aware of my place in it as labeled by others: "maverick," "outlaw," "street," or such contradictory terms as "avant-garde," "established," and "radical." At given moments I had either embraced or rejected those and similar labels, creating a couple of my own. A college dropout and working single parent between divorces, I had spent most of my writing life outside the mainstream, in the netherworld of independent presses and small magazines. I had little interest in piggybacking or social climbing, but a great interest in the politics of literary greatness in America. Were I to ever achieve greatness, I wanted it on my own very stringent terms. I wanted to earn it clean, my way, with full and fair recognition of my artistic work, which did not include book reviews.

New assignments from the *L.A. Times Book Review* had been extremely rare over the decade, and this was no less true after Steve Wasserman became editor in the 1990s. An assessment of

Audre Lorde's collected works was my first assignment, and had caused flak among her supporters [some of whom refuse to believe my distaste for her work is related strictly to matters of craft and not to her lesbianism]. Angelou's was my second.

Thinking back, I had agreed to review *Song* because the book was short and I could read it in one sitting. Singer-dancer Angelou was not an original or a challenging writer—essentially a one-book author with *I Know Why the Caged Bird Sings*, which was published more than thirty years ago. I had liked *Caged Bird* but had only loosely followed her career since it came out. She was said to be the first poet to "rise" from poverty to become a millionaire—a rise that had accelerated following her *L.A. Times* encomium of James Baldwin, published just after his death from stomach cancer, on November 30, 1987. I watched with my mother when Angelou moved Oprah Winfrey to tears on air during an early '90s broadcast. Nineteen ninety-three was a banner year for Angelou, who not only presented a poem at Clinton's presidential inauguration but had her poems featured in John Singleton's film *Poetic Justice*.

The sistuh's "pimp mack" was beautiful.

But when I finished reading *Song*, I was appalled. Not satisfied with being the doyen of African American letters, Angelou was attempting self-canonization as a political activist by standing on the backs of Malcolm X and Martin Luther King Jr.! *That* was to be the crown of a literary fraud she had been allowed to perpetrate magnificently for more than an entire generation. With *Song*, she was taking advantage of history's failure to accurately document the Civil Rights and Black Power movements. *That* needed to be exposed. Equally important, the failings in America's culture (with its postmodern anti-intellectualism) that had allowed Angelou's odious "rise" also needed to be exposed; but I was assigned to write neither a scholarly treatise nor an article on Racism in American Letters. It was a book review, contracted for either five hundred or a thousand words, for less than a dollar a word; the more I wrote, the less I'd earn. Knowing the dangers the reviewer faced when tackling an enormously popular writer, I felt like a hired gun riding into ambush. Therefore, if I were going to do justice, I could not afford to waste a single bullet.

When I turned in my take on Angelou's *Song*, I expected to be vilified in the letters to the editor, wanted the opportunity to defend myself, and requested it in my cover letter. I was confident, knowing I stood on solid writerly ground. I also knew most readers would be unfamiliar with my work and my hard-earned reputation—assuming they could appreciate the difference between a Maya Angelou and a Wanda Coleman. I suspected that few of my detractors had actually read her books or mine. I believed all of the ducats were on Angelou's side of the scale.

Purportedly, enough letters were received to paper an editorial cubicle, or to consume two issues of the sparse *BR*, which seldom exceeds sixteen pages. But not one of those letters was ever published in the *BR*, despite the deluge. Why ignore them?

The answer, so I assumed, came within two days.

"Have you seen this—it's unbelievable!" My husband rushed into my office waving the Los Angeles Times Book Festival schedule, listing events slated for April 27 and 28, the week ahead. "Look at this! Maya Angelou's the fucking main attraction!"

The explanation was now evident, I believed. I had been put into a trick, to use street parlance. Invited to participate in the Festival months earlier, I was slated for two panels and a poetry reading. When asked to review *Song*, it had not occurred to me that Angelou might have also been invited to participate. *What a setup*. But while Angelou would be given the Queen's treatment, an interview with NPR's Michael Silverblatt before a capacity audience in the best hall, I would be shuttled opposite her to the tacky Poets' Corner, to read to empty seats under a wind-battered canopy on the UCLA campus site.

We were stunned.

That scheduling was no coincidence. I felt used—had the old it-takes-a-Niggah-to-get-a-Niggah con been run, and had I gone for the okey-doke? Two African American women writers had been *pimped* in a ploy to generate a carefully anticipated controversy that benefited no entity save the Los Angeles Times Book

Festival. My husband and I discussed whether or not I should cancel my participation. I knew very well the embarrassment I faced, but quitting was not in my bones.

My two dreaded days of Book Festival activities unexpectedly turned into fun, my disappointment neutralized by the atmosphere of subterfuge: snide whispers, knowing giggles, and the nonstop congratulations for my review of *Song*. Rumor circulated that Angelou's editors at Random House, too, had noticed the specious timing of my review and had complained. It was the talk of the event. I was pleased that I hadn't backed out, even if the poetry reading went exactly as I'd predicted. One harried Festival staffer informed us that supreme efforts were being made to keep me and Angelou from crossing paths—an effort that nearly went awry when a golf cart in which Angelou was riding stopped our cart, which was going in the opposite direction. My son, my husband, and a novelist who happened to be sitting in the rear of my cart, all became hysterical with suppressed laughter. I smiled politely as Maya Angelou addressed her question to our driver. We exchanged a look. She did not recognize me (she hadn't seen me since 1992, at the Schomberg in New York City), we did not speak, and our carts went along their separate ways.

On the evening of the 28th, we left the Book Festival fête in a state of dazed euphoria. It was over and we were exhausted. My jaw muscles ached from the continuous smiling. Time to move on.

Oh—but—there was to be more: I was soon to be banned from EsoWon.

Co-owned by James Fugate and Tom Hamilton, EsoWon Books is one of the best of the independent Los Angeles bookstores featuring African American authors. That may not have meant much on the White side of town, but L.A.'s African American world is teensy—Blacks making up less than 9 percent of the population. EsoWon is an important part of maintaining the Black community in L.A. against the corrosiveness of economic disparity. People travel from all over Southern California to shop there for items unavailable elsewhere. I had patronized EsoWon myself, even though I knew they did not carry my books. James Fugate had once presented me with his card (still on my Rolodex), apparently pleased that I was spending my money on his premises. Over the years 1981 to 1996, my husband, Austin Straus, and I co-hosted *The Poetry Connexion*, a poet-interview program on KPFK/Pacifica radio, Southern California, on which we had championed them and all local independent bookstores.

It was on or around May 13, 2002, that I received a blind e-mail from Randy Ross, president of International Black Writers and Artists, L.A., to the effect that one of the authors in IBWA's latest anthology of short stories, *Griots Beneath the Baobab*, was no longer welcome at EsoWon. *Griots* included many noted Los Angeles writers, from Donald Bakeer to Jervey Tervalon. Ross asked "Should we: (1) ask the writer if he/she would be willing to opt out of the reading? (2) cancel the event? or (3) other? I need your feedback ASAP." Blind copies of this note were also sent to fourteen individuals, including IBWA board members and contributors to *Griots*.

The majority voted to cancel the *Griots* signing at EsoWon for May 22. I voted with the majority, but also urged Ross to take the incident to the press. Later, I insisted that Ross name the writer in question. He phoned and said it was me, and that the reason for my being banned was my negative review of *A Song Flung Up to Heaven*.

I sympathized with Ross and IBWA. They were caught in a complex and unsavory middle. The big book chains were not likely to carry their anthology. Considering that there were so few surviving independent outlets that would carry *Griots*, this was B-b-biiiggg.

Following my mother's timeworn adage, "You may go down, but go down fighting!", I got on the horn and left messages coast-to-coast that I was "banned from EsoWon." A day or so later, columnist Tim Rutten called. His piece about the flap—"'Flung' into Controversy by Negative Book Review, Bookstore Appearance Canceled"—appeared in the Friday, May 24, issue of the *L.A. Times*.

However, closure to this matter remains elusive.

A recent call from an enthusiastic young man reassured me that "this Angelou thing is hot," has taken on international proportions, and is all over the Internet—even if the literary mainstream that supports Angelou has remained silent. It isn't difficult to imagine what might come next, having once had a taste.

My mixed review of Audre Lorde's collected works in the August 31, 1997, issue of the *BR* caused similar if less intense fallout. I received no letters of support, and only one phone call —from a Black Studies department chair, taking me to task for being too rough. I agreed that perhaps he had a point. (Having heard my private critiques, one friend considered my Angelou review "Wanda Coleman lite.") But as critical as I was of Lorde, I never questioned her sincerity as a poet and writer. In my assessment, Lorde was flawed but still the genuine article.

A few days later, a fax came in, not intended for me, yet informing me that I was being boycotted (whatever that meant). The boycott was being led by a Black journalist—an immigrant—who not only took issue with my analysis of Lorde's craft (although he later admitted others had made like criticisms) but was also upset with my characterization of Lorde's late-career militancy as "tinged with defensiveness and guilt" typifying "the immigrant of color, an occasional enemy within the ranks who fattens on the sufferings of African Americans yet sides with Whites, believing we home-grown coloreds are inferior." He felt that I had gone overboard. To protest my review, he e-mailed well-known Black immigrant writers nationwide, his closing words: "Wanda Coleman must be stopped!"

I thought this was ludicrous—at first; however, the names on the e-mail were impressive, and included writers whose origins I had not known, some whose work underscored my point, others whom I admired, and still others who reminded me that "the Black immigrant of color" may also be a friend within the ranks.

Ironically, this journalist-boycotter had once contacted me through a mutual friend, in 1992, following the April 29 riots. She had asked me to help him keep his job by assisting him with an assignment for his Midwestern newspaper. He had to write an article illuminating the Black perspective and was stuck, trying to satisfy editors who, despite their liberalism, thought of Blacks as a monolithic group. I had graciously done so without a dime going into my pocket or requiring that my name be mentioned.

When I learned that he was boycotting me, I phoned him. We talked amicably. He said he remembered how I had helped him. He even agreed that my statement about Black immigrants of color was largely true, pointing out that *The New Yorker* had recently published an article precisely on that subject. Nevertheless, he was not going to return my kindness and would continue his boycott. I told him that I would stand by my words, and hung up.

Would any of this ultimately matter in the spectrum of American letters? I was too busy to worry, my private woes demanding attention. What could I do about it anyway? If anything negative had happened to me as a result of that so-called boycott, or if I had been denied any grants or invitations as a result, I wouldn't try to find out if I had the means. To engage in paranoia would be self-defeating. Besides, rejection had been a constant staple in my literary life and in the shaping of my intellect. In some respects, I found it could be liberating—particularly when it came to truth telling. I was beholden to no one, and to nothing save my own sense of duty.

I let the matter slide.

Now here I was in the swamp again—up to my dreads.

No sooner had my review of *Song* appeared than my phone began ringing off the cradle. One woman got my unlisted number from her boyfriend, a local D J, and called me screaming with ecstasy, repeatedly thanking me for the review she'd waited years to read. The thank-yous and congratulations poured in. But beyond the back slaps and laughter, there was the undeniable undertone of fear. This was often expressed as "That took courage," and "Somebody needed to say it," and, when in person, eyes shifted or rolled, and there was a change in skin pallor.

Whites were afraid largely because if they said anything about Angelou, they'd be dismissed as racists. Blacks were afraid, because

getting grants, reviews, and literary prizes was tough enough without making the kinds of enemies who might end up on the committee judging their manuscripts or books, or on the faculty of
the department in which they want to teach, or on the staff of the
poetry center where they want to present their work. Whatever
freedom I thought I had as a writer could be seriously curtailed by
Angelou supporters, as Fugate and Hamilton had demonstrated.
But the strongest odor of fear came from the IBWA.

If I was driven by moral imperatives, and come the hell of
crucifixion by Angelou fans, the IBWA response made it obvious
that not all were eager to climb up on the cross and bleed with
me. On June 10, I received the IBWA newsletter update with its
roster of events and ongoing call for membership. Under the title
of Griot Watch, it reminded members not to miss out on the first
edition of *Griots Beneath the Baobab*. "Word is that it's going to
be a collector's item . . ."—this followed by a list of where to purchase the anthology statewide. Under the section for Southern
California, EsoWon Books was listed.

Whatever circumstances may govern a writer's rise to fame in
America's murky literary world, excellence is too often a volatile
variable, if not a valueless quality altogether, particularly when
it comes to those of us who represent ourselves as African
Americans. Too often, Ebonics and the Oral Tradition are used as
justifications for bad writing rather than as modes of enrichment
for standard American English. As a writer who grew up in the
1950s and '60s, I still hear the strident words of those valiant
Negro teachers who risked their livelihoods by keeping us after
class, out of the earshot of Whites, to hammer these words into
our psyches: "You have to be three times better than *them* just to
stay even."

Whenever I pick up a pen, sit before a monitor, or peck at
a keyboard, I hear those voices and hold them dear. To hear
them is to honor them—whether what I write is a poem, a (non-
commercial) script, a story, or a book review. And in honoring
them, I crave true recognition for my acts of creation—those works
that I have sacrificed and bled for. I want to be heard—but by

an audience capable of appreciating what they hear. It has not escaped me that, to date, I have received more attention for my review of Angelou's *Song* than for any poem or story I have ever written. Anyone who assumes that I derive any satisfaction from that fact, other than that of a job well done professionally, is grossly mistaken.

Will I ever participate in the L.A. Times Book Festival again?

Yes—provided there's no scheduling conflict, and provided I'm asked.

Did I wage a personal assault against Maya?

No. All facts in my review had been published elsewhere. Angelou had written about her past in the sexual twilight years before.

Will I ever go back to EsoWon?

No. Nor will I recommend that anyone shop there. And whenever it's mentioned to me, I will inform that party that I have been banned from the premises.

Will I be writing anymore on this subject?

It depends. I'm not sure.

What is my current relationship with IBWA?

The same as always. When they ask me to participate, if I can, I will. They shouldn't be penalized for my personal or professional decisions.

Suppose something else happens, related to this?

I'll deal with that bitch when she slaps me.

Will I ever do a book review again?

Yes—if asked.

Will I censor myself if I do?

Niggah, please!

Boos & Reviews

The Angelou–EsoWon Contretemps

When African American sports fans gather ringside, it is the tradition to support those athletes who exemplify our greatness—"Air" Jordan, Tiger Woods, or the Williams sisters—and to defend them against any unfair manifestation of racism that might stain or limit their careers. Those all-Americans, and others like them, past and present, regardless of the controversies or conflicts surrounding them, have been hailed universally as world-class sports figures. Their sustained achievement has been rewarded with riches equal to or greater than any White athlete's, something that could not happen for a Jesse Owens, a Joe Louis, or an Althea Gibson.

When it comes to the creative writing of Black authors, the opposite is more often true. The complex nature of what is and is not literary among African American writers raises difficult questions that have been debated throughout our history, since the days of Phillis Wheatley. The discussion of excellence and quality raises issues about language and race our society and our people have yet to fully examine or address. Simply put: if Jordan played basketball, Woods played golf, or the Williams sisters played tennis on the level that many lauded African Americans write, no one would have ever heard of them.

152

I, a Black book reviewer, was banned from EsoWon, a Black-owned, Black-interest bookstore, for publicly criticizing the work of a famous Black writer. The possibility that I could be censored this way had occurred to me while I was writing my negative review of Maya Angelou's *Song Flung Up to Heaven*, just as it had occurred to me every time I've reviewed a fellow Black writer. (Keep in mind that no one asks me to review White writers.) Ebonics and matters of sheer craft aside, there are many complex factors that come into play whenever a critic ventures to judge such a book. Was it written for Blacks or Whites? Both? Anyone? What region is the author from? Is the author's voice authentic? Does the material presented jibe with the known facts? But the most powerful of these factors has little to do with the actual writing itself. That factor is what I call—for lack of a better term—*race-defense*.

Race-defense is an impulse that has grown out of our need to rightly protect ourselves against the relentless and ugly assaults of American racism. It has become a necessary part of our socio-psychological armoring, vital to our survival. We cheer on and support every "splendid" spokesperson and representative of our race. We have our own parades and our own heroes and heroines. We count them on every finger, pleased as the numbers increase from one to one hundred—hoping that someday, by the sheer force of those numbers, we will be granted full social parity with Whites. We announce the prizes won and the awards received. With pride, we keep the lists that define our historical progress. And in the last half of the twentieth century, during the Civil Rights and Black Power eras—and because of the sacrifices of men like Malcolm X, Medgar Evers, and Martin Luther King Jr.—we became quite vocal when presenting our important facts and figures to a predominantly White society that still continues its efforts to defame our accomplishments and keep us marginalized as a people.

However, as human beings, we too are imperfect. Under the frequently perverse pressures caused by the bizarre situations that we often encounter (DWB, racial profiling, red-lining, etc.), our *race-defense* can likewise become perverted. It may become a *race-defensiveness*, in which we become overly sensitive to any kind of criticism from anyone—even one of our own. When we are *race-defensive*, we attempt to draw unwelcome attention away from those deficiencies that we are embarrassed by or feel guilty about—ironically, most of those rooted in racism from the beginning. This is, to use the vernacular, a psychosocial double whammy.

The main problem with *race-defensive* behavior is that it is blind to valid criticism and will defend what is indefensible, what is harmful and irrational, to the very parties or persons presumably defended.

When I wrote my negative review of Maya Angelou's *Song*, I exercised my right and privilege to present my perspective on any author and his work, regardless of reputation. My right to do so was not simply a freedom-of-speech matter but a freedom gained by the hard work and sacrifice of millions of African Americans before me, victims and fighters alike, who dealt with racism by whatever means they had. Those people—*my* people—endowed me with the right to express my opinion, *without racist reprisals*, whether celebrating or criticizing *anyone*—including one of my own.

Therefore, when the owners of EsoWon Books banned me from the premises, they were not only engaging in *race-defensiveness* but they were also unwittingly going against the very hard-won freedom we African Americans have suffered to obtain, the same freedom their bookstore represents by its very existence. They were buying into the racism African Americans have made a tradition of fighting.

The May 30 issue of the *Los Angeles Sentinel* said that my review of Angelou's book was unfair; on the contrary, it was restrained. It was not a personal attack; it was an accurate, professional, and mild exposition of my opinion of the book and had nothing to do with my opinion of Maya Angelou—who I do not know personally, and neither like nor dislike. My criticism of Angelou was within the bounds of decency, or its publication would have made me liable for slander or defamation of character. Except for my analysis of the writing, there was nothing in my review that was not previously written about, in other newspapers or by Angelou herself.

I think that Maya Angelou is a one-book author in bad need of a ghostwriter. Her fairly engrossing *I Know Why the Caged Bird Sings* is, in my estimation, probably more fiction than fact and is flawed by hyperbole, but it found a popular readership among both Blacks and Whites. The book made her a literary celebrity, and in the wake of the book's success she has been adept at playing the race card for trumps. Angelou is a gifted gamester (a fact I admire) who is not above pimping her own people (a fact I do not admire). Her acceptance by the literary mainstream is predicated on the fact that she does not threaten the racist status quo. A White author writing on her level could not earn a cent.

Independent booksellers, even those with an eye on what sells, have always stocked their stores with whatever literature they love and support, usually giving their establishments a theme or a character that readers enjoy when shopping. These bookstores are paying the unfortunate price of extinction for that freedom of expression, as the giant book chains and online booksellers drive them out of business by offering speed and reduced rates to customers who rarely have the leisure or the patience to browse or the money to pay full price.

As one of those independents, Black-owned EsoWon is willingly taking a risk in arbitrarily banning African American authors like myself from its stores, but then—ironically—it has the legal right to do so, just like those many White-owned bookstores that have chosen not to carry the books of writers of color. The further irony is that those White-owned bookstores have made Black- and Chicano-owned bookstores necessary. As long as the independents, or the hipper outlets for the big chains, carry my books, I won't be needing the *race-defensive* EsoWon.

Following the cancellation of the *Griots* booksigning, the IBWA issued its June newsletter, announcing that EsoWon is among those booksellers offering copies of the *Griots* anthology for sale. EsoWon is doing so without recanting its banning of me.

Since few if any of the large book chains will carry *Griots*, I do not fault IBWA for seeking a compromise. For IBWA to be punished for my opinion of Angelou's book would be unfair.

I would like to believe that my being banned from EsoWon is the worst that can happen as a result of my April 14 review. But I know otherwise. The workings of literary influence occur outside public view, and are as subject to brown-nosing and cronyism as any other pursuit. Therefore, there is no way for me to know what trouble I'm in unless, as in the incident with EsoWon, the damage announces itself. I have long suspected that literary politics explains why some publications, like *Publishers Weekly*, do not always name their reviewers. It is a policy I can appreciate.

From where I stand, *race-defensiveness* is the root cause for the controversy that has brewed since my review of Angelou's *Song* appeared. I believe this *race-defensiveness* unfairly creates the demand for a greater level of excellence on the part of Blacks than it demands of anyone else claiming status as an American writer. By the same token, to give less than my best—whether I'm writing an essay, a poem, or a book review—would be to betray those African Americans who have practiced a healthy defense of our race in the name of liberty, freedom, and justice. Whenever I am called upon to be a book reviewer, literary-peer panelist, or cultural activist speaking out for my community, I believe it my duty to offer my best—not only in the service of my African American constituency, but in the service of society as a whole. It is the ultimate irony that I have been censored by those who, by their very nature, are parasitic on the peculiar circumstances of race that govern literary commerce in our age.

Hunt & Peck

Book Reviewing,
African American Style

As discussed above, my critical rip of Angelou's *Song* caused an immediate furor in the African American community. End of story? Not quite. I am still banned from EsoWon Books. The message?

Critically reviewing the creative efforts of present-day African American writers, no matter what their origin, is a minefield of a task, one complicated by the social residuals of slavery and the shifting currents in American publishing. Into this twenty-first century, African Americans are still denied full and open participation in the larger culture. Thus our books remain repositories for the complaints and resentments harbored against the nation we love, as well as paeans to the courage, fortitude, and sacrifice of peers and forebears.

For those who need reminding, books by writers of color were still largely found in the anthropology sections of libraries and bookstores until the Civil Rights movement was well under way. (The glory rush of pride, wonder, and dismay I felt whenever I stood before those sections has never been forgotten.) In grade school, circa 1954, the year "under God" was inserted into the Pledge of Allegiance, works by Negroes were treated as contraband and confiscated by White teachers or administrators. Out-side of home and church, creative writing by colored people did not seem to exist except for those authors who were assigned as classroom reading during Negro History Week (Black History Month since 1976). Of those, James Baldwin, Ralph Ellison, Langston Hughes, and Richard Wright were invariably our des-ignated spokesmen.

Getting hold of their books, however, was problematic if not impossible and meant leaving the ghetto to visit public libraries or borrowing from friends and relations—on one's solemn oath to return the precious tome. Few Los Angeles bookstores then fea-tured Black literature, even in the sociology section, and few pub-lishers braved carrying more than one or two African American authors. Black-owned presses, sans White patronage, led short lives. Books by Blacks had even less of a shelf life when reviews—good or bad—failed to appear. Good reviews written by Whites were the ideal, but bad reviews were welcomed if they generated enough controversy to sell copies. The few Black reviewers were usually among the ranking spokesmen of the race, and between them lay an ideological divide—those writing for Whites and those writing for Blacks, with the former receiving far greater attention.

The truths of our daily lives defined the truths for our litera-ture: we were constantly discriminated against, monitored, and censored. In defense and support of our writers, book clubs, dis-cussion groups, and writers' organizations emerged—in L.A., the Black Writers' Guild (later absorbed by the Writers Guild of America), Vassie May Wright's Our Authors Study Clubs, and, eventually, International Black Writers and Artists, Inc., and the World Stage in Leimert Park. But the majority of "folks" were reached via the grapevine (a.k.a. "the drum"); word of mouth was the primary news-and-review resource. If gossip, rumor, and spec-ulation were its liabilities, it was swifter than radio and TV and—best of all—was uncensored by the White establishment. (Any posture resembling that taken by EsoWon made a little more sense in those days.)

In 1963, Arna Bontemps published his *American Negro Poetry* anthology, which reintroduced older poets such as Gwendolyn Brooks and introduced the more racially conscious scions of education, miseducation, and self-education that converged in the Muntu Group, or the Black Arts Movement—Nikki Giovanni, Ted Joans, LeRoi Jones (Amiri Baraka), *et al.* Outside Bontemps' radar, writers and journalists like Ishmael Reed were making a name for themselves. And by the end of the '60s, popular fiction writers like Alex Haley, Donald Goines, Chester Himes, Iceberg Slim, and Frank Yerby were reaching audiences both Black and White, as a constellation of once-silenced voices exploded into print and onto screen and stage.

Following the August 1965 riots, Budd Schulberg's Watts Writers (Quincy Troupe, Kamaau Da'ooud) reinforced racial pride and spirited entitlement to unfettered speech. But the price paid for this newfound freedom was often scorching reviews by White book critics and the slight of being overlooked for literary grants and prizes. Knowing they were not exempt from the currents affecting all writers, Black writers became as adept as Whites at playing the literary games of cronyism, favoritism, and patronage. Impatient with the racist criticism that truncated their literary careers, they demanded same-race interviewers and reviewers. Supported by the leading Black celebrities of the day and underwritten by a riot-singed loosening of cultural constraints, African American reviewer-journalists began appearing in the mainstream print media.

Meanwhile, what had begun with *Brown v. the Board of Education of Topeka, Kansas* (1954) and public-school desegregation resulted in the boon of Black Studies programs in American colleges and universities throughout the 1970s. Since then, America has produced the largest educated population in its history, racism aside. New writers have emerged from workshops and from MFA and Ph.D. programs via whatever means necessary—affirmative action, grants, student loans, and scholarships. The publish-or-perish mandate of academic life, in tandem with increases in the Black middle and under classes, accelerated the outcry for cultural redress. An explosion into print of new kinds of writing to satisfy this boom market followed, meaning an inevitable diversity of Black authors across genres—from Samuel "Chip" Delany to Walter Mosley to Gary Phillips to Terry McMillan. Simultaneously, a fourth generation of fiction writers, social critics, and academics has emerged, along with a burgeoning Black avant-garde claiming influences from the Absurdists to the Surrealists, including rap/hip-hop writers flavored by Gil Scott-Heron and the Last Poets, the Nuyoricans, the Slam writers and acculturated others. The depth and breadth of writing across disciplines by those who identify as African American is now so staggering it outstrips the available review media.

It is thus incumbent upon any book reviewer to grasp the multifaceted broadening of what was once simply summarized as "The Black Experience," and it is the duty of the African American reviewer to accurately portray, critically assess, and convey this to potential readers. The ironic complexity of this task, no matter how savvy the reviewer, is best illustrated when the quality of the work produced by Black writers is measured against that of Whites using the criteria of excellence governing standard written English. Ideally, the social context within which the work under review is created should be factored in, but should that be done to the exclusion of evaluating the quality of the writing?

By applying my own standards to Angelou's *Song*, my answer was—and is—a resounding "NO!"

All literary criticism is, at root, biased, because each reviewer must bring to the act his or her individual worldview and aesthetic sensibility. Each must decide whether the social values of a text as a political record are more important than its literary values, which is often the case with books by African Americans. But to foster an illusion of excellence where none exists, regardless of the writer or subject matter, is to do a democratic readership the ultimate disservice. Saying amen to the going cultural directives without offering a true analysis—whether out of guilt, fear, or the desire to compensate the author for the social ills that shaped his or her existence—is as morally suspect as voicing a bigoted opinion. It is with this understanding that I write when-ever I assume the role of reviewer.

In post-9/11 America, where suspicions and the fear of terror-ism threaten long-coveted individual freedoms, a book review seems rather insignificant until the twin specters of censorship and oppression are raised. What keeps our nation great, despite racism, are those citizens who persist in honoring those freedoms. It is what allows me to voice my expertise, be it praise song, mixed bag, or dissent.

An Interview with
Wanda Coleman—2002

by Priscilla Ann Brown

I first became aware of Wanda Coleman and her work on July 16, 2002. One of my friends and I were talking about writers who were "funky" and "pushing the edges" of several genres. I was fascinated to learn of a writer who had been creating for decades and who had received several accolades but who was not yet a staple in the African American Literature canon. . . . The breadth of the topics she explores (gender, race, urban society, connectedness and disconnectedness, psychological hurting and healing, and love in all its many facets) . . . deserve deeper, scholarly exploration. . . . As a part of that deeper exploration, I flew from Washington, D.C., to Los Angeles on Halloween 2002 in order to interview Wanda Coleman on November 1 . . . What follows is [an excerpt from] that conversation. —*P.A.B.*

BROWN: Recently, I showed my students the film *Brother Future*; we've just finished up this unit on the Underground Railroad, and in the film, the Denmark Vesey character tells one of the other characters never to try to reveal another person to The Man, as it were, and at this point, I want to go to Maya [Angelou] for just a moment.

COLEMAN: All right. The Maya Situation.

BROWN: I have read your review of Angelou's book, and I have read many of the criticisms that have come back. As the culture at large tries to put Blackness, the Black Experience, the Black Voice, and Black people in general into one box under one label (and your voice is a voice from outside the box), what—if anything—is the responsibility of those Black voices that are being allowed to speak?

COLEMAN: Not to blow somebody's game? Because I say that in an *Another Chicago Magazine* interview. But you find that sometimes, when you blow the game, the people you're blowing it for are not going to be able to appreciate it. ... That's one level. ... I'm a professional. I do my J–O–B. I have pride in my work. So ... it could have been anybody. ... I reviewed Elaine Brown ... Monster Cody's book ... Garrett Hongo's poetry anthology [*The Open Boat*]. ... So that transcends that race thing ... my obligation is to the reader out there. On the second level, I might have been a little bit kinder if I had felt that I was dealing with someone who wasn't exploiting the race ...

BROWN: That's the sense that I got from the review, that you were taking Maya to task.

COLEMAN: You know, to me this woman was committing the ultimate betrayal. She was ... parasitic on her own people and on things that are important to her own people. I don't care about a parasite. I'm going to put salt on her, so she'll dissolve. [*Laughs.*]

BROWN: Dry her up? Now ... [*Laughs.*]

COLEMAN: Like a slug.

BROWN: Exactly. That's the image I just got.

COLEMAN: You know ... She can pimp White people up the yingyang, and I might not say nuthin'. Unless—I might pull the coattail of a particular White person that I like and say, "Watch out for Maya. Watch your back when you get to Maya." [*Laughs.*] You know? But I wouldn't say anything necessarily in public to out her. I would let her go on about her pimping. But when she starts pimping my cousins and my daughter and my grandbabies, then I gotta say something. And when she is pimping the young people in the inner cities, when she's running the same game on them as she's running on the White folks, then she's gone too far. So when she goes into the big White universities where they've got all that Grand Theft Dough, and she wants to hold them up for godzillion G's ... wants them to send the stretch limo, and get her fresh flowers, and pay for first-class roundtrip tickets for herself and her assistant—when she does *that* to them, that's fine, but when she does it to young Black students coming out of the ghetto at some rinky-dink community college—when she does it to them, and then won't autograph her books, even for them? When you do that, then you are something perverse and ugly ...

BROWN: And, as you said, that transcends race?

COLEMAN: In this case, I think it's all about race. Because like I said ... she was going to climb on the back of Malcolm X and stand on his shoulders, when she didn't deserve to touch the hem of his garment. And here we are talking about it in November 2002.

BROWN: That's right. There was an article still addressing the issue in late September.

COLEMAN: It's still explosive.

BROWN: Exactly. That this debate is still going on speaks to how deeply rooted the group mentality is in the Black psyche, how deep the "us" and "them" perceptions still run.

COLEMAN: That, to me, is a statement about how much work

164

remains to be done in the culture. That—contrary to what some might say, like a Ward Connerly—it's still all about race, and we still haven't done enough work.

Heavy Duty Postscript

Rereading the snippet from the Priscilla Ann Brown interview, it occurs to me that, in my relaxed chattiness, I failed to consider those readers who are incapable of grasping anything beyond the level on which Angelou writes, or those African Americans of Slave Origin who lack insights into the social circumstances that define and redefine their existences. Nevertheless, as of this writing, my posture is essentially unchanged.

Two weeks after that interview, around Thanksgiving 2002, I received a cautious telephone call—an intercession, by a friend of a friend, both of whom shall remain anonymous. I agreed to a meet and they dropped by my home on the appointed afternoon. Their mission was to hip me to their take on The Maya Situation. Immediately they warned me that I was in *serious danger*. I had assumed that Angelou and her supporters would take the high ground and dismiss me—since, if the EsoWon owners were any example, her supporters would not desert her.

Not so, according to my friends.

My review of *Song* and my subsequent articles had jolted our Black subculture like Krakatoa had jolted Java. There were tsunamis all through the south and shock waves in Europe *and*

166

Africa. (I mentioned that I had received responses from Australia and Thailand.) The subculture was now polarized pro against con, with those few who liked both Angelou and Coleman in the uncomfortable middle. Disagreements over my review had broken up longstanding friendships and thrown English departments into disarray. The fallout was so great, allegedly, that Angelou had finally "put out word" that she had to "make a move" against me. What, I wondered, could possibly happen, short of some *phenomenal* maniac taking me out like Malcolm X, since Angelou and I live in writing worlds that rarely intersect.

Word is out, was the comeback, *that anyone who shares the stage with you will be ostracized.*

Thus the fatwa was decreed, but in what country could I seek refuge?

Before departing my porch that November afternoon, among the things my anonymous friends reported were the efforts of several enterprising literary movers-and-shakers who had attempted to arrange a public forum in which Angelou and I would appear, presumably to debate or discuss issues of writing and censorship. No one had ever contacted me. Angelou was obviously the determining factor.

Grateful for their concern, I thanked my friends as they departed. But what could Angelou do to me, I wondered, given that our writing worlds were so far apart?

Eventually, the phone stopped ringing and I whirled on about my usual business.

Soon it was spring again.

Three years earlier, I had been invited east by a college English department, to be their distinguished lecturer in 2003. I was to spend several days on the beautiful university grounds, participate in a panel discussion, lecture, do a poetry reading, and hold several sessions with students. The honorarium was moderate, the lodging free, and I was provided with a tour of the campus, meals, and the generous camaraderie of faculty and staff. Events went along apparently well, as scheduled, judging by general responses. But I was barely on campus a day when was someone raised "The

Maya Situation." At first, I was complimented for my courage and forthrightness; then reluctantly, faculty members informed me that Angelou would be arriving on campus the very afternoon I was scheduled to return to Los Angeles. She was being flown in by the Associated Students for twenty-seven times the honorarium I was receiving to perform one tenth of the activities.

This, too, was no coincidence.

Perhaps, I later mused, I should ready myself for like events in the future—Angelou descending from the clouds to scarf up the grand-theft nuggets whenever and wherever Coleman is scheduled to appear for virtually naught. If this was supposed to embarrass or wound me, it couldn't and didn't. If there has been other so-called sabotage against me, I am, thus far, uninformed and unaware.

Driven by the love of language and the power of the word, I have made personal choices and career sacrifices that I doubt few persons, including Angelou, could appreciate or understand. Because of those sacrifices, I am fearless. Angelou, the one-book celebrity author and "inaugural poet," may make twenty times the filthy lucre—but I'm satisfied that Coleman is, and will go down in history as, twenty times the griot.

You can't convince me that life doesn't spring from neon, that sunlight isn't glitter, that the ocean's roar ain't that bad ol' tenor sax blowin' sideways in heaven's underpass to earth . . .

IV

MY FUTURE IS IN MY PAST

Dancer on a Blade

Deep Talk, Revisions
& Reconsiderations

i take the eleven to San Pedro's exit on Gaffney
thru town to the cliffs the sand the sea
where palms bear witness this midnight
as i take this final drive
my dreams of water the roar the foam
played back against the violet vista
i find the unmarked gate and take the hidden road,
park at tide's edge and kill the headlights
                    —from "Death 101," May 1984

There are moments when I'm inclined to believe that trying to define poetry is as fruitless as trying to define love. It simply can't be gotten right. Experts and sources abound, and some of their definitions ring true, but the ringing soon fades away into an embarrassed silence. As soon as a provisional consensus is reached, some small qualification or new sensibility emerges to throw all absolutes out the window. After years of thinking about poetry—about what it is and what makes it work—I've come to no conclusions. All I know is that the reader who appreciates poetry, or the work of a particular poet, is drawn to its sound and sense out of some profound and often indecipherable need, and that because it has an impassioned reader, the poem, with time, may transcend its author and all critics. But to say this is not to define poetry. Circumscription continues, just as it has since the Sophists.

What little I've been able to contribute to this ongoing discussion has been said not in formal essays but during informal interviews. When teaching workshops or in classrooms, I'm quick to admit that I'm a poetry bigot, believing it the highest form of human dialogue.

> *hand story: once upon a time i laid hands in love*
> *the sinister and the dexter*
> *in the hope of a man. to give him*
> *light by which to see me. once*
> *upon a time i laid hands in love*
> *to cure his flesh in the fire*
> *mine. burning together. once upon*
> *a prayer*
>
> *these hands*
> —from "Hand Dance," August 1983

My published interviews have only rarely been dialogues. Rather, they have been monologues wrung from me under difficult and sometimes bloody-odd circumstances. Sometimes, in the course of talking to me, the interviewer discovers that he or she doesn't much care for me or what I have to say. More often than not, I'm interviewed after having been up two or three nights working at one job, project, trauma, or another. (I have always lived in a rest-broken, sleep-deprived urban zone of endless stress and dissatisfaction.) In most cases, the interviewer cannot imagine the unsettling gyrations I had undergone mere minutes or seconds before at home, on the job, or outside on the streets. (Once, en route to a radio interview, I bodaciously committed a score of traffic violations simply to arrive on time.)

And yet I am always expected to sit down, comfortably, and

present myself coherently, answering questions with as much
bravado as I can muster and in the manner appropriate to a
"modern-day Langston Hughes" writing "movingly of the double
oppression of being both a woman and an African American." I
am expected to be a font of "straight-ahead, award-winning, and
powerful perceptions," an "uncompromising" and "skilled teller
of tales," an "L.A. Blues Woman," the "Billie Holiday of Poetry."

where are you
i'm trapped on sunset
the purple haze of headlights and laughing latins
roar past. something has snapped.
the thing won't run anymore.
i push it to the curb myself—
half a ton of useless metal,
open the hood and tinker around until
i conclude it has to be abandoned

talk about China?
i can't get out of Watts

where were you
when they broke into my pad
raped me and i was going crazy hoping
they wouldn't touch my kids?

talk about liberation
i can't get out of debt

and the time the LAPD jacked me up
for cop killing—a natural suspect
in my black leather jacket & jeans
they cuffed me and sped me off to jail
where were you & your checkbook?

talk to me talk to me
talk me to death
                    —from "Dear Sergeant Jack," March 1981

Literary publications usually give me the latitude to stretch, to say as much as I want in any fashion that I or the interviewer desire, because there is no hard cash exchanging hands. The disadvantage, I've come to discover, is that sometimes these interviewers aren't always interested in my poetry per se. Instead they are interested in the music they've heard in my poetry, in the "oral tradition," or in my "electrifying" performance style. Or in rubbing elbows with someone considered a cult celebrity. What I don't have the time or ability to do is to convince them of the intimate relationship between my two disparate gifts—the writing and the presentation of the writing. Early on, I wasn't too certain of the distinction myself.

Mainstream and alternative publications have either tried to protect me (from myself or the reader) or tried to fit me into their given agenda. Serious Black American writers of African descent have always been a rarity in the western United States; you can count them, past and present, on two hands and one big toe. Therefore, when a West Coast publication "needs a Black voice" and budget and timing are major limitations (meaning they can't afford to fly in a big-name Black from the east), one of us test-proven issue-ready local spooks must suffice. We come easily recyclable and almost interchangeable, and are used without consideration of differences in national origin, style, content, or point of view. And whether we get along or not is irrelevant to those who view the Black subculture as monolithic.

It used to be, however, that when someone was looking for a tough customer, particularly a "fearless womon poet" able to conduct a workshop in San Quentin, visit a Skid Row substance-abuse rehab house, or read at an ill-reputed Youth Authority facility—in short, an "artist" who wouldn't wince when told her audience consisted largely of murderers and child molesters— Wanda Coleman was summoned. But this presumed toughness, rooted in a racist reality in which I too was stereotyped, was not the glamour stuff that local newspapers wanted. Therefore, I was pushed, prodded, and spanked into either more "positive" postures or the acceptable kind of shock-value controversy easily

absorbed and dismissed by a power structure no longer threat-
ened by a passé '6o's Black militancy or any kind of American
social militancy.

At some point during the mid-1980s, I began to tire of osten-
sibly talking about myself without talking about myself deeply,
struggling to retain the grits and gravy of my existence for some
imagined future memoir. Presenting myself in what I considered
a recharged and powerful light became an unbearable pressure.
Yet, I had convinced myself that I needed every modicum of
attention I could garner because writers of all stripes who took
root west of the Mississippi and south of the Sacramento were so
terribly neglected by the rest of the English-speaking literary
planet.

> *dense opal fog obscures her black os*
> *entry, a navigational feat*
> *strong persistent undertow*
> *distant cry. another ship anchors*
> *horn sounds. lights & beacons define a*
> *cool welcome. February and the end*
> *of a troubled voyage*
>
> *dock and the rank pungence of oil spillage*
> *San Pedro tourista traps, bars & Marineland*
> *the blemished old royal Dame Mary*
> *stars appear like teeth lost in a barroom brawl*
> *bleed on the floor of sky*
>
> *travel these streets more tortuous than Sargasso*
> *nor can one be more lost than drive her*
>
> *uncharted promise*
> *home at last for a price*
>   —from "Port Angeles," May 1981

By 1991, a little over twenty-one years after sending my fledgling
manuscript to Black Sparrow Press, a deeply entrenched, un-
exorcised rage had "calderized" despite my having crisscrossed

the nation doing more than five hundred readings, my having published more than five hundred poems, and my having been blessed with a few honors along my circuitous route. The deep-rooted reasons for this anger were tangled beyond unraveling, yet it continued through the days that followed the fires in the name of Rodney G. King and persisted long after the sociopolitical eruptions died, burning as apparently cool as *pahoehoe*, or liquid lava crusted over in volcanic ash.

This anger, I began to realize, was my long-festering subliminal response to a surface-addicted world in which any remnants of in-depth journalism and serious literature were being rapidly subsumed by the cash-and-carry sensationalism of voracious tabloid exploitation driven by a new breed of pernicious corporate profiteers. I was not alone. The average citizen of the *fin de siècle* U.S.A. was awash in a ceaseless flow of controversies, crises, catastrophes, and celebrity trials.

one day a sapling broke ground
grew high enuff to start to block the view
between my neighbor's terrace and my window
good. more privacy, i thought

four years later it matured and gave birth
sweet firm orangy apricots good to eat.
we picked them, me and my kids
sometimes neighbor kids stole them

but knowing nothing of trees
(anyway, i didn't have time to know)
it went untended and grew wild while i enjoyed
the dance of leaves in late afternoon sun

my unkempt tree bears fruit less frequently
and what it bears is sharp tart pulpy

my fruit. stolen no more
—"tree of my planting," May 1984

By 1988, after a thirty-year struggle to mature as a writer (my first poem was published in 1959, at age thirteen), I seemed to have arrived when my first collection of stories, *A War of Eyes*, was favorably reviewed on page one of the *Los Angeles Times Book Review*. But I was just one hop ahead of the tsunami which had been building behind mainstream media's declaration of war against poetry, the quixotic charge led by the *L. A. Times Book Review* just the year before. Although the then editor provided evidence that poetry could and did make money, and an editorial stated that "poetry is not naturally a nurturing pursuit; as an intense form of self-expression, it requires a professional attention to the self that is as far from conventional selfishness as a clown's attention to the red spot on his nose is far from conventional vanity," this lame defense did not alter policy and followed the announcement that the *Book Review* section would no longer review small-press volumes by contemporary and unknown authors. (Now, a decade later, that policy has been shelved. But the harm to notoriously frail literary careers of the period can't be undone.)

This blatant and unfair reactionary censorship was more ice on the mushrooming cultural chill as states' arts funding collapsed nationwide and a corresponding assault on the National Endowment for the Humanities and National Endowment for the Arts loomed on the sociopolitical horizon.

> *a cross red and gold with flame*
>
> *a nation sleeps undisturbed beneath the bleeding*
>
> *moon where black flesh glistens, freshly hung*
>
> *black & anguished*
>
> *what would it have been like equal/free*
>
> *a child whose mother's apron is the red white & blue*
> *of a flag, her rhetoric of "wash those hands,*
> *your face and those dirty ears"*
> —"All the Hate Hate Is," March 1981

We Southern California poets, a motley generation of Whitmans forced to toot our own leaves, tremulously relied on regional publications to, at minimum, mention our names. When the culture wars broke out, many poets were casualties, though a handful of heavyweights who had breached the limits of regionalism were left standing. Fortunately, I was among the latter. But the wars had done their damage, contributing to my complex rages made public, the hurt and impotence long tempered to create the fabric from which I fashioned my poems, the good, the bad, and the rhetorical.

> *the walls sway and quiver*
> *my pulse thumps at the lip of my left ear*
> *i stare inward, mind focused*
> *on everything i thot we shoulda woulda coulda*
> *had love worked*
> *i blame me i blame him i blame the world*
> —from "The Aftershock," October 1984

In 1980, I was among the local literati invited to a salon at the West Los Angeles home of English drama critic Kenneth Tynan and his wife, Kathleen. That afternoon stands out in my memory as one of the rare times I've ever felt "in society." Mr. Tynan was ill with the cancer that would soon end his life, and Kathleen was assisted by friends, one of whom took charge of introducing me around. At one moment I found myself face-to-face with the gorgeous, olive-skinned, gray-haired P. Armando Fernandez, the cultural ambassador to Cuba, who was twenty years my senior.

He promptly and scathingly asked, "Why is it they introduce you as a Black poet and not as a poet?"

Knocked speechless by his unexpected arrogance and his enormous question, I groped to recover my tongue. He abruptly turned and walked away. Greatly disturbed, I left early, barely able to concentrate on the drive home. I remember little about the rest of that afternoon, everyone and everything else blotted out by that man and that staggering, cruel question to which my very existence was the answer.

> *we don't marry women like you*
> *your nappy head too dark skin*
> *even if in vogue*
> *turns us off*
> *and cookin' food and havin' babies is all*
>
> *we want you to do. and i can tell*
> *by lookin'*
> *you ain't ready for that*
> —from "Song for Some Sistuhs," 1970–72

In retrospect, I've speculated that Fernandez's infuriating question has been the subtext for my every interview since; therefore, in this literary moment, I've excerpted from some of my best interviews, selecting certain questions to be addressed in greater detail. As a result, I hope to make these moments re-speak me in a brighter and perhaps slightly less charring luciferosity.

ELECTRUM

"Coleman's poetry is personal, written with an eye for detail. That's not to say [that] Wanda's not especially conscious of being Black and a woman and a poet in a world where none of these categories constitutes an occupational asset."

That statement is as true now as it was in the mid-'80s when it appeared in the introduction to an interview conducted by writer Ben Pesta for the late, lamented *Electrum,* one of the few Southern California literary magazines to survive more than a few issues without support from a university or other patron. I had met Ben at a salon for the local Los Angeles literati given by poet Nancy Schiffrin. The L.A. poetry scene that had cohered around Beyond Baroque Literary Center in 1969 had mushroomed from infinitesimal to teensy, and it was, and still remains, virtually impossible not to know or bump heads with everyone active. My comments to Ben, as they tend to be when face-to-face with the interviewer, depended on my mood, and were pithy and to the point.

"When I was in Diane Wakoski's workshop," I told Ben, "she used to say, 'I'm not a political poet. My poems are nonpolitical.' That's okay [for her]. Her history [as a White woman in America] validates that. But I can't be 'just a writer who [happens] to be Black.' Not in my lifetime, anyway. If I sneeze, it's political. If I breathe, it's political."

My memory of the specifics is vague, but in 1972 I attended Diane Wakoski's poetry workshop at California Technical Institute, in Pasadena. I had met John Martin, the publisher of Black Sparrow Press, in March of that year, and he had strongly recommended I study with his "superstar" poet, author of *Motorcycle Betrayal Poems*. I was drawing unemployment insurance at the time. I had also dropped out of college, partly for financial reasons but mainly because I believed the chair of the cinema department, with whom I had studied, was a racist. Unluckily, he taught every course critical to my cinema major.

> *we don't hire black women as a rule*
> *especially with looks like yours*
> *skin flicks, maybe, TV rarely*
> *except when it's comedy haha*
> *unless you can coax the sex out of a note*
> *like Lena Horne or Billie Holiday*
> —from "Song for Some Sistuhs," 1970–72

In those days, I liked to consider myself a "Jane of all trades" or "Renaissance writer." I wanted to master all forms, from poetry to playwriting to scriptwriting, and eventually go into filmmaking. In spite of my impoverished reality, that of the divorced mother of two children, I viewed the world through lenses tinted fire-engine red. I had taken on a writing partner, actor and part-time preacher Christopher "Big Brutha" Joy, and we had enrolled

together. Unlike me, Chris was not having problems with our professor. I pointed out to Chris that while we were both Black, he
was fair-skinned and male, and didn't stand out as much as I did
among the forty-odd students. In favorable contrast, Wakoski's
workshop was minuscule with no more than three or four students
present at any one session. The benefits were greater intimacy,
attention to detail, and in-depth analysis. The drawback was the
increased pressure on me to produce fresh poems.

During this time, I was still processing my feeling of being "left
in the lurch" at the end of the Civil Rights, Free Love, and Black
Power movements. I had tried, repeatedly, to get my frustrated
militancy into my work. I had learned to aptly mimic the strident
Afro-American voices that had emerged during the Black Arts
Movement, those of Ted Joans, Shirley Steele, and my favorite, Joe
Goncalves. But less than a handful of these poems were ever published. After peaking at three thousand rejection slips by 1969, I
had concluded that I was doing something very wrong no matter
how closely I followed *Writers' Digest* and the other guides. I suspected that it had more to do with my approach to content than
with style and form (not to mention bad spelling and poor gram-
mar). John Martin had already forced me to begin examining this
problem, passing along literature he considered excellent and
that he considered "dreck," engaging me in arguments about my
approach.

> *we hire negresses like you*
> *to clean our bars at Sybil Brand or C I W*
> *try suicide again, it's one year in the slammer,*
> *said the White judge in Black robes*
>   —from "Song for Some Sistuhs," 1970–72

Diane Wakoski took me steps further toward enlightenment, as I
kicked and ranted, unable to fully articulate my point of view,
stubborn in my stance but absorbing as much information as she
could supply, doing my own comparative analysis, going home
nights to read and study as many of her books as I could obtain,

as well as those by the authors (Robert Kelly, Garcia Lorca, Sylvia Plath) whose work she lectured on in class. Once I left Wakoski's workshop, our disagreements would continue to set the tone for each poem for a number of years. Eventually, maintaining Wakoski's posture in constructive opposition (if that makes sense), I began to fine-tune my side of the argument, distinguishing between mundane issues-oriented party politics and what I considered the higher political reality organic to the circumstances of my existence as an African American of slave descent.

Not least of the benefits of participating in Wakoski's workshop was my friendship with poet Sylvia Rosen, a bond that has lasted more than twenty-five years. A dark-haired wife and mother and a former New Yorker, she drove into Pasadena from Canoga Park, a post-WWII suburban community twenty miles away in the West San Fernando Valley. Often we arrived early, and as we sat alone, waiting for Wakoski and the rest of the class, we talked about our lives as girls, as women, and as mothers. With Sylvia I felt like a human being instead of a social problem.

When Wakoski's workshop ended, we continued our friendship, made easier when I left the Watts I'd returned to in 1971, moving back to South Central in 1975 and then to Hollywood in 1976, communities well within Los Angeles proper. We continued to critique our poems, talked about our children, exchanged information about books (Kenneth Patchen, Adrienne Rich, William Carlos Williams, and Denise Levertov), joined other workshops, attended readings, and eventually shared the podium. Sylvia was my first poetry buddy and the only friend with whom I could share that part of my life devoted to literature.

> *sylvia with shocking brown eyes*
> *writes poems of dream worlds and weaves*
> *purple platinum quilts of warm motherhood: inspiring*
> —from "Some Women," May 1975

I had just wrapped up a divorce, finished a new book manuscript, and was in the throes of an intense new romance at the time of the Ben Pesta interview, working the usual two jobs to keep every-thing afloat. *Imagoes* (1983) was my watershed book. In it I acknowledged my full womanhood and attempted to place child-hood in perspective.

I grew up in the South Central of the Fabulous '50s, which was in relentless flux as a steadily increasing Black population demanded more access to financial, health, and recreational facilities and an end to housing restricted along racial lines. My parents left Watts proper when they bought their first and only home in 1949, when I was three. We were the first Black family in the tiny working-class community where many of the streets remained unpaved, the ragman drove a horse-drawn cart, and a pushcart vendor hawked tacos for ten cents each. Milk was still delivered to the front or side porch doors, there was this new in-vention the neighbors had called a television, and when you made a 360-degree turn, you could see the tall buildings and trees miles away. No one was talking about smog, and evenings were spent snuggled up on the floor, near my parents' bed, listening to radio programs like *The Lone Ranger*, *Gangbusters*, and my favorite, *The Whistler*. There were two Spanish-speaking families on the block, and a family of Gypsies. But in time, these families disappeared and the entire neighborhood became Black.

> *mass migration began in the 50s*
> *we observed their withdrawal and kept note*
>
> *we lived in their midst*
> *the ones in the house on our left, a strange pair*
> *they always crossed their yard on tiptoe*
> *children, my brother and i watched them*
> *through the thick barrier of morning glory vines*
> *and peach trees*
> *the female always wore an expression of dread*
> *and kept peeking over her shoulders*
> *in our direction*
> *the male seemed less afraid but nevertheless*

cautious. one time they saw us watching
and stood stark still, frozen
in the light of our
amazed inquiry
— from "Flight of the California Condor (2),"
September 1982

One morning, during the fall of 1957, I began to feel ill. But I didn't want to stay home that day and went on to South Park Elementary School. It was a cold morning, but I was inordinately cold, and before class started, I developed the chills. I became so sick that the teacher became concerned and sent me home. After a few days I began to hallucinate, unable to distinguish the real from the unreal. Having developed myriad allergies after birth, I was prone to illnesses, particularly horrible skin rashes, coughing spells, bouts of hay fever, and hives. An insect bite could swell as large as a saucer. But this was something new. Eventually, I would be hospitalized for what one doctor called "African sleeping sickness." At that time, children across the state were coming down with a mysterious type of encephalitis. Once I recovered, I began to notice that my motor skills were slightly impaired but my facility for language had increased. Always a poetry lover, writing in general began to dominate my interests. When answering Pesta's questions about being a writer, that seminal period was relived in a flash. I even remembered having left a Christmas gift, my leather-bound illustrated copy of *The Arabian Nights*, in the trunk of Pop's midnight-blue struggle buggy. He sold that old Plymouth while I was in the hospital. The loss was devastating. It came at a time when I had begun to regard books as friends.

oh little black girl baby
welcome to the world, wide brown eyes

never be happy in it

you will hear Pop say he wanted a manchile
as firstborn

184

you will sulk as he confines you
to the house & kitchen sink
and Mom instructs you
in the ways of cook, maid & seamstress

you will rebel
hungry to reshape everything to suit you

you will envy men their power
sometimes hate them
worse, sometimes love them

—"Greetings," July 1984

"I wanted to be a detective," I continued. "I had read a lot of Agatha Christie (*And Then There Were None*) and Earl Derr Biggers (creator of Charlie Chan)" on my way to Mickey Spillane (*Kiss Me, Deadly*) and Ian Fleming (the James Bond novels). My Uncle Kenneth, the perennial photographer at family gatherings, had been a private detective before becoming a bridge champion. The fictional life of the gumshoe aroused in me a serious interest in crime fighting until I began to tackle science textbooks on criminology and its history, going all the way back to the days of the Inquisition and the Knights Templar. I was finding life unfair and wanted to see the scales of political and poetic justice tipped in my favor.

i move forward in ecstasy
know what's ahead
i have chosen my fate
culled it out between the keys of my
electronic cohort
i have chosen my fate
and the knowledge of what i am
what i do will remain
in my heart unspoken
soldiers do not question

*they act and are judged by those actions
am i deserving of more?*
       —from "I War," February 1974

"Then I wanted to be a musician. Under the spell of Max Bruch's *Violin Concerto No. 1* and *Kol Nidrei*, I played piano and violin. I was starting to make progress, enough to do solo performances and recitals, when I contracted encephalitis. I was in bed for nearly seven weeks and fell behind in my music lessons. Music requires rigorous physical discipline, and when I got well I just couldn't do it anymore." Although I didn't completely give it up until high school.

My childhood was a culturally rich palette of ballet lessons, piano lessons, and Jascha Heifetz–inspired violin studies at a storefront music school. Mr. DiPinto was my Italian violin teacher, until Mama's money ran out. I became accomplished enough to play in one of Leonard Bernstein's Youth Concerts, representing Gompers Junior High. My working-class parents scuffled to provide as many activities for their children as possible. I quickly abandoned ballet after sustaining several unsubtle insults about my body type and size, let alone my inability to pirouette. My father, a visual artist and advertising man, had long ago taught me the rudiments of drawing and graphics. "He carried a pad and pencil wherever he went. He drew caricatures in the doctor's waiting room, everywhere he had a minute and a place to sit down. Now, I carry a pad and pencil with me everywhere."

Time being so precious, I resented being forced to "hurry up and wait" endlessly at the post office, in supermarkets, at social services, at human resources, at gas stations during the gas crises of the '70s, on autoshop parking lots for inept or fake repairs made at a snail's pace, at the bank, in department stores where consumers were predominately African American; and in heavy traffic during rush hour. Rather than succumb to numbness, I jotted down lines in a journal or on a steno pad, ideas for poems or stories, sometimes entire poems and bits of stories.

186

the children are asleep/
dreaming
they used to worry
but i told them what to do
in case the ride should go on forever

i reassured them
our love will go on forever
the dying makes it all fun
—from "Late Night Drives (2),"
January 1978

Often my poems are literally quilted together as montages from dog-eared pages torn from various notebooks. Over the years, my demanding life ("under the gun," "on fast forward," and "seldom without a break," as per past descriptions) has denied me the contemplative time I've long coveted as my convolutions have invariably developed complications. This has caused me to make mistakes. But to the better, I've developed my signature version of a time-worn technique of weaving poetic strands into complete works, as if writing the one poem over years of fits and starts.

Caught between the inhumane circumstances of poverty and a poetic compulsion, I began keeping a book of lines, a habit that I've found invaluable to my published work. I've kept notebooks of poems I'd be embarrassed to publish as initially written, and have come to regard such poems as "keys" (as suggested by John Martin) with which to unlock a publishable poem or story. Sometimes a single key will unlock several poems yet remain unpublishable itself. Over time, I've noticed that I never actually lose a poetic idea and often unconsciously rewrite or revisit a poem written years earlier.

Sometimes when editing my work, a vague, disturbing familiarity sends me plowing through old notebooks to find its unsettling but unsuccessful predecessor. Thus poetry, frequently assisted by music, has helped illuminate the workings of my memory.

My Future Is in My Past

i take the shortcut to the butt end
to the edge of industry past
where blue-collars are bleached in July sun
i stop at Jack's for ice-cold nostalgia
to cut the dust and clear my thoughts

it's all boarded husks of home, now
along this wide and strangely green boulevard
illusions as fat as bronzed-cheeked
bubbled-eyed brown babies at play on lawns

this is the avenue Mom & Pop always took
to visit Auntie & Uncle before they died
and i too am a ghost, passing thru
at the Lou Dillon crossing to recycle my life
—"Nadeau," July 1984

"Both my parents wanted to be poets," I told Ben Pesta. "So I am realizing some of their dreams. My father, in fact, wanted to start a magazine. He even taught me how to dummy . . . magazines and newspapers."

"A fairly esoteric skill to teach a little girl," was Ben's response.

A boxer, an insurance salesman, a janitor, Pop worked tirelessly to keep his South Central print and sign shop open, in the garage if necessary, moving from location to location over the decades once Mom tired of the struggle and insisted he vacate the garage. She settled for the back-and-eye-breaking dolor of a seamstress and was exploited by sweatshops in exchange for the steady paychecks that would keep our household together.

In his lion years, my father was in constant motion, always on the run, friends and associates coming by the house, men and women engaged in a ritual I've come to call scheming-and-dreaming. For many years there was always a printing press in the house or garage, an easel or drawing table set up, the rumblings of the airbrush motor drowning out the TV, my father under his visor, with his T-square, straight-edge, and X-acto knife, the air around him an aura of paint, ink, and rubber cement mingled with sweat and aftershave lotion. My brother George and I were eager apprentices, quick on command to grab a giant eraser, roll of masking tape, or paintbrush.

My mother had a socialite's tastes and ambitions, and supervised a roster of family activities including church socials, family picnics, and parties. She too had dreamed of being a journalist and a poet. But in the Los Angeles of their time, there was no place for my parents' creative talents.

Mom spent many long hours helping Pop chase his dream, accompanying him on interviews of Black celebrities like Sarah Vaughan and Archie Moore, setting cold type, stapling numberless brochures, booklets, and leaflets. I helped too, taught to handle "the ABC blocks" or ink the rollers on the old letterpress.

Until his death in 1991, my father kept trying to get a Black this or a Bronze that going. He and his buddies created a professional mock-up of a Black *Esquire* magazine way back in the '50s, and in doing so proved to themselves that they could produce a quality gentleman's product even if they could never convince a distributor. Pop died with his unrealized gospel intact, his belief that forthright entrepreneurship was the key to the Black man's ultimate success. What I learned at my father's knees as he cut and pasted would sustain me when I entered the '70s California subculture of sex-oriented magazines as copywriter, proofreader, and editor. It sustained me as a freelance editor of literary magazines and editorial consultant. His hard militaristic lessons on discipline sustain me still.

Mom had a beautiful singing voice. She sang in the church choir and around the house constantly. An upright piano was always against the east wall of the living room. She played the piano, took lessons, and sometimes accompanied herself. She had a lilting way as she spoke, especially when her moon was right. She half sang, half talked stories on those rare nights when, still unable to read for ourselves, she read us to sleep. She listened to the radio while working around the house, sang along to her favorite songs. Years later, as I honed my performance style, I would unconsciously begin to borrow her style.

Around the age of thirteen, I had voice and pitch training. Over the decade that followed, I quietly built a repertoire of over a hundred songs and was actually able to accompany myself on some of the gospel, Christmas, and folk songs, timidly thinking I might pursue a career as a latter-day chanteuse. But I had a problem. When listening to playback, I hated my recorded voice. I sounded more like a little girl than a woman, nothing throaty or smoky about it. My voice didn't sound as powerful as I felt I was becoming, and, at that point, I was unable to imbue it with the innate physical and inner personal power that was emerging on its own as I matured. Near the end of the '60s I would find the answer to this problem in the world of experimental dance and theater.

POISON IVY

whispers
voices in the radio that won't turn off, say
"i'm lonely"
music—i hate the music of lonely notes
drip
drip
drip off the dial
    (if i touch it i'll get burned
    so i just listen)
—from "And You Say You Used to Sing the Gospel," 1966–70

In the process of discovering Los Angeles, newcomers interested in poetry occasionally delight in discovering me as well. Twenty-eight-year-old Leslie Price, the brown-haired, personable editor of the raw "grrrl zine" *Poison Ivy*, seemed to fit that category. When she phoned, there was something in her manner that coaxed me into consenting to another (ugh) interview, although I was picky about who did the interviewing. Leslie finally opted to conduct it herself. It was February 1995 when we met at the Chateau Marmont, legendary hotel of the stars, haunt of actor Christopher Walken, and site of actor-comedian John Belushi's untimely exit.

"At what age do you feel your course of writing developed?" Leslie opened.

"I had my first breakthrough in [late] 1974. That was the year I lived or died, and I did both. After years and years of rejection and (mainly) bad work, the breakthrough came. I kept all of that work, by the way, and it's so bad that it's frightening."

"That will be encouraging to our readers."

"Nobody's ever seen it. I wouldn't dare show it to anybody. I keep it because it represents a period that was very important . . . the '70s were [my] big transition years . . . 1973 through 1976 were years when I began to know who I was . . . and say, this is it, this is me, I'm grown now, baby . . ."

I was being cavalier with Leslie, because the memories of those excruciating days were interred far deeper than I cared to delve. I was not only a poetry bigot in those days but also arrogant in my bigotry, often flaunting it to my detriment as by-product of my dissatisfaction with crummy jobs paying crummy wages, the long hours it took to earn bubkes.

Women's liberation and equality were on the lips of everyone except the Molochs who doled out the ducats, no matter how many bras were burned. And I was equally furious and disappointed that so many of my West Coast feminist literary peers apparently had a hidden agenda and seemed more interested in tête-à-têtes than profound social change for working-class women. All of the political correctness in the world could not prevent me from loudly expressing my disdain.

when the door cracked open
i thought there would be space enough for me
prejudice is evident even though
the faces lack five o'clock shadow
and macho digs

191

there's no doubt
what their ideology is about
seems to me most sistuhs of the pen are
not above the literary bullshit of their fellow men
            —from "The Feminist Press," August 1978

When the Equal Rights Amendment went down for the count in 1982 my tongue bled profusely. And again, I found myself cramming my rhetoric into my verse, feeling hemmed in by the color-blind social myopia of the Fatuous '80s, a twisted rerun of the Fabulous '50s. (Off the record, I explain all of this to Leslie, wondering if and how much so-called Generation X women will profit from their foremothers' mistakes.) In expressing my rage poetically, eschewing the essay that was the more appropriate expository form to contain it, I knew I was taking a risky short-cut, placing broken spoken words in the stead of prose more deeply considered and more skillfully crafted.

Clayton Eshleman had taken me to task for exactly that kind of "easy, tossed-off" writing during the workshop sessions I attended in his home circa 1974. Again at the behest of John Martin, I had enrolled in yet another workshop with one of my future literary siblings, determined to "get the poetry thang down cold."

My sessions with Eshleman would come near the end of a quest for the magic of language that had begun at age five, in kindergarten, when our teacher brought to class the first secular poems I'd ever seen. While I don't remember the poems themselves, I remember the 3-M paper they were printed on and the gooey purple ink they were printed with, and the chills that coursed over me as I held those pages, overcome by the power they transmitted. This, I knew absolutely, was the power I would seek to possess all the days of my life.

the river
opened his mouth to me
today
            —untitled fragment, April 1981

Even as I vacillated between my other gifts, poetry was always with me in one form or another. I always excelled when writing that Father's Day or Mother's Day poem, carrying it home proudly to show off.

My junior high school years, 1958–1961, would be fairly un-remarkable vis-à-vis poetry except for two tremendously magnetic Black English teachers, the honey-toned fine-framed Mrs. Brewer and umber-skinned hefty Mrs. Covington, the tough-love tag team of Gompers Junior High, which was, in that era, the most violent and dreaded co-educational campus of its grade level citywide. They were loved by the strivers, feared and hated by the slackers and not a few of the White faculty members. Armed with every American hero and heroine of African descent they could name and a slew of rah-rah adages, they waged exceptional battles of inspiration yet conducted themselves as no-nonsense splendid Ladies of The Race, able to mow you down or build you up in an instant. Counting myself among the strivers, I was eager to get into the class of Mrs. Brewer, the less intimidating of the two. But instead I wound up cowering two aisles away from my secret crush, Oscar Lopez, under Mrs. Covington's stern tutelage.

Mrs. Covington did not give out A's. Students had to earn them by doing an assignment well—and within one evening. On the second evening you received a B, on the third a C, and so forth. I was eager to score one of her nearly unattainable A's and worked overtime at home, burning the midnight light bulb, envy-ing the perfectly composed Oscar, who never failed to turn in everything the first day, the only A student in class. But the most I could achieve was an A minus. The occasional B minus and rare C drove me to smoldering exasperation. Then came that part of the course devoted to poetry. Along with the poems of Paul Dun-bar, Robert Frost, Langston Hughes, and Carl Sandburg, Mrs. Covington introduced us to William Ernest Henley's "Invictus." Cagily, she did not tell us the name of the author or mention his race, creed, or color; baiting us with supposition, inviting her dark-complexioned students to leap to the conclusion that "pole-to-pole," the author was likewise Black. I dove heart first into the gap. This time, when Mrs. Covington asked who had memorized the poem in one night and was ready to get their A, my arm inched upward, trembling across the room from Oscar's confident salute.

Surprised, Mrs. Covington gave me a skeptical look but I reinforced my right arm at the elbow with my left hand. She called on Oscar first, who leapt to the front of the class and gave his usual sterling delivery while my pudgy knees knocked under my desk. Her soft officious summons by surname preceded by "Miss" made my stomach flip-flop. But I rose and faced my classmates, focusing on a point on the back wall, just above their heads; a method I would rely on in the future to counteract butterflies and jitters. I started off with a bang, stumbled a bit during the third stanza at "...yet the menace of the years/ Finds, and shall find me, unafraid," lifting my voice to compensate with a rousing finish. As the class applauded, I shyly shot Oscar a sidelong glance to catch his curt congratulatory nod. My A at last.

High school presented the first testing ground for what were becoming my two primary areas of interest, performance and poetry. Drama was one of the most popular classes offered at John C. Fremont when I enrolled in the fall of 1961. Fremont was in a school system that rigidly classified students by rather specious and stringent criteria, inadvertently promoting divisions, dissension, and low self-esteem. It measured student intellects in tiers, which, if memory serves me right, went something like this: triple X was a genius, double X was gifted, X was superior, XY was above average, Y was average, YZ and Z were below average, and R was remedial, non-English-speaking, etc. Mixed classes were offered, but students were largely channeled into college preparatory or job-skill courses according to their ranking. These categories would eventually be phased out, but when I arrived I was promptly slotted as an X and as a math-and-science major. At that point, I had segued from action comic books to science fiction and fantasy, consuming as much Robert Heinlein, Isaac Asimov, E. E. "Doc" Smith, and Arthur C. Clarke as I could access, to my parents' growing dismay. Yet I continued to gravitate to poetry and performance.

194

Unable to get Drama for an elective, I opted for the next best thing, Public Speaking and Debate, the Forensic League. There I would come under the significant influence of my hawkish Irish debate coach, Mr. Robert Bruce Newsom. In my first tournament, I entered the dramatic interpretation and impromptu competitions but didn't do very well. Studying the various categories, from humorous interpretation to dramatic monologues, I was thrilled to find "original oratory." As a debater I was only so-so, finding it difficult to organize my thoughts in a linear fashion, bombast my way through an argument, or destroy my opponent with rapier wit. When interpreting the words of others, I did fairly well, and that skill improved markedly with practice. But as writer and presenter of my own material, I began to take more and more first place medals and trophies.

Recognizing my love of poetry, another English teacher, Mrs. Clark, took a personal interest in me, and with my mother's permission took me on cultural excursions, to museum openings and art galleries and to my first poetry reading and book signing. To double the pleasure, the poet was a Negro. Mrs. Clark was a member of the local chapter of Our Authors Study Club. I came away with the line "tongues of men and angels" thrilling my ears. I remember the heady air of expectancy and delight, the satisfied applause. As we descended the stairs, I stopped so Mrs. Clark could catch up to me, turning back to see the gathering around the poet as he stood poised, pen in hand. That, I decided, was the life.

> *Swing up, swing down*
> *no one swings here anymore.*
>
> *Here lie naked ashen bones*
> *mocking flesh,*
> *ah flesh*
> *Loves gold splendor days.*
> *Horrid holes*
> *of death once*
> *sprang a kiss*

a loving gaze ╻
a breath.

Phalangeous scabs caressed,
dismembered ulnae held.
    Gone
    gone
    gone.

Memories of childhood
hang upon my bedroom wall.
    No one loves here
anymore.

—from "Memories of My Childhood Hang
Upon My Bedroom Wall," 1966–70

By the time I graduated from John C. Fremont High in summer 1964, I had decided I wanted to be a writer of poetry and fiction. Weeks before school ended, I was invited by a professor to share my latest work with her class of slow learners at California State University, Los Angeles. She had seen me perform "The Epics of Infinity," my fledgling masterpiece, of which I was extremely proud. The class consisted entirely of Mexican Americans and Mexican immigrants. They listened respectfully as I was introduced and gave me a standing ovation when I took my bow, offering a hand here and there. One young man raised his hand then rose to address me. His English was broken but his message was clear. He wanted me to know that he believed I had a greater opportunity to realize my American dream than he, that my work was important to the world. I managed to contain my tears until I got home.

I took the words of this young man as my guide and enrolled as a journalism major on that same Cal State campus that fall. Of the five classes I would eventually drop out of, I managed to attend the poetry class of poet Dr. Henri Coulette the most faithfully.

During that first session, we sat there, terribly intimidated by this smoking wraith who was demanding that volunteers cough up their beginner's work for his critique. Supremely self-confident, I raised my hand. Dr. Coulette smiled wickedly as I handed over my barely-typed reading copy of "Epics." Without missing a beat, he went to the blackboard and, as he read it aloud, began a scathing dissection of my grand clichés and aureate phrases. I sat there in the very front row, speechless with embarrassment. Every point he made was absolutely on target. Why had I never seen that myself?

I felt destroyed, yet illuminated. How could that be?

After the session, Dr. Coulette returned "Epics" and thanked me for being a volunteer victim. He studied me closely, a hint of concern in his voice telling me he was aware of his impact on my ego. He suggested I might consider revising it once I had absorbed the shock. When I got home, I looked it over, seeing it with a new and searing light. It didn't read the same anymore, and I would never read it aloud again.

Work had to be done. But what work and how would I do it?

Slowly, steadily, I began writing the new poems as they emerged. They were slightly different, closer to the earth, less high-flown. But I was fated to leave Dr. Coulette's class and abandon college. In the interval between leaving Fremont and starting at Cal State, I had fallen in love.

My new marriage and first pregnancy, however, did not deter my pursuit of The Muse. Blessed with more than enough spare time, I kept writing, typing up new poems on my old typewriter, a Christmas gift. But what was I going to do with these poems? Were they any good? Did they show any real potential? After days spent arguing with myself, I determined to send my fifty-odd pages of work to Dr. Coulette for his opinion. Mid-spring, an envelope arrived in the mail. After a long silence, Dr. Coulette returned my poems with a few comments and corrections but, to my disappointment, nothing more specific. Days later, I received my report card. Among the withdrawals and incompletes was a solitary grade glowing like a diamond in coal dust, my C in poetry.

Give me a gun, I'll shoot to kill.
I'm destitute, hungry and poor.
I can't get a job, I've got no skill
and I'm too old to learn anymore.

Give me a match, I'll light a fire
And burn this city down.
Life in this world is no life at all
when you live in Riot Town . . .

I'll take some loot, some lives to boot,
life's a meaningless thing
when you're cast on a reef of state relief
and each check adds to your shame.

Show me a place where bigots thrive
in the sweltering heat of hate,
where poverty, fear and unrest are alive
and negotiations too late.

—from "Riot Town," 1966–70

Watts burned that August summer of 1965, the baby had arrived, and between motherly and wifely duties I harbored my writerly desires. When an article on the Budd Schulberg Writers Workshop appeared in the *L. A. Times*, I knew I had to find it at all costs. Convincing my then-husband to babysit that evening, I left the house and took the bus down to 103rd Street. In my excitement, I had neglected to get an address. When I reached a crossroad, at Grandee, I didn't know whether to turn left or right. I turned right. Which was the wrong direction. But the steps I took would lead me to the next important stage of my development.

tremble before the weight
this life
the others
but this life especially

tremble before the weight
lovers piled up like bricks on the construction site
it's a heavy load for such a weak back
my hands tremble at the key
locking out the old. turning the key
in this new door
this life. . .
such a tremendous weight
i tremble

—from "Watching My Hands Shake at the
Typewriter," April 1974

My post-riot associations with a Great Society–era teen canteen and Watts creative arts center would lead me along three different paths in the same direction. Encouraged to write plays as well as poetry and short stories, I would be offered my first writers workshop, become editor of the house newsletter, and participate in several other workshops at the site. During this time I was introduced to Bliss Carnochan, Professor of English at Stanford University. He took an interest in my short stories and offered to look at them. He was commuting between the Bay area and Los Angeles to conduct research at the USC library. On those Saturday mornings available, we would meet early for coffee, gingerly talking content and technique.

But as my sessions with Bliss were ending, my involvement with Anna Halprin's San Francisco Dancers Workshop was beginning. In response to the riot Anna had divined a project, a dance statement of racial harmony, "The Ceremony of Us." After an audition, I was selected to join the group of eleven Whites and eleven Blacks from whom the project would be culled. There would be two performances, one at the Mark Taper Forum, the other at the Workshop's 321 Divisadero address. I would come away from this experience with a new and profound grasp of my physical and artistic strengths. When participating in Forensics, I had glimpsed inklings of what I suspected was a subliminal *dialogue* between the performer and the audience. What had then seemed tenuous became a certainty with Anna's instruction. How one entered a space, where one stood, how one posed; these were a few of the vital elements of establishing one's authority. Listening to the audience was vital to receiving the audience. The information I came away with eventually provided the link I needed between my two gifts; those moments when writing itself became the performance and when the performance became the writing.

> *it comes, the sheaf of scrawlings*
> *begging eye and ear*
> *a cry, the long yowl of a two-legged critter*
> *lost in the mean dark of unread pages*
> —from "A Literary Misunderstanding,"
> October 1982

BACHY

> *I'm older than you were when you died*
> *by umpteen years.*
> *It makes me wonder why I'm still alive,*
> *why any of us*
> *are still alive. We should all be somewhere*
> *dying in*
> *bloody beds or alleyways, all somewhere*
> *plotting against*
> *racism, laying open our souls to*
> *the commitment*
> *that does not stop at the grave.*
> —from "A Fan Letter to Fred Hampton,"
> February 1972

As the energy of the '60s Black Arts Movement waned, I had begun publishing in soon-to-be defunct African American magazines including the *Journal of Black Poetry* and *Body & Soul.* Simultaneously, I had begun submitting new work locally, and soon my poems were appearing in short-lived Southern California literary magazines such as Michael C. Ford's *Sunset Palms Hotel* and the combination anthology and program for Jack Grapes's *Alley Kat* reading series. By the end of summer 1979, I had published my book *Mad Dog Black Lady*, and had established my reputation as a fiery performer, jokingly calling myself "the Sidney Poitier of the L.A. Poetry Scene."

Poet, actor, and typesetter Lee Hickman interviewed me on August 26, 1979, on the veranda of the tore-down Hollywood 4-plex where I rented a unit on the upper floor, across the street from the Los Angeles City College parking lot. I had first spotted Hickman in 1969 at a Beyond Baroque reading, but we wouldn't meet face-to-face until late summer 1975, at a salon given by actor-poet Harry Northup to bring together the new generation of Venice Beach workshop writers orbiting the burgeoning literary center.

Lee had become the editor of *Bachy*, a hefty and substantial magazine published by poet John Harris out of Papa Bach, a West Los Angeles bookstore and counterculture hang. *Bachy* would lend cohesiveness and validation to the evolving mid-'70s scene of independent bookstores, poetry venues, and literary magazines that had begun to emerge. A small manuscript's worth of my poems had been rejected by *Bachy*, but my persistence to the tune of twenty submissions ultimately paid off and I became an occasional contributor. By the time Lee and I sat down to laugh and gab over coffee, my poems had begun appearing in small magazines nationally and overseas.

"So you published your first poems around the age of thirteen?"

"I was a kid—yeah."

"How about your first stories?"

My summary was fast and loose: "I didn't publish my first stories. They were really never publishable. I started getting away from writing when I got married. About 1966, I decided I wanted to go back to it. I really wanted to accomplish something in that area. And the Movement was ... building ... momentum at that time, and I said 'I want to write for the movement,' man. I want to get out there and I want to write propaganda. You know, do the thang . . ."

(Actually, I published "Watching the Sunset," one of my fledgling stories, in *Negro Digest* in 1969, the last issue before Hoyt Fuller rechristened it *Black World*. Excited by the change to a more militant tone, I was confident that more of my work, particularly my poetry, would be accepted. But my poems were returned so rapidly and without comment that I began to suspect they weren't read, merely opened and placed in the return self-addressed stamped envelope. Confounded, I retired my efforts and sent my work elsewhere.)

But "the thang" was over by the end of 1969, before I was out of the box. The post-riot enthusiasm for revitalizing Watts and all of Black Los Angeles had collapsed in a morass of false economic starts and empty social promises. As the urban madness returned to usual, Black gradually went back to being unbeautiful.

I divided my time between the Watts arts workshop and a drama class at Mafundi Institute further down 103rd Street. Within days of my fateful bus ride, I met members of Budd Schulberg's Writers Workshop, who invited me to attend class. But after a handful of sessions at The House of Respect, I was stymied and disappointed by the blatant bullcorn and boisterous cronyism that dominated the sessions and promptly took a powder. I was too serious to high-sign, and while I didn't mind the hang with the gang, I had no patience for posturing and pretense. Dr. Coulette was the standard by which I was coming to judge all mentors. I wanted nothing short of the difficult but informative criticism he had offered. I did not need to be coddled or to have my ego stroked. L.A. had neither a solid Black community nor a solid core of Black literati with whom I believed I could constructively interact. I was as angry as the next militant over, but my parents had provided me with an unshakable sense of self-worth long before Watts burned.

My involvement with Anna Halprin demanded so much time, including considerable travel between San Francisco and L.A., that I was forced to drop the Mafundi workshop. Once "The Ceremony of Us" ended, I again began to seek mentors, to cruise through intermittent evening workshop sessions at Beyond Baroque's 1969 location, to drive across town to attend other workshops, like the minority Open Door workshops at the Writers Guild of America, west. Ever eager to enhance my writing skills, my chance would come when my brother George left home to attend Otis/Parsons art school. When he rented a basement room from one of his professors, I went out to visit and stumbled into the grit-licious reality of writer Charles Bukowski.

> *a drawer of forms awaits the typist's eager*
> *black fingers—the color of death or a subculture.*
> *she's hidden behind the stack on her desk.*
> *around the corner from the filing cabinet*
> *comes muffled gossip and the drippings of the*
> *water cooler. no one invites her for lunch.*
> *plants clamor at the plateglass, soak up sun*
> *and there's a panoramic view of the city below.*
> *she spanks her nervous heart to be still.*
> *there's a room full of charts to be organized*
> *and months of neglected billings. they'll never*
> *find her idle here, they'll never find her at all.*
>
> —"Evasion," June 1977

"How did you find out about the L.A. poetry scene?"

My answer, in retrospect, should've been "But Lee, we *are* the Los Angeles poetry scene," but I hadn't yet come to that realization. Who came to mind were poet-in-exile Tom McGrath, the late Stuart Perkoff, and the *Coastlines* holdovers from L.A.'s Beatnik and coffee-house era. Between that generation and the post-WWII Baby Boomers loomed one figure all by his lonesome, Hank a/k/a Charles a/k/a "The Buk" Bukowski, whose alter ego, Henry Chinaski, had made Black Sparrow Press one of the top alternative presses in the country.

One summer afternoon in 1970, I braved one of those steep

hills off Alvarado Boulevard in Echo Park to visit George. I was curious to meet this "strange White dude" he kept telling me about, Bukowski's friend, a poet and calligrapher who actually made his living ripping off corporations for free goods from fur coats to stereo equipment. When George tried to describe his new whereabouts, words failed. "Doi-Doi, you have to see THIS to believe it." When I arrived, George gleefully led me upstairs to meet poet John Thomas. I could hardly contain my amazed shock. The hillside hideaway was a riot of photographs (the only one I remember, Lenny Bruce, slacks-down on a toilet), paintings, rare books, knickknacks, and a simply staggering amount of well-organized stuff.

On subsequent visits, sometimes with my first husband in tow, we'd wave a brief hello at Thomas as he watched us from an up-stairs window. We'd then go down and around to George's base-ment door, which was occasionally left unlocked. One night when I dropped in, George was gone and the door was locked. I vaguely recall a sense of urgency. I was upset and had to see him, so I decided to wait outside on the grounds. After a few minutes, the door opened behind me. Rose, George's teacher and John's wife, invited me inside. Sensing that something was wrong, Thomas tried to amuse me with small talk. Drawn out of myself, I was fas-cinated by the huge man with the Orson Welles voice, particu-larly when we got around to our mutual interest, poetry.

Within weeks, I was returning on a regular basis, on my own, not to visit George but to brainstorm with Thomas. Eventually, he grew to trust me enough to lend me rare books from his col-lection of Ezra Pound, T. S. Eliot, Charles Olson, *et al.* Finally I worked up enough nerve to ask him to review my freshly-typed manuscript of poems. Thomas was reluctant, but I reassured him that I wanted the absolute truth and that he was not to spare my feelings. He took me at my word. Excited, I took the marked manuscript home and began poring over each precious page.

Barely nineteen but passing for twenty-one, George went "carousing" with the considerably older Thomas, hanging with "these crazy old White guys," and filled me in on their anarchistic shenanigans. The wildest of the bunch was this Charles Bukow-ski. Suddenly, I was hearing Bukowski's name on the lips of all my peers. His controversial stories were starting to appear in the underground, alternative, and European press. Everyone had something to say about Mr. Bukowski, most of it negative.

After I separated from my first husband, I continued to drive up from South Central or Watts to frequent Hollywood rock, soul, and folk clubs. I was particularly keen on the impromptu per-formances that occurred during an open-mike session before the main audience had arrived or after it had gone home. One of my favorites was a bookstore and headshop performance venue called The Bridge. The young owner, declaring "it was no longer happening in L.A.," had sold The Bridge to Peter, a German-born tool-and-die maker, and had taken off for Boulder, Colorado, "where all the Hippies are going." As the story went, Peter was one of Charles Bukowski's drinking buddies. However, my attraction to The Bridge was Peter's Black girlfriend, a singer-songwriter, and the handful of women who stayed after hours to share their musical gifts; singer-songwriter Judy Sill, an amazing auburn-haired singer named Natasha, and Shurli, who, six years later, would become my mother-in-law when her son became my sec-ond husband.

Buying books was a great luxury in those days. What I couldn't borrow and return, or obtain from the public library, I read straight off bookstore shelves. I took every opportunity to study the numerous small-press magazines I couldn't afford to buy, and jotted down the addresses of potential places to send poems. Most of the presses that had produced the beautiful limited edi-tions Thomas lent me were either defunct or published by invi-tation only. Of all the writers Thomas and I had shared, I gravitated toward Bukowski most (Black Sparrow's Diane Wakoski, Jack Spicer, Sherril Jaffe, Paul Bowles, and Fielding Dawson would come later). Peter carried an ample sampling of Black Sparrow books, especially Bukowski, at The Bridge. Eager to read more, I'd stand around the stacks, to Peter's annoyance, gingerly devouring the wonderfully printed Bukowski, trying not to break the spine, as per Peter's exasperated instructions, because, as he knew, I couldn't afford to pay for them.

> *i am trapped in the office*
> *the Xerox has broken down*
> *my nails have been chewed off one by one*
> *by the IBM. the artificial air has given me the flu*
> *my legs cramp from filing charts*
> *this special art of the clerical drone*
>
> *what union do i organize*
> *with what time with what army*
> *and in the meantime who will clothe my back*
> *and feed my brood?*
> *who will hold me close, say "it's all right"*
> —from "Dear Sergeant Jack," March 1981

The more I read, the more excited I became. Dare I wonder if the publisher who likes Charles Bukowski would like me? I dared, and mailed my painfully retyped manuscript to Black Sparrow Press. In March 1972, the manuscript was returned. Disappointed, I set it aside. Days later, an unsigned postcard arrived at my mother's address. It read simply: "Please call me right away (phone number)." After vacillating back and forth and consulting with several friends, I decided I had nothing to lose, and the call was local.

Thus began my thirty-year association with Black Sparrow Press. Responding to my eagerness to learn, publisher John Martin steered me first to Wakoski and, months later, to Clayton Eshleman. In the meantime, I had become a Bukowski fan, trying to imitate his style, going to his readings, and hanging out at the infamous Bukowski parties, invited along by Peter's girlfriend.

But it didn't take long to realize that my approach to language was, at root, radically different from Bukowski's. I had no qualms about his fast-paced bare-bones prose. But it lacked music. Bukowski was tone deaf. And I loved the musical lyricism of writers like Neruda, Robert Louis Stevenson, and Brother Antoninus (a/k/a William Everson, who would eventually displace Bukowski as my favorite). I was also enthralled with the plays and poetry of Amiri Baraka (LeRoi Jones). Bukowski was no stranger to poverty and class arrogance, and I related to that aspect of his writing-psyche well. But as a Black woman, I had a perspective Bukowski couldn't fathom and I was starved to articulate it. I was extremely self-critical and knew I was still far from my goal.

Apparently sympathetic, John Martin encouraged me to join yet another workshop, handing me a copy of Clayton Eshleman's just-published *Coils*. I liked what I read and agreed to join Eshleman's workshop. Off and on the record, I've explained to interviewers that my cultivated public persona of an "imposing," "outspoken," "uncompromising" Black poet has its disadvantages and contradicts my private nature as a rather inarticulate introvert. Over the years, I've come to refer to myself as a "functional extrovert," driven out of shyness in pursuit of life's necessities. My major peeve has been my failure to bust through the going dominant culture stereotypes that others use to define me. These days I'm instantly a Whoopi Toni Maya Oprah, ready to hug at the drop of a tear. But this is a major improvement over my '70s image as dope-fiend prostitute gangster thief. Poet and intellectual was never the assumption. And this was often the sorry case in workshop settings.

> i do not know the right people
> who is it i hear listening to my phone calls?
> I was educated in the wrong schools
> why doesn't my mail arrive on time?
> i sent my resume to the united of
> these United and it came back with coffee
> stains, boot marks and a squibble
> in the lower right-hand corner
> complaining about my bad spelling
> —from "Polemos (3)," October 1985

In Halprin's dance workshop, I had learned how to get in touch with my feelings and release them. But once they were released, I couldn't get them into my work satisfactorily. The few instances that worked were accidents. I wanted control. I wanted my internal rages to snatch readers into the page and never let them go. I wanted my anguish to move readers so greatly that they had to close the book and rest. I wanted readers to experience my text viscerally. I wanted to wring the blood out of language. Clayton Eshleman was the answer. It was during his workshop that I would discover the rage beneath my rage.

In his kitchen or dining room, over freshly ground gourmet coffee, the members of the sizable workshop, divided nearly equally between men and women, gathered to read and critique each other's work. (Usually, women dominated poetry workshops and readings.) I had more on the romantic front than I could handle, and was not looking for a man. But I found one, Wilhelm Reich, the Austrian psychiatrist. At that time, Eshleman was an enthusiast of Reichian therapy. I got myself to a library and began reading Reich. Eshleman's cathartic approach to discussing one's "material" was valid. But the machinations of Black urban ghetto life was something I was not equipped to share with my workshop fellows, some of whom were snidely racist. During one meeting, I was flat-out called a liar.

After that particularly nasty episode, I decided to leave the workshop. I had tired of struggling to conceal how shaken Eshleman's sessions left me. Sometimes I became so upset I could barely make the long drive home. I would pull off the freeway and park until I could get myself together. Yes, I had to acknowledge, I'm angry about the indignities my people have sustained. And yes, I'm terribly enraged that racism still stymies our best and cripples our brightest. But the subtext to all of this was the hell my life became the day I entered the Los Angeles school system. I may have developed a love for poetry at the age of five, but I also developed a profound hatred for racism (and anyone of any stripe who perpetuates it).

So I dropped out of Eshleman's workshop. I was becoming

afraid of what it would mean if, as I was encouraged to do, I actually vented my hatred. This is an easier assessment in hindsight, but at that time, all I had to offer the perplexed Eshleman was confusion tantamount to no explanation. I had yet to develop the means to express my truth.

What I had learned about myself is exemplified in the following incident from my kindergarten year:

In the Los Angeles of 1951, the African American population was so insignificant that classroom integration seemed more or less an organic process. Even Watts was a largely White community. If you lived in a certain neighborhood, you went to the neighborhood school. Whenever my parents needed time alone, George and I were taken to stay, sometimes for a weekend, sometimes for weeks, at the central city home of my grand aunt and uncle Douglas. When I became school-aged, my mother enrolled me in the elementary school nearby. The measure was stopgap. She found a babysitter and housekeeper through our church, a matronly woman who agreed to visit our home during work hours. Mom then had me transferred to the school within walking distance from our new South Central home.

At first, Mom would drive me to school, dropping me off at the entrance. But when she changed jobs, that became a luxury. She took me by the hand and walked me along the strict route I was to take each day, cautioning me to look both ways when crossing intersections, and to never speak to strangers. I was not to stray, tarry over a candy counter or comic book rack, or visit the homes of new friends without her permission. If someone tried to kidnap me, I was to run into the nearest open door and scream for help. And if a strange man in a car offered me candy, I was to keep walking, looking straight ahead as if no one spoke. I was to do the same with barking dogs.

But I was a stubborn study. When the first day came for me to walk the route alone, I refused to leave our front porch. Infuriated, Mom resorted to the peach limb and drove me off the porch into the driveway. But once she went back inside, I followed. She locked the screen door and would not open it, staring stonily at me through the smoky grid. Then she closed the big door. I had no choice and started walking.

My kindergarten class was mixed, boys and girls, Blacks and Whites. But the girls were separated from the boys on the playground during recess and tended by monitors on the lookout for scraped knees, thumbs with splinters, and precocious expressions of puppy love. Anyone had access to the monkey bars, slides, and swings in the giant sandbox. The younger boys played truncated, supervised versions of baseball (catch) and football (tackle). The girls were relegated primarily to hopscotch, jumping jacks, and jump rope. But everybody played dodge ball and four square, a forerunner to basketball. To play four square, each player stood within one segment of an orange square divided into quadrants. Each player had a turn to start a round and pass the ball. One's partner stood in the opposite quadrant. The object of the game was to get the ball to one's partner without stepping on a line or having it stolen by the opposing team. It was my favorite game.

Shortly into the term, Gail, whose Catholic family had moved to Los Angeles from Texas, was solicitously introduced to the class as "the new girl." Ours was a prim, lace-trimmed teacher, a rigid, thick-bodied and grimly distant White woman. Watching Gail turn her into gushing, smiling jelly quickly caught our attention. Mrs. So-and-So's harsh milky hands, infamous for pinching ears, actually *touched* this newcomer with affection! We were impressed right out of our little ribbed cotton socks. Her parents drove a sleek new convertible and Gail loved to flaunt it by tossing her head as she climbed into it every day after school. Gail had status.

Gail also had what was called a peaches-and-cream complexion. On extremely hot days Gail and the other fairer-skinned White girls inclined to faint or blister were given bench privileges, the best seats in the shade reserved to protect them from the sun's rays. We tougher, dark-skinned girls were allowed to play on. Gail's skin was flawless and she flushed at the neck when angry. Her effusive mop of sable hair was, for a few weeks, a beautifully coifed mass of Shirley Temple curls. Before bangs and ponytails became the rage, Gail would sport them.

While there were several girls and boys I gravitated to, everyone got along as children do, with the usual childish territorial conflicts. The coyly manipulative and beautiful Gail, self-confident beyond her years, was about to change all of that.

Within days of her arrival, the boys, who had seemed indifferent about sex, began fighting among themselves about who would be Gail's partner during co-ed games. One boy was injured so seriously he was taken away by the school nurse to see the rarely seen school doctor. Gail also seemed capable of likewise upsetting the girls and pitting them against one another. When a commandment failed, Gail was not above lying and cheating to get her way. Wary, I kept my distance, watching these jealousy-inspired skirmishes wax and wane. When she had dispatched everyone of even vague interest, Gail turned her attention to me. Before the entire group, I was drafted as her Truly Best Friend. So friend it was. When Gail discovered I could match her brain power, we became inseparable. And when it came to the boys, I had dibs on her castoffs.

Our bond, though, would come to an inauspicious end over a game of four square.

Always the center of attention, Gail had managed to likewise seduce tall, lanky Susan and round-faced, Italian American Maria. These two dark-haired staffers, barely in their twenties, aspired to be full-time elementary school teachers. They devoted an inordinate amount of time catering to Gail's needs and I got the spillover. But that morning, Gail and I ended up on opposite teams on the four-square court. And my team was winning.

Before the game was over, Gail began her game of distraction and threw a temper tantrum, seizing the ball out of turn at every opportunity. Thoroughly intimidated, the other girls gave up the ball to her. But when my turn came, I refused to give it up. Screaming and stomping, Gail instructed the other players to take the ball away from me. They tried, but I wouldn't let go. As they backed off, I stood mid-square, the ball tucked at my waist, impervious to threats. Gail gathered the other two girls into a huddle. Monitor Susan was standing nearby, saw trouble, but assumed our tiff would resolve itself. Gail altered her body language for a fresh approach. I was a head taller, but she put on a smile and, on tiptoes, put her face so close to mine, we were nose-to-nose. Surprised at this dramatic change, I assumed that Gail had decided to apologize.

"Are you sorry?" I asked.

"Yes," she lied sweetly, but I saw the glint in her eye.

"No."

Instantly livid she hissed, then stammered, searching her vocabulary for an epithet strong enough to hurt me. "You you're nothing buttabuttabutta nigger!"

I bounced the ball in her face and caught it again.

Furious, Gail dashed after Susan, who was trying to recover from her shock. She had heard Gail call me nigger and, her illusion of Gail shattered, was reluctant to come to Gail's defense. Sensing a fight, the other girls stopped playing and circled our square. Gail begged the reluctant Susan to make me give up the ball. Maria joined Susan and took over the situation, coaxing me to give up the ball. I refused. One girl leapt at me, attempting to knock the ball away. I held it fast. While Susan stood back with arms folded, Maria grabbed me. We struggled for the ball. I curled my body around it, and weighted it against the ground.

Worried that they'd attract the displeasure of the school's vice principal, Maria and Susan tried reasoning with me. I insisted it was my turn and that I was being treated unfairly. Maria turned my own word against me, pointing out that it was unfair of me to prevent the other girls from playing by keeping the ball. I looked at their faces. The girls agreed. Fair or not, I was now the bad guy. I gave the ball to Susan. As the crowd dispersed, Susan gave the ball to Gail who promptly turned to me and stuck out her tongue.

I was left standing alone in the middle of an empty square.

At some point, I had repressed the childhood rage that had begun with Gail. But in Clayton Eshleman's workshop, I rediscovered it. Nearly two years would pass before I would succeed in channeling it into my poems. Now that I had tapped into the source of my rage, all I needed was the discipline.

Midway through our *Bachy* interview, Lee quoted a review of my first book, *Mad Dog Black Lady*: "'. . .whoever would rather not walk in the predawn ghetto, or live there daily, faced with a sordid ferocious reality, might look into this book for a painful amazingly spirited glimpse of an underside of our culture seldom addressed in polished/published verse, much less in terms so mercilessly lucid . . .' Many of your poems take place in the ghetto. They seem to be in contemporary times, not out of your childhood . . . Is this you or a dream of you?"

"This is me. . . ."

"Do you use personae in your work?"

"Yeah."

"How much would you feel that the reader should have to work to be able to distinguish between the fantasy and the reality?"

"They shouldn't, because it's insignificant. I use other voices, but they're not fictions. Most of the dialogue I use is verbatim. I . . . pride myself on having an ear for dialogue. That's why I like scriptwriting . . . I have a memory for what people say and how they say it."

The last element needed for my poetic breakthrough came as a direct result of work as part of the writing staff for the daytime drama *Days of Our Lives*. I had met scriptwriter Pat Falken-Smith circa 1969 while she was engaged in a movie project with Howard Hughes. Six years later, she would lift me from the morass of men's magazine editing and take me on staff. The world of television moved at ten times the pace. Deadlines were mercilessly final. I was placed on a work cycle of ten days on and four days off. Nearly a generation younger than my fellow writers, and Black, I had no choice but to drop my literary pretensions in the name of bread and butter. The poetry I was forcing myself to write during this eighteen-month period was the worst I had ever written. Stubbornly, I insisted. When Falken-Smith lost her contract as head writer, her staff was let go, one by one, during contract negotiations. Last hired, I was the first fired.

Prior to my days with *Days*, I had written my poems, draft after draft, in longhand. Now that my soap-opera script career had ended, the poetry returned. But with a major difference. I could now compose on the typewriter. All those painful, handwritten drafts suddenly disappeared from my life. The hours and days it had once taken me to write a poem were reduced to minutes, and within an hour, I could write several poems, most of them excellent.

It had all come together. At last.

> *this is the ritual of the whole becoming the hand*
> *shaping a certainty*
> *i am rooted in a tree of hands where i nest*
>
> *give birth. stretch my arms to take the wind*
> *here. a forest of hands where the only fauna are*
>   *my eyes*

—from "Hand Dance,"
and the book by the same title,
Black Sparrow Press, 1993

NOTE

Following the birth of my third child, in March 1979, my second husband and I welcomed two feminist filmmakers into our home. They had eagerly hustled me during pregnancy to participate in their documentary on young marrieds raising newborns in poverty, but balked immediately upon meeting my husband, having assumed that, like me, he was dark-skinned. Even if we identified as a Black couple, they explained, the disparity in our skin tones raised the specter of racism, which would overwhelm their pur-pose-of-persuasion. They took their cameras and split, leaving behind our disappointment and shock and my eternal contempt for American feminism.

I Was a Stand-In Diva for June Jordan

Feeling caged and brutish, I descended at midnight, via 747, from the Palm-lined Nightmare into a squee-gee wielder's hallucination. An unenthusiastic young sistuh-lady, a Poetry Project assistant, had set me up at this Washington Square hotel recently taken over (or fronted off) by Ethiopians. I was on a National Literary Network tour, substituting for an ailing June Jordan. I was sharing the gig with Antler at the behest of his supporters, though I desperately needed every niggling ducat.

The minute they SAW me, the Ethiopians tried to jack me up for more jack, even though we all knew my bunk was prepaid by Poetry Project. After having to LOUDLY threaten to stomp butt, embarrassing them in front of White clientele, I was keyed for a room.

It was the stuff screams are made of.

I went downstairs and DEMANDed better digs. Got them. Nevertheless, the sheets were fax-paper thin and the quilt hairs were like dead insect antennae. After I unpacked, I decided to check out the neighborhood and found a kissy Sicilian pizza hang within a hop-and-skip. Along the way I stopped for a minute, for a bit of amusement, as a Brutha-of-the-Grape was struck mid-spasm by a bus. As I exited the joint with my pepperoni and three-cheese breakfast, the Revelations-spouting brutha was being hefted into an ambulance to the cheers and jeers of observers.

Things had somewhat settled into jake, as I was lulled to sleep by a campus radio's stokings of Lady Day.

The blankets started biting me through the sheets at three A.M.

I turned on the light bulb and looked at them closer. I ran my palm across them. Wool. This, after I'd troubled a ridiculously complex form that wanted too much information—including all my allergies, the primary one listed being WOOL. (Why the refusal of, in this racist society, even MY OWN PEOPLE to acknowledge that being large, dark, and delicate is not a contradiction!?) I immediately hit the elevator, clowned with the management, and was handed an armful of scrawny cotton blankets and quilts. Fortunately, I had my burnt-orange fake-fur coat to throw across my feet for ballast.

That late morning, I did one of my best readings for the women at a drug-rehabilitation halfway house near Avenue C. The space was imperfect, the room cramped, but ears and hearts were hungry. Hettie Jones was present. I had read her autobiography, *How I Became H. J.*, only months before, and thanked her for being there for me. I began to feel half human.

The next afternoon, I ran into Antler and we walked the waning sun to Poetry Project's St. Mark's Church. I was uptight, wondered if we'd draw. I had just learned all the Rebel Angels were in town for a weekend Naropa Beatnikfest featuring Ginsberg *et al.* with kick-off scheduled simultaneously with our assumption of the Poetry Project podium. When we got to the church, I was pleased to see a few old friends from Los Angeles—mom-of-friend, a partner's lady, and someone who heard me years back at the Knitting Factory with Lydia Lunch—among a number of interested strangers. By the time we started, ours was a respectable assemblage.

Antler went first, shunted his polemics, and floored everyone (including me) unfamiliar with his boy-love and late-in-life-I-found-woman-love anthems. I went next. Ultimately, the applause and ovation were satisfying.

Afterwards, sistuh-lady trotted us over to The Fez, plopped us down in a booth across the room from a gilded stage, and split. Between Gong Show acts of verse, Antler and I mulled over the nature of regionalism and exile on the margins of things literary. We exchanged tales of rip-offs by Hollywood scriptwriters (one of Antler's camp adventures, one of my best lines from *African Sleeping Sickness*); how sickeningly strange it is when one's stolen lines jump out from that Big Screen; how poverty, coupled with The Trivalization of Poetry in America, victimizes those who aren't presidential *dahhhlings* or anointed by the poetry establishment.

Early the next morning, as our taxi to Newark pulled into traffic, the cabby braked to avoid a stumbler. In silent consternation, I recognized the Brutha-of-the-Grape, who, this time, sported a plaster cast and sling.

It was spring of 1994.

I knew life as I was ambivalent about it was coming to an end.

Letters to E. Ethelbert Miller

It was Ahmos Zu-Bolton who introduced me to the work of Wanda Coleman. This was back in the early 1970s, when Ahmos and I were running "poetry" back and forth across the District lines. Ahmos had come to Washington from a number of places, many as small as DeRidder, Louisiana. He was editing a publication called HooDoo *and wearing the same coveralls one would associate with a farmer or maybe a member of SNCC. What I immediately liked about Ahmos was his love for poetry. From his tongue, he dropped names I'd never heard of; he could have been talking about catfish or trees growing along the Mississippi for all I knew.*

When Ahmos mentioned the name of Wanda Coleman, he would get the kind of look in his eyes that wives see when their husbands come home late on Saturday nights. It was obvious that Zu-Bolton thought this woman was special. But how special? What kind of work was she writing? I respected Ahmos's taste in words because he had passed me the bottle from which I sipped the work of Lorenzo Thomas and Yusef Komunyakaa.

Unfortunately, it would be almost ten years before I could actually meet Wanda Coleman. Our letters and correspondence began in 1984, when I invited her to read at Howard University as part of my Ascension series. I was hoping to put a few students in the orbit of this West Coast woman. That's how I think of Wanda: she is a writer who can claim her space the way SunRa saw himself connected to planets such as Jupiter and Saturn. I sometimes think of Wanda claiming all of Los Angeles and moving outward to seize the imagination of what is left of the rest of America.

It's difficult to define who Wanda Coleman is. I think her letters reveal her genius, anger, humor, hurt, pain, ego, and blackness. I think it would be incorrect to refer to her as a writer who has been overlooked. She has produced too many books for our eyes. Her letters offer insight into how she sees the world.

Literary letters are footprints. They leave an impression, a path down a road where one can sit under a tree, waiting for a person's return. I think of Wanda Coleman "returning" each time I read these letters. I see her sitting in my house eating a good meal prepared by my wife. It is evening and Wanda, our laughter, sits at the table, holding her head high. "Girl . . . you know you can't say that. What will people think?" She has that look, which reminds me that Ahmos was "crazy" not to warn me. "HooDoo, Baby." "HooDoo."

> *E. Ethelbert Miller*
> *Washington, D.C.*
> *January 4, 1998*

July 28th 1984

Dear Ethelbert,

When I wrote you earlier about my visit to the East Coast I had no idea fate was about to TKO me and 86 my aces. It is painful but necessary to cop to a sob story. There is the sudden horrible reality of terminal illness in my immediate family circle. I will spare you the gory d's just to say I am still numb somewhere inside and have not allowed my emotions to get loose at my mind, yet. (Tearing up a very anguished missive I'd written to you earlier while in the initial shock.)

I cannot tell you how strange a state of mind I'm in. As you

219

will be reading in the papers this A.M., a man went berserk in the affluent west L.A. college town of Westwood, near UCLA, and killed (at this point) one person and injured many others, 40-to-60, by driving his car down the sidewalk in the late-evening heat. I might have been among the victims, as would my lover, my daughter, and my son, had not my daughter been so slow to dress last night. We went out to obtain the last available copy of a book of poetry by an acquaintance. The bookstore was just across the street from where the mayhem took place. This in the wake of the San Jose Shakey's shoot-out and the San Ysidro McDonald's massacre, not to mention the strange aftertaste of the Democratic convention accompanied by torch fever & Olympicytosis as "the games" kick off this very day. California seems more bizarre than ever, and I speak as a native daughter.

Anyhoo, I expect you'll write when you have news. A call from a hysterical friend interrupts this letter. She has just beaten another female acquaintance severely with a chain and I must go to the spiritual rescue; police, outraged landlady, the whole banana . . .

October 14th 1984

Dear Ethelbert,

Can't thank you & Denise enough for that wonderful meal. It was the best "grease" we had while on the East Coast. I've been searching and searching for a little "thank you" that would be appropriate and when I find it I'll send it! And thanks for the work you put into trying to get an audience for me at my reading. I know you did your best, guess there's just some things time will have to take care of.

We took the train to Philadelphia, then the bus to Atlantic City on the 28th. After losing about $200 at the roulette table, we decided to call it quits. But I discovered $8 in chips in my pocket. We went back to the roulette table and won it all back save $32. But what really made this little side trip worthwhile was meeting Bishop Desmond Tutu, the Anglican priest from South Africa who is using the Bible to fight apartheid. We were in the Atlantic City bus terminal; apparently he was en route to some conference and is presently here in Los Angeles to address the World Council of something-or-other. It was quite a thrill to touch this man and shake his hand and wish him well. He seemed quite startled that we recognized him, and quite pleased.

New York was just as I expected it with few surprises except the delicious water and more "short" buildings than I had imagined. We ate our way from one end of Manhattan to the other. I was impressed by the degree of hardness, depression, and "hard life" that mark the people there; as well as the "laid back" nature of the police, nothing like L.A.'s cowboys. Anyway, I'm back in L.A. and back to "schemin' & dreamin'." If you ever find your way to this coast again, be sure and look me up. And I'll cook dinner. . . .

October 31st 1984

Dear Ethelbert & Denise,

Unable to select any particular item of thank you, I decided these four items would have to do. I've put together a California Care Package designed to assist you in understanding life in "the horizontal hell zone" where Disneyland, Hollywood, and the *Los Angeles Times* reign.

First is a box of See's candy. This fantastic phenomenon is found only on the West Coast (that I know of) and, in my considered opinion as an authority on obesity, diets, and fat attacks, is the best candy in the world. I have enclosed a representative sampling, which you may share with intimate friends & relations. Let me assure you that this wonderful taste treat is the nemesis of every actress and model who has ever aspired to the perfect size 8.

The second and perhaps most important item is the mandatory California stream-of-consciousness transcendental wood prayer beads which were hand strung by a local hoodoo woman. These can be used under most any meditative circumstances by members of almost any cult or religion. These come with a spiritual guarantee without expiration date and may be used in times of serious soul searching as well as when calling forth the powers of positive thinking, etc. They should be kept in a cool dry place.

Third is a photo book on Los Angeles itself, featuring the peculiar customs of the natives, quaint commercial architecture, and erotic cultural trends. While the overview this book provides may initially appear somewhat superficial, it can, when placed in conjunction with item four, take on a significantly greater depth.

Fourth and last is *Neighborhood Rhythms*, the third in a "limited edition" of spoken-word albums documenting the complex social/cultural fabric that shapes survival in L.A. It has been suggested that the best preparation for listening to this album is the smoking of at least one joint of high-grade marijuana. Allow me to assure you that this is not necessary in order to appreciate *Neighborhood*—although one may certainly need to smoke a joint afterwards, as well as have a couple of good stiff drinks.

Well, this completes my little Care Package. I hope that you will derive moments of intense musing, pleasure, and fun from this little box. Remember, Los Angeles isn't such a bad place and is as enjoyable as any major metropolitan center once you learn how to glibly answer that dreaded question: "But what have you done lately?"

Thanks again for your warm hospitality!

October 29th 1990

Dear Ethelbert Miller:

First, I hope you are well and deeply into continuing establishing your literary career. Mine is sagging a bit these days. I've recently/finally quit my job to see if I can "make it" once and for all. Working on more stories, novel, etc. But being my own secretary demands more of my time than I would have imagined. Sigh. Am trying, again, for foundation support and hope you can help me out by writing a letter—or, at least standing by your previous letter. They should be contacting you if they haven't already. I've enclosed a postcard for your quick reply, knowing how horribly busy everyone is these days in the face of The Recession. My timing was impeccable—Austin, my man, is trying to fill the void the absence of my steady paycheck has created, but thangs are tough.

Otherwise, the poetry business is brisk—requests for material I can't possibly fill, lots of speaking engagements I'm too exhausted to really care about—including finally going EAST in the dead of fall to perform twice, at the Knitting Factory in the East Village, Maxwell's in Hoboken. Then I'll be back in N.Y. on December 9th for a stint at the Caribbean Center. Funfunfun.

L.A. is as hellish as ever, more so. I know you hate travelin' WEST, but I'd like to treat you to din-nah whenever. . . .

April 4th 1995

My Dear E. E.—

When the smoke clears, and there are only two Negroes left in America, there will still be a war on about who is going to be Spokesperson for The Race—and what's going to be The New Black Aesthetic.

February 4th 1997

Dear E. E.:

Today is the sixth anniversary of my father's funeral. Funny. The day he died, I had been scheduled to do a reading for some African women's group on the California State, L.A. campus. They called and canceled me because they preferred an African-born immigrant writer instead. I was outraged beyond reason. As it turned out, I ended up having to go to New York to do a reading the following morning, on January 29th. And I returned on the morning of the 4th and went straight to the mortuary for Dad's service, arriving just as it started.

Perhaps you might say, the topic of this letter is value or the lack of value; measurement, or the lack thereof.

School was always a nightmare for me. Which is why I resisted teaching for so long. I was a misfit then. And it seems I remain a misfit; misunderstood in all my endeavors, regardless of who my detractors are or who my supporters are.

One of my old schoolmates has been on my mind these past few days. Kathleen was a honey-skinned, befreckled, sandy-haired young woman, who, luckily, was a rather pretty version of what was usually considered a crone-face, most such types having a large jaw and gross overbite. Kathleen wore glasses, sexy frames selected to stop any insults about having four eyes. She was also the la femme class clown, pulling pranks on our predominantly White unhip teachers and doltish boys and girls. I liked, even admired her from a safe distance, but when she made overtures of friendship, I went for the okey-doke. Little did I realize that she counted me among the doltish.

I was extremely lonely, to such an extent I'm certain I was unable to conceal my pangs. So when Kathleen wanted a pax, I went for it, suspicious but quelling those suspicions to enjoy the sunshine of her jokey behavior. At the best moments, I managed to fool myself into thinking the best part of her soul found me likable. I was to discover otherwise one day, when I was nastily confronted by a group of girls I liked but who had nevertheless declared themselves my enemy. They couldn't understand who I was or why I was so different. They were all lighter-skinned (I was third darkest of my entire peer group, meaning there were only two girls darker than me and they too were considered outcasts, one being too tall and heavy, the other being too black, "retarded," and having a huge toothy overbite). I had had a new disaster with my short, stingy hair. It had been freshly pressed and curled in one of the new styles my mother kept trying in her desperate attempts to make my looks more acceptable. She would never succeed. And when I got to school, it was all I could do to tolerate the stares and the mockery. But, as usual, I was handling it. But this visual affront (remember, Black was still a long way from being beautiful) was even too much for Kathleen. And rather than be seen with and identified with me, she openly sided with my girl group enemies—the ones with good hair. I'll never forget that moment, watching her on the landing, climbing the stairs with laughter, turning towards me as I lumbered behind her on my way to class.

"Wan-da," she said, with exaggerated melodrama, " when are you going to let your hair down?" The roar from the girls crushed my heart.

When I saw the first reports on Karposi's sarcoma circa 1980, I knew that a deep trouble was coming my way. And when my homosexual son rebelled and left home, I was even more certain what his future would be. It didn't take a seer to know what his rebellion would cost. Knowing what was coming, I worked tirelessly, 14–16 hours a day, two jobs for diddly pay, to try to secure my place in American Letters as a writer. I went without sleep forever. But I couldn't get the kind of support I needed. I wanted desperately to earn money, for my son's sake, for all our sakes. But I couldn't compromise who I was in order to do so. I didn't know how, and whenever I thought I had gotten the idea, circumstances intervened to prevent any compromise from taking place. So I was doomed to be who I had to be, regardless of outcome. But I knew what was coming and I wanted to be as ready for it as I could be.

When I met M.D., I thought a prayer had been answered. She was an intelligent young lady and I thought she would be extremely helpful; in fact, I thought we would be helpful to each other. This seemed to be the case at first—but, like Kathleen, somewhere in her soul she may have liked me, but my agenda was secondary to her own even as I paid her money I could not afford. I did not know that she wanted to displace me, with my man and my career. (In my heart, I couldn't imagine anyone wanting to nail themselves to my particular cross.) I did not tell her about my son, or any of my personal motives, because I didn't want to use my sob stories for gain. I kept my personal pains private. I was a true believer in merit being rewarded. Likewise, when M.D. steered me off my chosen path through introducing me to the University system, I convinced myself that compromise might be possible; understanding and acceptance might be possible. But, as it turned out, that wasn't so. Within that private-sector system,

I was expected to play the very games my lifelong refusal to play had made me an outsider.

Suddenly, after years of going nowhere, and just when it seemed that I was arriving at an artistic plateau, I found myself under assault from various quarters. I learned this, after an unpleasant (and, as far as I know, unmotivated by me) confrontation with several of my literary contemporaries. And any attempts I made to strike back were, for the most part, futile. It seemed everything I touched turned to shit. My new book of poems, *Hand Dance*, was ignored completely and barely received three reviews. During this time, I wrote a newspaper column, which I hated. All of this external "stuff" while my private madnesses raged as my son soon announced he was HIV positive and Mother had yet to accomplish anything vaguely resembling financial security after 30 years of intense poverty, no matter how good her resume seemed on the surface. By the end of 1996 everything was in shambles and 32 years of sacrifice to become a writer was tantamount to nothing.

When my 31-year-old son died of AIDS this January 24th, I didn't have the money or the insurance to bury him. In my grief, I replay and replay the scenarios of this, my life, that led to that moment when his breath and heart stopped so quietly simultaneously that we were stunned. I keep going over the reasons why I'm presently destitute, and why my pride, so far, keeps me from begging help. When I told one friend my story, in considerably greater detail, he marveled that I hadn't committed suicide.

I watch and I watch from the sidelines. And I marvel that I'm purportedly so famous that, when my girlfriend's daughter ordered commemorative flowers sent through some florist service out-of-state, the young woman manning the phones knew who I was, "a famous writer," because her friend was studying me in school. I watch and I watch from the sidelines as my thunder is stolen and others reap the benefit of my dislocation.

I am, tonight, in a place far beyond tears, unfamiliar and without boundaries. At the moment, I do not know how to find my way. But I wanted you to know some of the reasons I'm here, and why I was truly unable to make that lark of a trip to Vegas. And why I was not in Australia. And why I am not who I thought I would be by now. And why I will never be what I aspired to. And to give you an inkling of what has lain under the text of previous communications.

This is a groping . . . a groping . . .

April 14th 1997

Dear E.E.:

I returned from Nellie McKay's symposium celebrating African American anthologies last weekend. And I've had much to digest. When I first started out publishing and reading my work, particularly at a local Unitarian church where I was frequently invited to appear, men and women, Black and White, used to approach me afterwards and tell me they had personally known either Richard Wright or Langston Hughes—particularly Langston—and that these fellows had nothing on me, especially when it came to performance; that Langston was a particularly uninteresting reader of his own work. I had assumed otherwise and was surprised.

Now I return from Madison, Wisconsin, quite clear on why my fellow so-called Black intellectuals have never embraced me. At this point I have seen them all—the best America's top ten universities could nurture. And this po' chile me—this niggah womon off the streets of Watts—simply IS the best; she eclipses them in her light.

E. E.—*it wasn't the prizes*. Although they would've certainly helped my children. It was the being left out, the being rejected (that supercilious silence—or was it fear?) by those I considered my own. Stupid of me wasn't it? Such a naïf. I didn't know my own power/the strength in my own gift. Well. I know now. And the price has been dear, the lesson costly beyond expectations. But I know now.

I've had the sweat and tears. Now the blood is come.

April 27th 1997

Dear E. E.:

Sometimes I simply lose my mind. But, E.E., I understand Black Academia very well, have always understood it, and pity it—in all its stinginess, cowardice, and meanness. I reserve my vituperation for specific individuals, and the influence they exert when Black (as in African American) Literature is discussed in ANY of the few quarters considered legitimate. If W.E.B.Du Bois were resurrected he would instantly die of shame and shock to see what kind of backbiting nigger ignorati American universities consider the crème de la crème. I take that back. Those were exactly the type of niggers who *sent him to his grave*.

I've always dreamed—being as American as anyone else—of sharing my gift, my particular knowledge, with my folk. Well, after thirty years and ten books, eight of them substantial not teensy, I've decided it is time to trash that notion. Instead of embracing my genius, my folk have sniffed at it and run. I've published more poems than any Black poet in the history of verse—including Langston Hughes. But no one has ever noticed. Plus my powers are considerably greater than those of Hughes. A few here and there have noticed. (But then—I've been able to function without the constraints of form and language which reigned in good ol' L.H. All that beside the point, because I've never been in competition with Langston in anywise. I don't think we would've liked one another had we met, but I certainly would be the last to denigrate his contribution.) Yet not a single Black has written critically (in this instance, meaning with serious depth) on my oeuvre.

Crying over the continuous omissions—the spilt ink—is a luxury I can no longer afford to indulge. Otherwise, thanks again for your awareness, E. Ethelbert Miller. I've spent whatever energy I've put into ranting over the bourgeois. As I age, I must be more judicious about where I focus my rage. Until . . .

June 11th 1997

Dear E.E.:

Rereading and reconsidering your *First Light* this week. This morning, rose at 5 A.M. and fed my head with Jeffers' *Double Axe* and writings on Jeffers. I was particularly struck by your "Poem Looking for a Reader" (pg. 160):

> if poems/could undress/you
> i would not/hesitate/to ask/or find
> words to place/in my hands
> sitting/in a room/trying to/write/is like
> daydreaming/about your/body
> a/comma/separates/your/legs
> the/problem/with paper/is that/it has/no openings
> i am/tired/of touching/the surface/of things
> there must/be other ways/to love

I understood profoundly, for I resolved my version of that weakness long ago. (When I teach, one of my lessons for students is how to break through—to mine the language beneath the language.) For what it is worth, I offer this more succinct and articulate response FYI gleaned from my readings this morning:

> For since the actual states of "being" the poet celebrates are registered with undeniable power, it follows that if that power is "crude and approximate" then crudity and approximation must reside in the states of being themselves. They are not failures of taste or defects of awareness, or else they could not be called powerful, for power in literature can only emerge from power in life.
> —Brother Antoninus/William Everson,
> *Roberson Jeffers: Fragments of an Older Fury*

Ahhh, E.E., paper—DOES have *openings!* But one must have the eyes! And there are so many many ways to love that the pain of the poet writer is in excess.

Until . . .

5 Years After

Discontent Festers in South Central & We Are All O.J.

Around midnight, the street traffic is light on the sweeping, modestly lit, palm-dotted boulevards except for an occasional black-and-white patrol car rounding a corner or cruising slowly past a darkened, deserted cluster of cheap stucco buildings. All seems quiet in South Central.

Well, yes, Los Angeles has recovered according to city fathers and mothers—even though much of the happy-face private sector bluster about healing and recovery had ceased within two years of the April 29, 1992, uprising.

Then came O. J. Simpson's infamous June 1994 low-speed chase.

Within minutes of the criminal trial jury's acquittal of O. J. Simpson for the slayings of Nicole Brown Simpson and Ronald Goldman, the socioeconomic ills that had continued to plague South Central's predominantly African American community were thoroughly forgotten.

As I write, The Quiet Riot—the White backlash against Black claims on mainstream attention—continues to devastate South Central and its sparse landscape of marginal businesses, ethnic clubs, motels fueled by sex trade, churches, palmists, assorted

231

auto-repair shops, check-cashing places, public-storage monoliths, liquor stores, and a plethora of mom-and-pop concerns. But the more substantial needs continue to go begging as they have for over thirty years.

The first major coalition between concerned African American and Korean grassroots leaders had disbanded. The judge who acquitted Korean grocer Soon Ja Du for the killing of fifteen-year-old Westchester High School student Latasha Harlins over a container of orange juice, had been handily re-elected by a majority White electorate.

Koreatown continues to expand, transforming bordering Black and Latino mid-city 'hoods. Korean ideographs on signs and buildings in Hancock Park, one of L.A.'s wealthiest Zip Codes, signal rapid displacement of WASPs and Jews living there. African Americans are nonplused by the economic autonomy with which Koreans seem to operate as they exhibit the prosperity still denied Blacks.

There were Black–Latino artist collaborations, gang truces, and public spates of good will. But qualified Blacks continue to lose jobs to Hispanic bilingual applicants, as they have since the 1970s. Latino immigrants have become entrenched as a hedge against further Black population growth. Cultural wars over dress, music, and dance styles have polarized Black and Latino youth on local campuses. In the prison hierarchy, the Mexican Mafia has displaced Black gangs. In retaliation for their displacement, in an expression of their frustration, African American voters endorsed the anti-immigrant initiative Proposition 187.

Hollywood personalities, who had eclipsed concerned community leaders, had long tired of solution groping and returned to more lucrative pursuits. New police chief Willie Williams had settled in uncomfortably, and now will be unsettled and replaced in July. The local gangsta underground was being combed, fruitlessly, by political leftists for the next Malcolm X, MLK, or Huey P. Newton. An effective grassroots Black leadership transcending empty rhetoric and shallow amens has yet to appear, unlike the upsurge of pride, power, and activity which followed the Watts Riots.

232

Prosperity continued its White flight west, in patterns familiar since the mid-1950s. The renowned arts campus of Otis/Parsons abandoned its drug-infested Ramparts 'hood for the bedroom community of Westchester, to relocate within a mile of Los Angeles International Airport and the controversial marshlands site of DreamWorks (the Steven Spielberg, David Geffen *et al.* entertainment mega-conglomerate). But this post-Reagan-era West-moving boom has developed with a significant difference: the discontent in predominantly White enclaves has swelled. This vengeful movement of the spitefully shortsighted and the tacitly racist has come full fever in the classrooms and corporate boardrooms, where Blacks feel they are being divested of earned advancements, retirement benefits, perks, and scholarships as a result of anti-affirmative action hysteria. With the quick acquittal of Simpson, virulent White rage came to a puffy head. By this year's finding of liability in Simpson's civil trial, it had long burst. Whites cheered the civil trial verdict and the millions awarded as compensatory and punitive damages.

But for some African Americans, the dollar-per-dollar dissection of O. J. was the horrifying equivalent of Dred Scott being sold back into slavery. Last fall, the offices of The Brotherhood Crusade, NAACP, and local politicians were deluged by irate calls when black billboards appeared on which the words GUILTY and STILL GUILTY jumped out in giant white letters, particularly in areas of the city heavily populated by Blacks—a publicity stunt by a local radio station. Exacerbated by the soft anti-racist posture of President Clinton, who endorsed changes in the welfare system, and an even softer pro-diversity posture by incumbent Mayor Richard Riordan, re-elected in a lukewarm landslide over political activist Tom Hayden, who failed despite last-ditch support by Jessie Jackson and forages into South Central, a second groundswell of discontent has begun. Among African Americans.

"Cut-off of welfare got everybody all in an uproar now!" says Sweet Alice Harris, director of Parents of Watts, a community group that provides assistance to the students of South Central L.A., where a 60 percent unemployment figure has been constant for young Black males for more than three decades, welfare cut-backs ($565 to $594 per family of three in a city where the average one-bedroom hell hole goes for $500 a month) are viewed as genocidal.

Harris reports that SSI has begun denying benefits to crack-damaged recipients, including children. Community caregivers no longer know where they stand, either in advising their clientele or with city, county, or state governments. Children are being taken out of their homes without the pretense of an investigation as to the innocence or guilt of parents or guardians. A seize-first-and-ask-questions-later mentality has become the law's new order. When students get in trouble, the L.A.P.D. is apt to be called before parents. Cops on campus—under the guise of protecting youth, administration, staff, and faculty—have been charged with criminalizing students. "Somewhere down the line, somebody's got to stop," Harris warns. "I see another riot comin', a civil war comin'."

In L.A.'s Black community, tangible evidence of progress is limited to the Magic Johnson Theatre Complex near Leimert Park Village, where venues such as Fifth Street Dick's coffee house and The World Stage feature jazz and poetry. There has been rebuilding in South Central, but not enough. A local institution, the Aquarian Spiritual Center, was destroyed during the riots when its new mini-mall location was burned. Until the mid-'60s, it was one of the few places carrying Black literature and providing a podium for Black authors and lecturers. Young people were always welcomed and gathered there to share cultural interests, pursue spiritual quests, and engage in philosophical discourse. Owners Bernice and Alfred Ligon have suffered thousands of dollars in setbacks and may finally give up trying to rebuild despite letters of support from the community.

"The new building needs a lot of work, wheelchair access, parking lot and rest rooms, etcetera." Alfred is a survivor of the Chicago Riots of 1919, in which Whites attacked Blacks.

While the "loco" pundits are still scratching their heads over riot causes, a collapsed recovery, and myriad failures to rebuild, working-class and working-class-poor residents are being crushed under relentless economic pressures. L.A. is currently a city where the poverty level starts at $50,000 a year. Rents are astronomical and, as following the Watts Riot of August 1965, the promises of critical low- and middle-income housing have failed to materialize.

In South Central, real estate agents won't call back unless you speak with an accent. White gentrification geared toward reclaiming formerly Black neighborhoods, such as West Adams or Sugar Hill, is being encouraged while Black families are being run out of traditional 'hoods, public-housing projects, and middle-income housing complexes by Latino street gangs—and out of upscale communities by Whites.

In addition to providing roadside service and insurance, one automobile club now also offers courses on how to avoid carjackers, looters, and snipers.

The message from L.A. to its Black citizenry seems undeniably clear: *There is no place for you here.* Many Black families are heeding this warning as they relocate out of the city, rebuilding their lives in far removed locales like Victorville (which was established by Blacks), the Imperial Valley, and San Bernardino and Riverside counties.

Visitors to South Central by day are inclined to ask why there was a riot. It looks so middle class. After all, there are so many green trees, and all the little homes have lawns. The sky above is as beautiful as the Côte d'Azur.

In answer, locals do their best to describe the devastation, the toll in human expectations and lives. Visitors are invited to brave the streets after sundown when the blight takes on a hauntingly romantic quality, accented by red, green, and yellow neon. Remnants of spring fog misting inland off the Pacific Ocean deepen the sensation of restlessness beneath an exhaustion-inspired stillness.

They might observe an occasional walker in ski cap and jacket, who can be seen loping along the seemingly endless sidewalk, hands rammed into pockets—a prowler, a vagrant, a worker getting off late without bus fare to get home. A wraith-thin bronze hooker, cigarette to her smirking lips, appears suddenly at the intersection of Seventy-ninth and Figueroa. And traveling west on Manchester toward the Forum, their attention will be grabbed by giant letters done in cheap paint that scream "Black Owned" across the coarse charcoal-gray metallic siding designed to discourage looters of all stripes.

NOTE

As erosion of L.A.'s African American population continues, any post-1992 emergence of "effective grassroots Black leadership" is not yet apparent other than those already highly visible: actor Jim Brown, community activist Sweet Alice Harris, author Earl Ofari Hutchinson, former L.A.P.D. Chief Bernard C. Parks, and former Crip gangleader Stanley "Tookie" Williams (controversial nominee for the Nobel Peace Prize 2000). Fifth Street Dick's coffee house has closed. DreamWorks Studio cancelled its controversial Ballona Wetlands construction in July 1999, following Wetland Action Network protests. Bernice Ligon, who, with husband Alfred Lloyd Ligon, operated the Aquarian Book Shop and Spiritual Center, once America's oldest continuously operated Black-owned bookstore, died in November 2000. Alfred died on August 10, 2002.

Wearing My Maturity

Malcolm Boyd's Q & A on Aging

In July 1998, the gay/political activist and clergyman Malcolm Boyd, author of Are You Running with Me, Jesus? *and* Running with Jesus: Prayers, *included me among several writers he queried about getting old. It was the first time I'd ever been invited to discuss the subject.*

BOYD: Do you fear aging—growing older, growing old—in any way?

COLEMAN: No. I don't fear aging. Not that I've had time to do so. However, most of my friends are eight to twenty years my senior. I wonder/worry about being without them, particularly the ones I rely on heavily for emotional support. One of the ongoing difficulties during my adolescence was the unexpected death of highly valued Black male mentors.

BOYD: Do you feel prepared for it?

COLEMAN: I like to believe that I am, psychologically and philosophically. But there isn't any way to prepare for it, is there? And if there is, to date I don't have the luxury of time and money to do so in a materialistic manner. Isn't how one lives one's daily life a preparation?

BOYD: Have you any specific positive or negative images of it?

COLEMAN: Not really, but plenty of resentment for not having lived—metaphorically speaking. That is, having gotten very little satisfaction out of life thus far.

BOYD: Could it be the best time of your life?

COLEMAN: There isn't any "best time."

BOYD: Or, do you think it might be the worst time?

COLEMAN: Life has offered the worst of times, and I can't imagine death being more cruel. I had two near-death experiences during childhood. Whatever death is, it is not "the worst time."

BOYD: Daniel J. Levinson wrote in *The Seasons of a Man's Life*: The connotations of youth are vitality, growth, mastery, the heroic; whereas old age connotes vulnerability, withering, ending, the brink of nothingness. How does that resonate with you?

COLEMAN: This is a roundup of the usual clichés. I find that youths can be old before their time, well along on that brink of nothingness, and that the old can be vital and heroic. In my youth I was much more vulnerable, and stupid, and stupidly trusting. I would hope to be one of those heroic elders, withering in my mastery, vital and on the brink of possibility.

BOYD: Whether you're thirty, sixty, or ninety, are you consciously aging now?

COLEMAN: Usually, when I wake up in the mornings I am amazed that I woke at all. Often I find I had no awareness of being asleep. I've always had an active dreamlife. Remarkably: One of the best by-products of aging is that the L.A.P.D./the cops don't bother me anymore! What a relief THAT is!! The other remarkable thing is the number of Latino men, all ages, who suddenly find me attractive. A very strange cultural phenomenon Granny hasn't had time to investigate.

BOYD: If so, how does it affect your body, your mind, your spirit?

COLEMAN: I'm starting to look like my mother, to see myself through my child's eye more and more. Her legs, her buttocks, her face, her terror—her softness of flesh. I take my vitamins, exercise when I'm so moved, and keep stepping.

BOYD: Your memories, your plans, your dreams?

COLEMAN: I am more preoccupied with the past, because I'm angry about all my stolen and spoiled moments. My plans are unchanged because they've remained ill-realized. My dreams have consumed me.

BOYD: Does your spirituality or religious faith hold any relation to your aging process? If so, what?

COLEMAN: Probably. I attend church occasionally, any denomination, but I quit "going to church" as a teenager. I enjoy the human need for ritual. But any "religious faith" I harbor moves through me and works without my being conscious of it; therefore, I'm not sure what my specific beliefs are any more —when I have the contemplative time—just that they make themselves manifest on their own, in my work, for others to observe. Spirituality, however, seems more a deliberate matter. The characteristics many attribute to the supernatural have always been a natural/given part of how I am in the world. My intelligence. I have grown more comfortable with this as I've aged. Occasionally, I wonder if this is a false comfort. As a child, I feared "my gifts" greatly. I enjoy the "knowing" that time's passage has given me.

BOYD: What, if any, are the effects of aging on your energy? Ability to work or be creative? Sensuality? Sense of security?

COLEMAN: I'm uncertain. I don't think I'm old enough, yet, for it to have had much effect; although, I'm TIRED of doing certain things—certain minor rituals of private hygiene, and housekeeping—and have to force myself to do them. I don't think age has anything to do with this. I attribute it to stress. The stresses of this racist world have been GREATLY debilitating. Stress has aged me and affected my mental and physical health negatively.

I am at my creative height, and can work like a laser slicing through granite.

Fucking has seldom been better. Although, Granny gets pleasantly shocked when young men flirt with her. She's too tired to care when her peers or older men flirt with her. Married sex is better than chicken on the run.

Security? No such animal has ever lived in this jungle.

BOYD: What are your reactions to older/old people?

COLEMAN: I think they're fortunate to have lived so long. But it depends on the variables. Racial and ethnic differences become greater with aging. People of color handle it better; are less defensively imperial, demanding, and pissy; but then, they don't tend to live as long as their White counterparts. In the ethnic lexicon of my youth, old was synonym for a White person who got lucky. At one point in my childhood *the only old people I ever noticed were White* and racist authority figures. And I detested them. Especially the White women who insist the world is their private plantation and the rest of us are the slaves put here to do their bidding. There were older Black people, but except for the church sisters, no old Black people.

BOYD: Do you see them as role models of maturity, experience, or wisdom?

COLEMAN: No. Nobody's cornered the market on these. Regardless of age.

BOYD: Do you view them as embarrassing, second-rate, functionally poor, objects of pity?

COLEMAN: Only when they make themselves so.

BOYD: Do you expect to age well? How do you propose to manage it?

COLEMAN: If I live long enough, yes. I'm fifty-one. Except for weight gain, I'm not doing too badly. Haven't got a single wrinkle I wasn't born with. (The one wrinkle I *was* born with crosses my forehead on a diagonal, and has noticeably deepened with increased consternation.) I don't have the time or money to manage it.

BOYD: Do you plan, near the end of your life, to enter a nursing facility, a retirement community, or stay in your own home?

COLEMAN: I have no retirement, no expectations, and no plans. I'm living on the wing.

BOYD: How do you view your death?

COLEMAN: With trepidation. I hope there's no such thing as reincarnation. I want to stay dead. Once I'm out of this bloody effing world, I want out for good.

BOYD: What are the role models of aging in *your* experience— the ones you've witnessed, the ones close to you—both the Bad and the Beautiful?

COLEMAN: I met the great theatrical agent Audrey Wood on a social occasion a few years before she died. I'll never forget the moment she entered the room. She was what many would consider an ugly woman. To the contrary, she was magnificent! She carried herself gloriously. She has always been my standard of how a woman is to wear her maturity.

BOYD: What is your view of assisted suicide?

COLEMAN: Our MEAN SOCIETY of the greed-driven post-Civil Rights years has created a subculture of poverty in which survival is so fierce suicide has become a viable alternative. Weak individuals trapped in it frequently take that option (and/or a homicidal one) with or without help. Therefore, it is hypocritical of any American to deny another American THAT choice. It should be legalized and civilized, permitted on a case-by-case basis, each case documented and swiftly reviewed by a board of certified medical, legal, religious and psychological peers so that it doesn't degenerate into rampant legalized murder. With some religious folk the stigma/issue will remain unresolved. But those who want this service should have it, with dignity, rapidity, and at minimal financial and emotional cost.

9/11 Blues

—for Peter Reese of Youngstown, O.

Into the Valley of the Shadow of Death
Strode the Three-Hundred . . .

Getting my tongue around the events of September 11, 2001, is still more than I can handle six months after. Events of such magnitude deserve more than the *RoboCop* rhetoric and knee-jerk sappiness that has dominated whatever dialogues—beyond jingoistic amens—that have taken place in public thus far. America is a nation at war. And while I am as patriotic as the next soldier over, I take critical issue with many of the decisions my country and its predominantly White male leadership has made in its manic effort to address what it calls terrorism—its reluctance to acknowledge that the ideological horse has been a long time out of the sociological barn.

Complex emotions have governed my response to 9/11. *I am against your arrogant, bigoted, self-righteous imperialistic posturing, which you sanctify by evoking God and Jesus Christ. I am against your hypocritical foreign and immigration policies, which you have used to marginalize my people, your African American*

243

constituency. Now Osama bin Laden knows what it's like to be a Nigger in America, where a campaign of economic terrorism has been waged against citizens of color since Plymouth Rock. I am amazed at the resources galvanized against the Islamic world by Americans reluctant to eradicate the evils of racism and anti-intellectualism, and whose combat against the scourge of AIDS has been lackluster. I am amazed at the willingness of my fellow Americans to reach deep down into their pockets to financially compensate the victims of 9/11 and the City of New York—but who won't spend a penny in reparations to compensate the victims of American Slavery. Many of those same Americans have tolerated the thirty-year destruction and decline of urban centers nation-wide, forcing Blacks to flee by moving to the suburbs, yet they were subdued and welcoming and hopeful, investing their trust in a Colin Powell as U.S. Secretary of State and in a Condoleeza Rice as National Security Advisor to President Bush—individuals who are exceptional products of the very same racism that fosters nationwide urban blight. I'm not above my own rhetoric.

As a public person, an artist—more definitely, as a Southwest-erner, as an African American woman, as a Black writer, as a working-class-poor mother, as a poet sickened by the demographics that govern my participation in whatever cultural dialogue must take place—I have chosen to remain silent, absorbing the images of the days following the collapse of the World Trade Center and assault on the Pentagon. If I am certain of anything, I am certain that my true feelings would not be universally appreciated. With the exception of my husband and my children, I keep my truest opinions and observations to myself—beyond those re-vealed here. I am also reluctant to cheapen or to capitalize on the horrific experiences and losses of those at the epicenter of the collapse, those who died on the Philadelphia flight, and those who died in the Pentagon crash. (Not to fail to mention the innocents who have died in those anonymous anthrax killings, as the patho-logical rises to compete for headlines with the sociopolitical.) I know that many of their stories are yet to come, that theirs are the most poignant—except for those dozen or so individuals in the West, most notably in Arizona and California, who lost their lives to RACIST vigilantes who *rightly* read in President Bush's clumsy, Texas-cowboy rhetoric a declaration of war against Americans with dark skins.

One specific incident of violence comes to mind.

The victim did not die.

It prompted me to call my daughter and warn her to stay close to home, to not leave the house unless she had an emergency. (Status post-9/11, I tease the Mexican American driver who regularly delivers my UPS packages, cautioning him to beware of being mistaken for "an A-rab." He laughs, then says his wife tells him the same thing.) My daughter—trying to raise her three children—left virtually alone in their Lancaster, California, home, because, in order to make a living, her trucker husband is on the roads, crisscrossing the nation twelve days out of fifteen. My daughter, her husband, and their children make up a mixed-race family. My daughter, a complex mixture of Caucasian, African American, and Native American, has almond-colored skin. Her husband, a Nicaraguan and Puerto Rican mix, is often mistaken for Mexican American. Their children, my grandchildren, are olive-skinned variations on those ethnic themes. The Lancaster-Palmdale area in which they live is a former lily-White enclave whose promising future collapsed in the '80s when the aerospace industry failed to flourish in the High Desert when government contracts were awarded elsewhere. With that decline, homes intended for young White families were sold off to minorities. A hundred miles north of L.A., surrounded by mountains, the community became a magnet for those trying to raise families in South Central Los Angeles where Blacks are discouraged from buying real estate. As a result, constant disharmony and racial incidents characterize the High Desert. My daughter and her family live two doors down from a family in which one grandson was assaulted by a skinhead with a hatchet or machete. I remind my daughter of this, that certain *ignorant folk* might not see a Black person when they look at her, like that unfortunate man who was chased from his car by two young

White males. They were going to make him pay for the destruction of the WTC, and all those lives lost. They chased the screaming man into his home and through it, until they discovered their victim was not an Arab but a Mexican American.

See?

I have so much to say—and yet, I feel unable to be completely clear and cogent about it. And organizing it into a simple essay is more than I can handle right now. A riot of images plays across my eyes as I write. And I've never felt so *unable* to do a subject the justice I feel it deserves. I sense that I have not said all I need to say. But this must suffice for now. Until the events move through me, and, like the stuff of my poems, express themselves "organically" on some other page.

But of all the events that have moved me—most recently, the death of journalist Danny Pearl, his courageous pregnant bride of mixed racial parentage—there is one that stands out above them all:

My heart was pierced by that tiny little single-engine Cessna that crashed into the forty-two-story Bank of America office building in Tempe, Florida, on Saturday, January 5, 2002.

My heart was rent and collapsed by the solo flight of Charles Bishop—young, gifted, and White.

That little American boy, and the statement he made with his life . . .

The Riot Inside Me

A Statistic Speaks

Every time I think back on the summer of 1992, my head and heart ache. I am as reluctant as ever to write personally about the violence protesting the verdict in the Rodney King beating case. I took one opportunity when I guest-edited a special issue of *High Performance* magazine—an independent effort that went unnoticed outside Los Angeles. Rhetoric comes easily when speaking of "the issues," as I did— or attempted to do—at the forums, panels, and town meetings that occurred in the wake of the South Central Riots, the largest man-made destruction in the history of twentieth-century U.S.A. I am calling them riots because that is what they were. I have exhausted the politically correct jargon of "rebellion" or "insurrection." As I was a witness, people—of nearly every ethnic description—were in the streets, smiling as they looted. It wasn't going to be just a Black affair that time around, not the way it was when Watts burned twenty-seven years earlier. I did not engage in the looting myself—not in 1965 and not in 1992. For me, the fact that others were so engaged was spectacle enough.

Long after the flames died and the curfew lifted, the riot inside me waged on. It had been ignited three months before April 29 by a failed job interview. I drove the streets fiercely, struck the

247

steering wheel, and cried profanities aloud. The hissy far tran-
scended the incident that triggered it. I did not know it at the
time, but my systemic hypotension was becoming hypertension. I
wanted to single-handedly destroy the birthplace I hated yet loved.
In my stead, I asked that disaster strike it and that terror reign.
Thus, the riots, when they happened, seemed to answer a prayer.

My rage was a lifetime deep.

That life began one year into President Harry S. Truman's first
term (1945–1953). My tender years corresponded to General
Dwight D. Eisenhower's term of office—1953 to 1961. My parents, migrants from mid- and southwest farming communities,
voted Republican—they were Americans of African descent who
believed in "Abe Lincoln's Party." My mother worked as a
domestic in the home of then actor Ronald Reagan and wife Jane
Wyman; quit, eventually becoming a seamstress. My father
aspired to be a champion boxer. They hung on the periphery of
an ambitious clique that gravitated around "the talented tenth"
of coloreds who had seemingly gained entrée into the White
world as artists, entertainers, and sports figures—singer Sarah
Vaughan, painter Charles White, and Light Heavyweight Champion Archie "The Old Mongoose" Moore (who actually hung
around our house). Race aside, it wasn't *what* you knew, but
who—so went Pop's tried yet tired mantra on success.

My early days included parent-sponsored activities. They took
me into the world of 4-H Clubs and lawn tennis. I experienced a
wealth of cultural events, from concerts at Philharmonic Hall to
the Shrine Auditorium, including those in which my father per-
formed, singing Negro-spiritual solos in the grand auditorium at
the then dazzling Golden State Insurance Company building as
if he were Paul Robeson. Sunday mornings were usually spent at
Price Chapel AME Church. We were poor—although I didn't
know it—but not yet disenfranchised. A dollar, when one had it,
stretched a long way. Like many of their peers, my parents
scrimped to maintain a new automobile and a one-car-garage
home. This was done on my father's salary—once he gave up

boxing—as an insurance agent, janitor, and house painter cum ad man. However, what started as an idyllic Negro youth in the Southern California of the '50s would quickly be aborted. I was about to enter the Los Angeles School System.

My parents had avoided explaining racism beyond strong warnings that others "out there" might try and make me feel inferior. I, too, was an American, they insisted, anyone's equal, regardless of race, color, or creed—words taken to heart despite a reality that would soon shake my confidence.

These were the days before Black was beautiful.

Outside home, I lived in a White world, Caucasians whose parents or grandparents had emigrated from Europe—Franco-Italian, Scotch-Irish, Danish-Swedish, and the like. When I started school, the Black population was small, the student body in the schools I attended 80 to 90 percent White. Inside the classrooms, the children of immigrants received preferential treatment. The hands of teachers—females—were rough as they *snatched* my forearms to move me away from one spot or to another, one place to another, without any explanation except "You belong over here." In time, no explanation was required. The reason was obvious. I was soon a survivor of kindergarten and first-grade bouts of being called "nigger," increasingly sensitized to the White authorities and low-toned males who preferred Negro girls with small bones, long pressed hair, and "funny colored" eyes. Yet—the concept of racism remained amorphous, eluding my preadolescent expression.

This sad madness was compounded in 1952 by an influx of new schoolmates—the majority with lighter complexions—largely the offspring of migrants from Texas and the Old South, drawn west by jobs and a purportedly less racist social climate. Our Florence-Graham neighborhood housed several Rom (Gypsy) and Filipino families whose children also attended local public schools. The majority of migrant workers had once been Black, but that had quickly changed as Mexicans increasingly crossed the U.S. border to displace them. These new arrivals quickly adjoined Southern California's Negro subculture and its pecking order: if you light, you all right; if you Black, get back; if you brown, stick around.

By second grade, I had heard of restricted housing and Blue Laws but knew nothing about wards of the United States or second-class citizenship or the kind of hardships the children of these migrants had experienced. I had never heard of the paper-bag test or soul food, much less Jim Crow. Along with folkways, regarded by our White teachers as superstitions, these migrant children brought with them an unparalleled wave of self-loathing, shame, and a remarkable fear of Whites I did not share. I would pay for my independent or "s'ditty" *attitude* during recess and after school, with my ego and knuckles. Among these new school-mates, I would be branded ugly and undesirable.

I began to learn how to hate.

Likewise, I began to pray for freedom from hatred.

At school, as I walked the hallways or dealt with whatever bullcorn awaited me on the school grounds, I prayed to be free of the ignorance and race hate that smothered my love of learning. I prayed that one day I would find a way to wear my hair in a manner others would accept—free of the stink of pine tar and growth pomades.

I recall—once—standing in a near-empty hallway, tardy as usual, facing a double flight of stairs, dreading the climb. I knew that the second I entered the classroom, I would face the ongoing ridicule garnered by my kinky grade of hair, bright eyes, toothy smile, and dark skin—not from the White students, the few Mexican, Asian American, and Filipino students, or the teacher, *but from my Black classmates.*

When walking home alone after school, I would drift into crying jags that would end in dry retching and pugnacious resignation.

The only words that I had ever heard that approached what I felt came ironically from the villainous lips of the Thuggee cult leader (Eduardo Ciannelli) in the film *Gunga Din.* My favorite part was the soliloquy in which he deplored the subjugation of his people by the British. To abort his capture as hostage, he jumps to his death. In my imaginary rewrite of the script, the Thuggees were victorious against the colonialists, my role a faithful follower who inspired her husband's sacrifice, or as the goddess Kali incarnate. I longed to be able to articulate what I saw as the psychosocial subjugation of my people—internalized racism—what I saw of it then, in hope that such an articulation might, in the sheer power of utterance, dispel it.

At the public library I researched the Thuggees, finding little. There was less on Mr. W. D. Fard and the Black Muslims—a cult that had once been compared with the Thuggees in a newspaper article. I had found the item among papers in my parents' portable mahogany liquor cabinet. From 1948, it concerned a sect that touted economic freedom for the Black man. My parents had never mentioned the Muslims and, when asked, could not satisfy my curiosity. They talked about Thurgood Marshall, Adam Clayton Powell, A. Philip Randolph, and the like. They read and discussed James Baldwin, Richard Wright, and W. E. B. Du Bois. But these leaders and heroes seldom came west, and their rhetoric and actions seemed to have little effect on my parents. As their lives became bleaker, the blacker our neighborhood became—Whites fleeing the heart of the city, taking wealth and prosperity to the suburbs.

The hero I longed for did not seem to exist.

In August 1955, a fourteen-year-old Chicagoan, Emmett Louis Till, was lynched in Money, Mississippi. Photographs of his corpse, in state, and the lines of hundreds of mourners, appeared in either *Ebony* or *Jet* magazine or both—they graced our living-room coffee table along with *Life* and *Look*. It was the first time I had ever heard of Whites lynching a Black child, although the mysterious or suspicious deaths of Negro juvenile males were frequent here at home and, not rarely, at the hands of Los Angeles police officers. Those violences seemed distant, therefore abstract. (I was two years away from learning about Nazi death camps and the fate of six million Jews, including children, when Alain Resnais's 1946 documentary *Night and Fog* was screened for Gompers

Junior High seniors in 1960.) However, those photographs made Till's death brutally intimate. I stared at them for hours. His murder seemed harbinger of the social change I longed for at the beginning of each school day.

But by 1958, the only changes in Los Angeles seemed to be the arrival of the Brooklyn Dodgers, the destruction of Chavez Ravine's neighborhoods—L.A.'s first Jewish settlement turned Mexican American—and a remarkable surge in White flight. As the complexions of students in my classrooms darkened, I found myself in a constant state of inexpressible rage, Ping-Ponging between thoughts of mass homicide or suicide. My childhood diaries are full rant. ("July 20, 1961—Can I help it if my hair is short? Damn everyone who makes cracks at it ... I feel like hell.") I hated school. My stomach flip-flopped continually on my fifteen-minute walks from home to campus. My hatred had become physical. I did not know how to discuss this anguish with my parents, or anyone. I became moody and brooded about the house, to their consternation. My grades dropped and I began to get into trouble. A rage was blossoming within me fertilized by the insistent logic that any concept of self-pride must include skin tone and everything that went with it.

As much as I hated school, I loved the poetry I had been introduced to by a kindergarten teacher. Surely poems, even if poets didn't make googobs of money, were magically transformative—as was all art. I became the child who always excelled when writing something original, a poem for Father's Day or a story for Christmas. Somehow, I thought, if I could master my inarticulation, I could master my rage, and not only change myself through my writings, but transform the hateful world I knew into a place I could love. More important—a place that would love me back.

Then, in 1959, we watched a TV documentary titled *The Hate That Hate Produced*. My parents were shocked yet intrigued, although agreeing with the documentary's point of view. I was thrilled and electrified by the appearance of "fine-looking" (Mother's description) Malcolm X—who openly addressed the subjugation of Negro people with as great a fire as Mr. Ciannelli in his role as Thuggee kingpin. But Malcolm X was a real man. My hero did exist!

Malcolm X visited Los Angeles in 1961 (the year J F K was inaugurated) during a period when gang activity was so intense, the transit system was refusing to allow Negro students on public buses without passes guaranteeing they were not gang members. One morning, as I rushed to school, I forgot my pass. The bus driver actually closed the door on my ankle, trapping my foot inside. He did not drive away, but, after I took a few hops, released it. I walked the hour to Gompers, missing homeroom and first period. I was not in a gang but was paying for the stigma. I belonged, as I would say two decades later, to that larger "gang," the Black race.

As if coinciding with Malcolm's visit, rumors of an underground surge of Black pride began circulating through South Central. Freedom was increasingly whispered about on campus at John C. Fremont High, during recess, lunch, and after school at the clubs that met for extracurricular activities. It was spoken of in soft tones by adults in the neighborhood. It was confirmed by White teachers who stormed the school district by the hundreds with requests to transfer out of inner-city schools where the student body had become predominately Afro-American. We knew the White teachers who feared us. They had taught us well how to hate them.

On November 23, 1963, John Fitzgerald Kennedy was assassinated, and the promise of the "Affluent '60s" began to evaporate. By 1964, the Civil Rights movement was dominating headline news. But in private quarters and closed meetings, L.A.'s Negro bourgeois elite sniggered at Civil Rights activists like Martin Luther King. My parents sided with these conservative Negroes who did not want the associated violence in their communities, no matter how nonviolent they were supposed to be—those boycotts, hunger strikes, sit-ins, and marches. While the Civil Rights movement never reached Southern California, a militant political activism was emerging on campuses and in enclaves. In a May 1963 issue of *Muhammad Speaks*, an article appeared in which

Malcolm X accused L.A.'s Mayor Yorty of running a "Ku Klux Klan police force." It jolted the city. "Friends of" networks were organizing underground meetings and fundraisers. That year future mayor Thomas (Tom) Bradley would become the first Black to be elected to the city council. My worried parents broadcast their hopes and opinions loudly around the dinner table—for my benefit.

I listened quietly.

There was a strange new construction going on in the inner city. Our stately schools, built before WWII, were beginning to resemble prisons. Certain sections were sealed off, the green quads and courtyards placed off limits or paved over. Bungalows appeared as class sizes grew, decreasing area available for playground activities. Calculus, Greek, Latin, and Journalism were among the classes that disappeared from the curriculum. In the November 1964 election, a local Fair Housing Act proposition was defeated by White voters—which angered my parents, who still resented the restricted housing that had crippled their chances for economic stability in the early years of their marriage.

At home, my parents began to fail economically as the price of material things outclimbed their combined incomes. My father could no longer find fruitful employment, abandoned the Republican Party, and became a Democrat. My mother's paycheck as a seamstress was steadily eroded by bosses bringing in cheaper labor from Mexico. I was exiting puberty, and it was more than obvious that they could not send me to college. My hatred for Los Angeles increased exponentially.

Within six months, between June and November of 1964, I graduated from high school, started college, turned eighteen, left home, married, dropped out of college, threw away my hot-iron pressing comb and curler to go *au naturel*, and joined L.A.'s political underground. Nine months later, I would give birth to my first child. Days later, in August 1965 (the violence raging three days before being reported in local newspapers), Watts erupted in flames.

Black had become beautiful.

I lived in a Black world.

From the ashes in Watts sprang a series of arts and educational organizations that opened their doors to encourage Black writers and artists. I joined a creative-arts workshop, writing plays and poems. Whenever I ran into old classmates, they were usually embarrassed. Malcolm X was assassinated on February 21, 1965. Martin Luther King was stilled on April 4, 1968. In August of 1968, James Brown screamed "Say it loud, I'm Black and I'm proud" over the airwaves. My first husband and I were remarried as orthodox Muslims, but it would not save our marriage. The Civil Rights movement was declared over by 1969. Except for programs at the Watts Towers and Inner City Cultural Center, similar programs in Watts, funded during President Lyndon Johnson's War on Poverty (1963–69), would vanish by 1975—two years before the debut of my first poetry chapbook. My exorcism of old hatreds by writing had begun, but the transformation was elusive. A second marriage and a new child were on my horizon.

By the end of the '70s, I had again divorced to become a single working mother, dropping in-and-out of college while working full time. Whatever job sustained me—magazine editor, waitress, and proofreader—at whatever interval, I groped to fulfill the promise made to that younger self. I stayed the difficult course— as the years fled, no matter the diversion or distraction, through broken relationships and the ceaseless crises that attend the working-class poor. I became an accomplished writer, but the world I had known was disappearing under the relentless pressures of economic disparity—as the unresolved issues of red-lining, police brutality, poverty, and drugs continued to fester, and new, more voracious, youth gangs sprang from the asphalt.

Unable to get steady work as a scriptwriter, I entered the pink-collar working class, moonlighting as a bartender. Between 1979 and 1989, I had skipped vacations, sacrificed sleep and any available spare time to produce seven collections of stories and poems with Black Sparrow Press. But prestige is hard to eat. The boss who refused to give my mother a raise to feed her family had become President Reagan (1981–89). Mother had voted for him, despite her history. Toward the end of that horrific decade, during which my father's health declined, she would receive a rude cut in her Social Security check and regret her ballot.

I began teaching occasionally, traveling and lecturing with my poetry. But that was not enough.

In 1991, following the death of my father, I took a major risk and quit my "slave" as medical secretary, encouraged by my third husband of ten years. The pull of my gift could no longer be denied. I had to write—regardless. I was in my mid-forties. Other than temporary layoffs, it was the first time since 1972 that I had been without a regular paycheck. Ahead lay disaster—spun from the ever-complex machinations of race. Mother would soon re-marry only to become a widow for the second time. With the help of a friend, I scored a new script agent and began crawling Holly-wood's pitch dens. Renewed pursuits as scriptwriter and journal-ist, promising at first, did not work out. Then, on April 29, 1992, as I left a late-morning meeting at the Department of Cultural Affairs, the verdict by the Simi Valley jury in the Rodney King beating case was announced. Afternoon into evening, I drove the city from downtown to Hollywood, through the Crenshaw dis-trict, then through Westwood. By the time I arrived home the city was again in flames, after twenty-seven years—and for virtually the same reasons.

As I watched the coverage, I was struck by newscasters who repeatedly referred to rioters as "thugs." They didn't grasp the meaning of the word. I recalled Mr. Ciannelli's performance and wished. But like the headless hens I had once watched flop around the farmyard after my grandmother had wrung their necks, the various outcroppings of violence spent themselves and collapsed, leaving residues of fear and more hate. As factions struggled through curfew toward recovery, it was apparent that the issues of South Central Los Angeles, the same issues that had affected my parents in the postwar Los Angeles of the late '40s and '50s and that circumscribed my lifetime, would go largely unaddressed.

Yet another decade has passed. The new century my father did not live to see has begun.

As I write, the thirty-fifth anniversary of the Watts Riots has just passed and the tenth anniversary of the South Central L.A. Riots approaches. As I prepared this essay, I spent a week gathering various clips from my extensive collection from which to extrapolate and draw statistics. (I began keeping them in 1959, the first for a current-events report for History class on Fidel Castro's overthrow of the Batista regime.) I think of Attica (1971), Philadelphia's Operation M.O.V.E. (1985), and the O. J. Simpson Trial (1996). But the clips I favored were those documenting the twenty-seven-year terror of racism against African Americans in California, emphasis on L.A. They detail a multileveled domestic assault—economic, educational, financial, psychosocial—in law enforcement and entertainment, everything from the Bakke case to the People's Temple and Jonestown to an item on Black women as the favored targets of airport security searches. As I scanned them, I was again reminded of how much a statistic I had become. I put them aside to consider how this particular statistic should bring itself to life—*personally*.

Then, something unexpected and tremendous happened. On Tuesday morning, September 11, America sustained an assault on the Pentagon and the catastrophic destruction of the nation's financial heart, New York City's World Trade Center. Nineteen men—thugs—presumably of Arab or Afghani descent, martyred themselves, commandeering four jet passenger liners. Three of those transports-turned-bombs struck their targets. They extinguished the lives of an estimated six thousand innocent people on American soil, roughly 1/1000th of the number of lives lost in the Nazi concentration camps. I thought about the 64,000 at Nagasaki and the 135,000 at Hiroshima. I thought about learning that rocks bleed. I thought about my draft-age son.

The war against terror has been declared. The transformation has begun.

Like the majority of citizens, I watched—and still watch—the daily news reports, seeking signs of the tumult ahead. What role can I play, other than lighting candles, making donations, writing letters to friends? What does a poet do when poetry is the most under-appreciated art in a nation—even considered subversive —where the images manufactured in Hollywood (largely negative images of Blacks) are "its second largest export," to quote *Chicago Tribune* journalist Clarence Page. But . . .

Being who I am, I can't not make note of the ironies—of the arrogance governing our nation's rhetoric, its military and intelligence agencies, and the misology that governs the mindset of our predominately Caucasian leadership of immigrant descent. In an e-mail to a kindred spirit who resides in Washington, D.C., I posed rhetorically: "Did agism, homophobia, racism, and sexism die in the Attack on America?"

He did not answer and I did not pursue the issue.

After four straight days of round-the-clock viewing, I decided I had to get out of the house and drive out to the cemetery. I had not visited my father's grave in over a year.

I did as usual: took grass clippers, a rag, and bottled water, got down on my knees and tidied up, asking, as I always do, the unanswerable.

It was Saturday noon, the sky was overcast, and the grounds deserted. When I finished, I walked the hill overlooking West Los Angeles—Century City Plaza and beyond. This, I thought, is the city my father loved, in which he died unfulfilled, if well into his seventies. The plaque that marks his spot in the underworld was paid for by my book royalties.

Mother has never visited the site.

Sources & Acknowledgments

The epigraph is from the poem "Pico Blvd.," by Patrick Bianucci, published in *Alcatraz 2*, edited by Stephen Kessler (Santa Cruz: Alcatraz Editions, 1982). Copyright © 1982 by Patrick Bianucci. Reprinted by permission of the poet.

The quotation on page xiv is from *The African American West: A Century of Short Stories*, edited by Bruce A. Glasrud and Laurie Champion (Boulder: University Press of Colorado, 2000). Copyright © 2000 by Bruce A. Glasrud and Laurie Champion. Reprinted by permission of the editors.

"Jabberwocky Baby" appeared in *First Loves: Poets Introduce the Essential Poems That Captivated and Inspired Them*, edited by C. Ciuraru (New York: Scribners, 2000).

"For Dad, On What Would Have Been His 84th Birthday" appeared in *From Daughters and Sons to Fathers: What I've Never Said*, edited by Constance Warloe (Ashland, Ore.: Storyline Press, 2001).

"Love-Ins with Nietzsche" was originally printed as a limited-edition chapbook (Fresno: Wake Up Heavy, 2000).

"Angela's Big Night" appeared in the *Los Angeles Free Press* in March 1972.

"Primal Orb Density" appeared in *Lure and Loathing: Essays on Race, Identity, and the Ambivalence of Assimilation*, edited by Gerald Early (New York: Penguin Books, 1992).

"Looking for It" appeared as "An Interview with Wanda Coleman," by Andrea Juno and V. Vale, in Re/Search #13: Angry Women (San Francisco: Re/Search Publications, 1991). Reprinted by permission of the interviewers.

"Bobbi Sykes: An Interview" appeared in Callaloo, Vol. 8, No. 2 (Lexington: University of Kentucky, 1985). The poems "Ambrose" and "Racism/Many Faces" appeared in Love Poems and Other Revolutionary Actions, by Bobbi Sykes (St. Lucia: University of Queensland Press, 1979). Reprinted by permission of the poet.

"Remembering Latasha: Get Out of Dodge! Blacks, Immigrants & America" appeared in The Nation, February 15, 1993.

"Uncommon Courtesy" appeared in the Los Angeles Times Magazine, June 21, 1992.

"Coulda Shoulda Woulda: 'A Song Flung Up to Heaven,' by Maya Angelou," appeared in the Los Angeles Times Book Review, April 14, 2002

"Black on Black: Fear & Reviewing in Los Angeles" appeared in KONCH, an online literary magazine (www.ishmaelreedpub.com/konch.html), July–August 2002.

"Boos & Reviews: The Angelou—EsoWon Contretemps" appeared in the Los Angeles Sentinel, July 11, 2002. (It was written in response to the May 30, 2002 Sentinel article "L.A.'s Leading Black Bookstore Bans Popular Author Over Review.")

"Hunt & Peck: Book Reviewing African American Style" appeared in L.A. Weekly, July 25, 2002. (An expanded version appeared, as "Book Reviewing African American Style," in The Nation, September 16, 2002.)

"What Saves Us: An Interview with Wanda Coleman," by Priscilla Ann Brown, appeared in Callaloo, Vol. 26, No. 3 (College Station, Texas: Department of English, Texas A&M University, 2003). Reprinted by permission of the interviewer.

"Dancer on a Blade: Deep Talk, Revisions & Reconsiderations" appeared, with photographs, in Contemporary Authors Autobiography Series, Vol. 29 (Detroit: Gale Research, 1998).

"I Was a Stand-In Diva for June Jordan" appeared in The

World, No. 55 (New York: Poetry Project, St. Mark's Church, 1998).

"Letters to E. Ethelbert Miller" appeared in *Callaloo*, Vol. 22, No. 1 (Charlottesville: Department of English, University of Virginia, 1999). Introduction reprinted by permission of E. Ethelbert Miller.

"5 Years After" appeared as "Five Years After the L.A. Riots Discontent Festers in South Central" in the *Washington Post*, April 20, 1997.

"9/11 Blues" appeared in *September 11: West Coast Writers Approach Ground Zero*, edited by Jeff Meyers (Portland, Ore.: Hawthorne Books & Literary Arts, 2002).

"The Riot Inside Me: A Statistic Speaks" appeared in *Geography of Rage: Remembering the Los Angeles Riots of 1992*, edited by Jervey Tervalon (Los Angeles: Really Great Books, 2002).

The remaining pieces—"My Writing Life & Loves," "A Girl's Diary," "My Blues Love Affair," "Flung into Controversy—Indeed," "Heavy Duty Postscript," and "Wearing My Maturity"—appear here for the first time.

Photograph: ROD BRADLEY

WANDA COLEMAN was born in the community of Watts in 1946 and raised in Los Angeles. To support herself as a writer, she has worked as a medical secretary, magazine editor, journalist, and scriptwriter, and occasionally teaches on university level. In 1971 she began her thirty-year association with Black Sparrow Press, during which she published eleven books of poetry and prose, beginning with a chapbook of poems in 1977. For her poetry she has received literary fellowships from the California Arts Council, the National Endowment for the Arts, and the Guggenheim Foundation. Her honors in fiction include a second fellowship from the California Arts Council and the 1990 Harriet Simpson Arnow Prize from *The American Voice*. She received the 1999 Lenore Marshall Poetry Prize for *Bathwater Wine* from the Academy of American Poets, the *Nation* magazine and the New Hope Foundation. Her collection of poems *Mercurochrome* was a bronze-medal finalist for the 2001 National Book Award in Poetry and a finalist for the 2002 Paterson Poetry Prize. An electrifying presenter of her work, famed for her readings, she has become known as "the L.A. Blueswoman." In 2004 she became the first literary artist to receive a C.O.L.A. Fellowship from the Los Angeles Department of Cultural Affairs. She lives in Southern California with her husband Austin Straus and family. *The Riot Inside Me: More Trials & Tremors* is published by Black Sparrow Books/David R. Godine, Publisher.